Crime Fiction and the

This book opens up a range of important perspectives on law and violence by considering the ways in which their relationship is formulated in literature, television and film. Employing critical legal theory to address the relationship between crime fiction, law and justice, it considers a range of topics, including: the relationship between crime fiction, legal reasoning and critique; questions surrounding the relationship between law and justice; gender issues; the legal, political and social impacts of fictional representations of crime and justice; post-colonial perspectives on crime fiction; as well as the impact of law itself on the crime fiction's development. Introducing a new sub-field of legal and literary research, this book will be of enormous interest to scholars in critical, cultural and socio-legal studies, and to others in criminology, as well as in literature.

Maria Aristodemou, Fiona Macmillan and **Patricia Tuitt** are based at Birkbeck Law School, London, UK.

Crime Fiction and the Law

Edited by Maria Aristodemou,
Fiona Macmillan and Patricia Tuitt

Routledge
Taylor & Francis Group
LONDON AND NEW YORK

First published 2017
by Birkbeck Law Press

Published 2018 by Routledge
2 Park Square, Milton Park, Abingdon, Oxon OX14 4RN
711 Third Avenue, New York, NY 10017, USA

First issued in paperback 2018

Routledge is an imprint of the Taylor & Francis Group, an informa business

British Library Cataloguing in Publication Data
A catalogue record for this book is available from the British Library

Library of Congress Cataloging-in-Publication Data
A catalog record for this book has been requested

ISBN 13: 978-1-138-62433-7 (pbk)
ISBN 13: 978-1-138-81846-0 (hbk)

Typeset in Baskerville
by Apex CoVantage, LLC

In memory of Professor Patrick McAuslan (1937–2014)

Contents

Foreword

This edited collection grew out of a symposium on Crime Fiction and the Law, jointly organised by Birkbeck School of Law and the Birkbeck Institute for the Humanities in December 2012. The book, which is the result of the collaboration of a range of colleagues, has taken shape slowly but surely. The generosity of those who have contributed chapters is visible to the naked eye, but we are no less grateful for it on that account. We also wish, however, to express our gratitude to those whose contribution might not otherwise be evident. The students who have participated in our undergraduate module on Crime Fiction and the Law have had a special role in the development of our ideas, and it is our hope that this book will provide stimulating source material for future students on this course. We owe particular thanks to Henrique Carvahlo, who rendered us extensive assistance with the editing process. Colin Perrin and Laura Muir gave us unceasing help in getting the book into print – like the wise publishers they are they know exactly how to balance pressure and patience.

Our special thanks go to Dorrette McAuslan for permission to publish the chapter written by her late husband, our much-missed colleague Professor Patrick McAuslan. Most within the academy would have known of Patrick for the way in which he revolutionised teaching and scholarship in the fields of land, property and planning law. All will know that he was at the forefront of three significant experiments in legal education – having founded the Law Schools in Dar es Salaam, Warwick and, his last affiliation, the Law School at Birkbeck. However, few would have known of his passion for the crime novel – especially for the contemporary police procedural. Involved in the early design of the undergraduate Crime Fiction and the Law module, Patrick was working on his chapter, which appears at the end of this collection, at the time of his death. This volume is dedicated to his memory, not only with inevitable sadness for his loss but also in celebration of his extraordinary energy, productivity and enthusiasm for life.

Maria Aristodemou
Fiona Macmillan
Patricia Tuitt
London, April 2016

Contributors

Maria Aristodemou is Reader in Law, Literature and Psychoanalysis at Birkbeck, University of London

Chris Boge is Honorary Research Fellow in Law at Birkbeck, University of London

Peter Fitzpatrick is Anniversary Professor of Law at Birkbeck, University of London

Oscar Guardiola-Rivera is Reader in Law at Birkbeck, University of London

Fiona Macmillan is Professor of Law at Birkbeck, University of London

Patrick McAuslan was Professor of Law at Birkbeck, University of London

Janet McCabe is Lecturer in Film and Television Studies at Birkbeck, University of London

Anton Schütz is Senior Lecturer in Law at Birkbeck, University of London

Patricia Tuitt is Professor of Law at Birkbeck, University of London

Barbara Villez is Professor in the Département d'Etudes des Pays Anglophones, Université Paris 8

Chapter 1

The introduction didn't do it

Maria Aristodemou

1 The invitation

'The English', writes Jorge Luis Borges (1999, p. 11), 'live with the turmoil of two incompatible passions: a strange appetite for adventure and a strange appetite for legality.' Both passions, he claims, find satisfaction in detective fiction. A collection of essays on crime fiction and the law, following the teaching of a course and a symposium on the subject at a London law school, may appear to lend strong support to Borges' claim. The purpose of this introduction is to examine this claim by interrogating the desires that animate not only crime fiction, but the teaching, symposia, and writing of such volumes. The claim, contra Borges, is that these twin passions are neither incompatible, nor (only) English: they are animated by the same limiting and limited human condition which seeks solace in law and, failing law in its symbolic manifestations, seek satisfaction in law's imaginary depictions.

Several decades after the law and literature movement took off on both sides of the Atlantic, crossed the Channel and took firm roots in old and new worlds, it may seem anachronistic if not reactionary to begin by questioning the movement's purpose and achievements. This is, nevertheless, what this introduction hopes to do. A school of thought, after all, is only as relevant as its continuing contributions, and a school that has ceased to question its purposes and consequences (intended or unforeseen) is no longer a school of thought. Let's rewind then to some of the ideas and ideals that spearheaded the law and literature movement and animated its enthusiastic participants, who, timidly at first, then more and more boldly entered the legal curriculum to the extent that, several decades on, the study of law and literature is not only tolerated but positively encouraged in the academy.

2 Terms of endearment

There is no doubt that in its early manifestations the law and literature movement had much to address, and much to complain about. The woefully dry nature of legal education, faithful to legal positivism's dictum that what the law is can be and should be separated from what the law ought to be, produced not only disheartened and cynical students, but equally cynical and despondent teachers: law divorced from its social, political, historical and literary roots, was law, they did not dare to admit, in its final stage of impotence.

The enthusiasm with which law and literature (and variations on this theme, such as law and film, law and culture) were welcomed in the legal academy was owed to the fact that until recently, legal education on both sides of the Atlantic was an admirable manifestation of the influence of positivist philosophy and the reliance on observed, empirical facts to the exclusion of supposedly unverifiable statements of value or causes. Legal positivism's tenets determined both the perception of the nature of law and the methods of its instruction. While historically (and despite Plato's infamous attempt to exclude poets from his ideal state) law, politics, humanities and religion were intellectually as well as professionally interdependent, with modernity legal study became more specialised, technical, and increasingly utilitarian. The insistence was that law is a science unto itself, one that could and should be studied in isolation from external influences and from other disciplines.

Injecting literary works onto tired legal syllabi had, initially, a two-pronged rationale: on the one hand, proponents claimed, works of literature would teach lawyers how to read and write more effectively, more persuasively, more beautifully even. For what is the use of a lawyer armed with an arena of legal precedents, if her rhetoric fails to convince judge and jury? In arguments that were reminiscent of Plato's *Gorgias*, law and literature advocates insisted that their teaching would produce more accomplished lawyers, ones whose success at the art of persuasion would be enhanced and perfected.

At the same time as praising literature's utilitarian values, and without any seeming acknowledgement of the contradiction, law and literature advocates offered a parallel rationale for the use (and abuse) of literature. The claim was that legal education that confines itself to teaching law as it is without paying attention to what it ought to be leads students to ignore the social impact of law in their society: that it is only a short step from arguing that what the law is is separate from what it ought to be, to believing that what the law ought to be is irrelevant to legal education. Not only was literature 'useful' then, but it also furthered, the argument went, the pursuit of truth, even a higher truth than that offered by legal positivist education. What did this truth consist of? The hope, more or less loudly advertised by its advocates, was that the truth law missed would and could be found in the archives of literature. This, again full of hope, wasn't just any truth, but a truth with a mission and a goal: it was, to simplify if not generalise, to 'humanise' lawyers, make them, without a shade of irony, more attentive to the plight and suffering of others, starting, of course, with their clients.

So literature would broaden and enhance students' 'ethical consciousness' by exposing them to and reminding them of the value judgements implicit in their work. Assuming that great literary works are the repository of society's cultural values, literature, it was argued, would widen the dimensions of a problem, demystify law's claims, encourage self and social criticism, give an impetus for change and reform, indeed liberate! Literature would teach lawyers to understand and empathise with the problems of others, qualities without which they would not crave, much less attain, justice. So those engaged in the project confidently asserted, as the saying used to go, 'they would make a better man of the lawyer and a better lawyer of the man'. Not only would they teach lawyers to read and write more effectively, but they would also teach them moral values and make them better persons. At which point, some of us, initially excited by the invitation, started wondering, do we actually want to go to this party?

3 Cold feet

Both the instrumental argument, that the study of literature will produce better lawyers, and the humanistic belief, that the study of literature will make lawyers better persons, are problematic. Claims about the 'liberating' or 'humanising' potential of literature cannot be assumed without inquiring into whether morality can be taught at all and, if so, how. Knowing about morality, humanity must sadly admit, does not make us moral and understanding the 'moral law' does not necessarily lead us to act in accordance with it. The Socratic view that immorality is due to ignorance of the good must also be balanced against Plato's elitist view that only the wise can acquire knowledge of the good. It is therefore idealistic, if not dangerous, to expect, and there is no reason to assume, that lawyers immersed in literature will have better abilities to identify and apply moral values than other lawyers.

Above all, the view that education can have a transformative power cannot ignore the fact that both law and literature are part and parcel of society and that somebody will be educating the educators. Cultural texts, no less than legal ones, proclaim, knowingly and unknowingly, consciously and unconsciously, the ineluctable rules and mores that make up the social order, whether we are aware of them or not, like them or not, suffer them, tolerate them, or enjoy them. Far from standing outside or escaping the dominant ideology, cultural texts too often bolster, maintain and perpetuate it. To follow my own law and literature thesis over a decade ago, cultural texts are just as influential and norm-making, if not more so, than so-called 'real' laws (Aristodemou 2000). The fear, therefore, is that, dissatisfied with law, the law and crime fiction critic finds compensation and consolation in literature: in that sense, crime fiction and art generally serve not to critique, or undermine but to supplement and thereby bolster the legal edifice.

Janet McCabe's chapter in this collection takes us behind the scenes to uncover the business deals and negotiations that go into producing these cultural and legal 'fictions'; the vast (and lucrative) *Wallander* project, she quotes a producer admitting, 'was designed so that broadcasters would be satisfied'. What is produced, we must remember, is not just 'entertainment' precisely because no cultural product is 'just' entertainment: what is produced is ideas, views, values which are just as norm-creating and influential if not more so than the norms we find in law books. These supposed 'local' norms and values are tailored, as McCabe shows, for global marketing and consumption, following what she aptly terms a 'glocalisation strategy'.

Barbara Villez's paper addresses the popularity of French television crime fiction and examines how, while initially crime narratives stopped when the culprits were caught, with no view of the judicial handling of cases, new series *Engrenages* follows the criminal justice investigation in all its stages, including the trial of the culprits. In contrast to earlier series where the depiction of the French criminal justice system erroneously replicated procedures familiar from the American system, the new *Engrenages*'s fidelity to French legal procedures has led to critical acclaim, and even judicial approval. Villez examines the changes in the series and the reasons for its acceptance among judges and lawyers; fiction, after all, cannot successfully perform the ideological role of eliciting interest, as well as faith, in the system, if its televisual depiction is dismissed by the public as unrealistic and indeed at times, ridiculous.

4 The party

Despite our reservations, we have arrived at the law and literature party and indeed started enjoying ourselves. As one would expect at the start of the evening, food and spirits are plentiful. There is no doubt that in its heyday the law and literature movement delivered a plethora of analyses of the perennial jurisprudential questions on the nature and aims of law: the relationships between natural and positive law, between moral and legal obligation, between law and justice, justice and revenge, law and punishment, rule and discretion, law and power, order and hierarchy, were, after all, themes that literature had been addressing with as much persistence and for much longer than lawyers. We learned from these analyses not only not to take legal discourse for granted but also more methods with which to challenge it. We questioned insistently whether law was reasoned argument alone or does it (or should it) cater for other, perhaps irrational, elements of the human condition; whether legal definitions of guilt and innocence are universal or does law insist on its own standards and classifications by ignoring, and oppressing, alternative systems of values; whether law's claim to its own absolute legitimacy is justified, or is its domination achieved by collapsing every situation into its own mould? If the latter, what consequences does this have for those excluded from its empire? Above all, how do we account for the intimate, indeed incestuous, relationship between law and violence? If violence is the founding act of every order, including the legal system, what, if anything, explains, let alone justifies, law's insistence on a monopoly on violence?

Crime fiction was an inexhaustible reservoir for this party providing the music, drinks and drugs for its enthusiastic revellers. By inserting it into the legal curriculum, Borges' two supposedly irreconcilable enjoyments could be impudently and scandalously enjoyed side by side: students, and teachers, could enjoy law and its transgression, fidelity to law serving as absolution and the price for the illegal trespassing into fiction. In the process, attention to crime fiction could claim to draw attention to, as well as challenge, some of legal discourse's most treasured creeds: the idea, for example, that human beings are rational and self-interested rather than self-destructive and masochistic; or that human instinct is to resist rather than embrace authority; that legal language is used to exclude and oppress rather than include and liberate; the assumptions we make about free will and responsibility; the view that law is based on rationality and consent rather than oppression and fear. In classrooms we relished the paradox that while lawyers and legislators in debates about criminalising or decriminalising conduct assume there is a stigma attached to criminality, in many portrayals of criminals in crime fiction the criminal is depicted as a hero, a fascinating human being. Above all, crime fiction drew attention to the violence at the heart of the law itself, both at its inception as a system that monopolises violence, as well as for the maintenance of its supremacy in wielding force; a theme, as we will see, meticulously analysed by Macmillan and Boge in the final chapter of this collection.

5 In the kitchen

Slowly but surely the more obvious interrelation between law and literature, that is, the examination of how law and lawyers were depicted *in* literature, became both common and popular. While some revellers were enjoying themselves in the lounge and garden, dancing the night away, other, more introvert guests, could be found in the kitchen earnestly debating the latest developments in theories of language and suggesting that it's all very well for lawyers to examine how literature depicted law, but have we forgotten the much more interesting dimension that law itself was always already literature? From such humble kitchen chats began what came to be called the law *as* literature movement, particularly beloved by lawyers on both sides of the Atlantic craving to infuse their academic ramblings with certain continental *je ne sais quoi*, generously on offer in 1980s parties.

Ironically, while mainstream legal education had little trouble tolerating the revellers in the house, the ideas being conjured up in the kitchen met with more suspicion and outright condemnation. While, and as we just saw (and not without justification), the main party was perceived as harmless distraction for bored children, for many the stirrings in the kitchen were much more ominous: legal theory's resort to positivism to explain the binding quality of legal norms, was, after all, premised on the possibility of a scientific knowledge of the law. The desire for the 'scientisation' of law, and the insistence on distinguishing law from other disciplines, aimed to base law on a secure foundation with its promise of pure presence and essential, final meanings. The lawyer, the faith was, could search for and discover, like the detective or archaeologist, the origin and truth of the law. This origin, truth, or 'right answer', as Ronald Dworkin would call it, was not 'made' but 'found', and, once found, it was possible to believe in it in the same way one believes in one true God. The desire for a right answer, is, as Anton Schütz shows in this collection, and as psychoanalysts note, profoundly religious: even and perhaps because of modernity's so-called murder of God, the desire for a master who possesses the right answer, persisted and was displaced elsewhere. Where one once believed in God consciously, now one believes in god (with a small 'g') unconsciously: if in the court room this unconscious god takes the form of Dworkin's herculean judge, in crime fiction, as we will see, she takes the form of an eccentric but nevertheless unerring detective.

The work of critical legal scholars alerted us to the fallacies involved in the positivist enterprise and the losses incurred by their insistence on law as fact divorced from politics, history or literature. The analytic tradition's attempt to eliminate metaphor from legal discourse ignored the fact that law is also, even first and foremost, a text. In the same way that, as Hayden White (1978, p. 99) argued, the fetishism of facts led history to 'lose sight of its origins in the literary imagination', lawyers also craved for a law that was outside and beyond interpretation. Yet neither law, nor the past, exist 'out there' ready for us to appropriate: they arrive, if at all, through the traces they leave in texts. The lawyer's attempt to accord these textual sources with meaning cannot take place without selecting, hierarchising, supplementing, suppressing and subordinating some traces to others. This process cannot be other than literary and the lawyer's tools are no different from those of the literary critic.

The losses incurred from the attempt to banish the law's textual origins are not small: the attempt to distinguish law from fiction, the suppression of metaphor and the speculative led to the exclusion of what, had the same teachers taken their own masters seriously, was fundamental to law. It was Bentham, after all, who understood, and insisted that the nature of law was fictional: just as language is fictional, bringing something that is absent into presence through representation, legal concepts are fictional constructs whose existence depends on our collective belief in them. Take belief away (as even positivists like H.L.A. Hart appreciated) and the rules evaporate, bringing the system tumbling down. Peter Fitzpatrick's contribution in this volume draws attention to the fictive nature of law, the 'mysterium tremendum' as he calls it, which, once 'a transcendent and transgressive reference of realized being', was ignored in legal discourse. Drawing examples from Kafka's fiction, Fitzpatrick shows how that immanence is nevertheless recognised in literature. Literature's generative force, Fitzpatrick argues, typifies the genre of detective fiction, a genre, he concludes, which instances the fictive force of law.

6 Drunken promises

The dismay with which law *as* literature critics were received by the academy was understandable: to suggest, as some scholars did, that there is no such thing as a right answer to legal cases, that, as Allan Hutchinson (1989) once infamously insisted, there are as many interpretations of the US Constitution as there are readings of Hamlet, appeared anathema to the legal empire. As Patricia Tuitt argues in this volume, however, they needn't have worried: critique soon became stultified instead of blossoming under the 'no right answer' doctrine. In particular, as she shows, the 'no right answer thesis' proved least well-prepared to respond to the challenges posed by the twenty-first century's changes in legal education and services.

What was it that worried the academy then? Oscar Guardiola-Rivera's, Patrick McAuslan's and Chris Boge's contributions in this volume leave us in no doubt of the threat posed by this branch of law and literature: to lay bare the political nature of representation is also to lay it open to interpretation and appropriation by different groups. Taking their cue from deconstruction and postcolonial theory, these critics pointed out that the stories inherited from mainstream legal education, presented as final and definitive, often obscured the voices of the colonised, robbing them of the opportunity to tell their own stories and create their own norms. Colonial writing had assumed a universalist mantle, purporting to talk for an undifferentiated humanity and time, presenting texts and the values they promulgated as unchanging and universal. In Guardiola-Rivera's and McAuslan's chapters we see how postcolonial writers took up the task of reopening and questioning legal doctrine, thereby creating not only new histories but new norms for those individuals and communities.

At the heart of the texts Guardiola-Rivera and McAuslan address, is the appreciation that although the end of colonialism meant, in legal terms, a change of sovereignty, this did not mean the end of exploitation or effective self-determination. For that, the myth of white superiority and the pervasive influence of European languages, literature and laws had to be challenged. It is supremacy over the latter that was more difficult to dislodge and to which postcolonial writers turned their attention. The first task for these writers was to challenge the view of liberal humanist critics that law, and literature, reflected timeless values irrespective of place, colour or race. Instead, it was imperative to point out that, not only did Western writers assume the authority to speak on behalf of us all, but they also bestowed other oriental qualities they did not choose to acknowledge or repressed in themselves. So, where the white European was rational, the other was emotional, where the European was civilised, the other was savage, where the European was good and saved, the other was evil and lost. The European assumption of the right to speak the universal meant again that language in law and in literature was a major means of exercising domination. Only once such claims were exposed as serving the interests of a white, male, middle class rather than humanity as a whole could the colonised begin to find their own language and start reclaiming their past.

Guardiola-Rivera's analysis of Julio Cortázar's novella *Fantomas Contra Los Vampiros Multinacionales* addresses these themes and suggests that writing, in addition to acting as a witness to injustice, can also actively, prophetically, and radically perform 'the lack in the heart of society, that is, justice'. Behind Cortázar's novella are the events of September 1973 which resulted in the overthrow of the constitutional President of Chile, Salvador Allende. Cortázar was one of a number of Latin American scholars taking part in the second meeting of the citizen's tribunal first convened by Bertrand Russell and Jean-Paul Sartre. In his search for a new language to express the challenging realities confronted by the tribunal, Cortázar, argues Guardiola-Rivera, undertook the composition of a trans-genre work that combined the languages of literature, visual art, filmography and law. Guardiola-Rivera shows that Cortázar's experimental text corresponds to the novelty of the legal and theoretical concepts that the Latin American members of the tribunal created as they reinvented its legacy for times of military intervention and multinational financial violence.

Cortázar, like other postcolonial writers, had to wrestle with a language that had been used to repress rather than express difference. While military, economic and legal power enabled the oppressor to exercise control of the body of the colonised, it was language itself that entrenched that control by writing the values of the oppressor on the soul of the oppressed. Since these values were inscribed in language, injustice began and was instituted in language: language, that is, in law and in literature, was always a site of struggle and to express new values, not only new laws but a new language was needed. Furthermore, Cortázar appreciated that power and discourse, far from being possessed entirely by the coloniser, is also ambivalent and open to appropriation: Cortázar shows how the coloniser's language can be reopened and exploited to challenge, unsettle and subvert the values it inscribes and in the process subvert its authority. Well known legal concepts, once interpreted to confer a sense of the law as linear progression, and as revealing universal truths, are reopened, as Guardiola-Riveras's account shows, to reveal the raw violence of the law. In the case of *Fantomas*, such a challenge means that the beneficiaries of 'excess profits' from colonial exploitation cannot be let off the hook; writing here moves from passive witnessing to active participation in the struggle for justice.

Before his untimely death, Patrick McAuslan was working on an overview of the relationship between crime fiction, the criminal justice system and the reality of crime in Botswana, Kenya, Nigeria and South Africa, places where he had worked for much of his life. His contribution in this collection pays particular attention to colonial and postcolonial criminal justice systems and explores whether the approach to law and legal systems in the novels he selected differs depending on whether the authors are expatriate or African, colonial or postcolonial. For empires, as his text makes clear, aim to present their narrative as not just the only but as the true one, and crime fiction is enlisted to aid the process: empires are built, as McAuslan's lifetime work showed, not only on brute force but on words and images, and it is their appropriation and domination over language and culture that secures their continuing existence, in law, as in literature.

New empires are no different: Chris Boge's chapter on Christopher Nolan's *Dark Knight* trilogy exposes the hidden ideology of Hollywood blockbusters and their complicity in perpetuating, as well as glorifying, new empires. Where would the American empire be, Boge's text implies, without Hollywood's tall tales of valiant outlaws resorting to, and celebrated for resorting to, extralegal means? Today's Hollywood, Boge shows, performs the task of solidifying and disseminating the American empire's ideology: in a marketing ploy designed to maintain

American exceptionalism and propagate an image of the US as victim of foreign aggression, Hollywood's latest wave of superhero movies, he argues, refashions and promotes the concept of vigilantism. Christopher Nolan's take on one of the earliest characters to emerge from the Golden Age of American superhero stories depicts Batman as an outlaw vigilante who becomes a national icon. The *Dark Knight* trilogy, concludes Boge, 'ultimately seeks to place the US in a dramatic progressivist narrative that tells of Western manifest destiny, and the need for democratic governance to be complemented by private policing'.

7 The crime of crime fiction

Given, as these chapters suggest, cultural texts, far from escaping, all too often strengthen and maintain society's dominant ideology, how do we account for our fascination with literature generally and crime fiction in particular? For lawyers generally, and critical lawyers in particular, we must wonder: does the study of literature aid or stultify critique? The first step to critique, I suggest, is acknowledging the enjoyment at the heart of our own writing, reading and watching. In the case of crime fiction, 'the dead body', as Žižek (1991, p. 143) reminds us, 'is the object of desire par excellence, the cause that starts the interpretive desire of the detective (and the reader): How did it happen? Who did it?'. Crime fiction, more than law and literature in general, taps into desires lying at the root of both the lawyer and the reader. It is not only the fact, as critics of crime fiction appreciate, that any murder, is 'matter out of place', a stain on the general order that needs to be swept clean. It is also that in the very process of 'cleaning' another desire is excited and, more often than not, satisfied for spectator or reader: the enjoyment of making meaning, of 'jouis-sense' as Lacan would call it.

The classical detective story, as analysed by Tzvetan Todorov (1977), consists typically of two stories: the story of the crime, involving action and often blood, followed by the story of the investigation, involving enquiry, revelation and closure. Such stories chart the progress from a community whose order and stability are temporarily disrupted by a crime that breaks the rules, back to order and stability once the criminal has been identified and his/her crime explained by a suitable motive. In the first story, the inability of society's official agents to prevent or solve the crime threatens the validity of that order. An unsolved crime is an uninterpreted sign, resisting integration into society's system of meanings: its obstinate departure from approved rules threatens to discredit the validity of the system and therefore cannot be ignored. In the second story the first story is reconstructed and the aberrant event is integrated into society: the disrupted social order is restored and existing social norms validated.

Humanity's preferred way of defusing and integrating the aberrant event is through narrative: telling and retelling a story helps generate coherence and meaning. The assumption of the detective genre is that not only is there such a true meaning but that the detective can deliver it and narrate it in a form that transmits that coherence to the awaiting audience. The assumption that polyvalent signs are capable of being deciphered and explained into one true meaning is shared not only by the detective genre but by the legal system. Law also cannot tolerate indeterminacy, gaps or contradictions when faced with an act that challenges its supremacy. Since murder is 'dirt', 'matter out of place', the law and the detective-hero seek to clean up the mess of the murder and reduce aberrant signs into one true meaning.

Like the detective story, the law assumes that this meaning can be delivered through narrative: law puts its trust in language as the instrument through which polyvalent signs can be reduced to a single truth and deliver both justice and closure. Reason and language are expected to explain and dissolve mysteries, delivering the reassuring message that order and meaning will prevail over chaos and disorder. In the best examples of the genre the reader experiences the pleasure of believing she participated in solving the mystery, that the credit for cracking it is owed as much to her as to the writer. Classical detective fiction therefore not only reaffirms cultural norms and assuages the audience's anxieties, but it also affords a surplus enjoyment in the process of making meaning.

Importantly, more often than not in the classical detective story, the crime is not any indeterminate crime but one that meddles with property and inheritance laws: in that sense the crime is a direct threat to the privileges of the propertied classes. By uncovering the criminal, the private detective confirms not only the value of individualism but the class system's ability to preserve itself: the anxieties of bourgeois readers are appeased, property relations are reinstated and illegal acquisition of property is punished. Above all, the genre celebrates individualism reflected in the protagonist-sleuth: the detective of the golden era insists human reason can unlock mysteries and uncover patterns where previously there were disparate data. Like the positivist project in law, the ideological function of detective stories promotes a belief in the triumph of mind over matter, and of law over chaos; readers can rest assured that however chaotic the events, reason will prevail, guilty parties will be punished and order (especially class order) will be re-established.

It is the celebration of this human arrogance, and our enjoyment of this celebration, that we must interrogate: enjoyment is never free, and, if we are enjoying here, we are probably paying the price elsewhere. Detective fiction, we mustn't forget, came into its own as a distinct as well as popular genre at the same time as a certain doctor in Vienna was developing a practice called the talking cure. Freud often likened the work of an analyst to that of a detective looking to uncover the causes of the crime. For Freud, Oedipus's story charts not only the development of the human psyche but also the method for uncovering the roots of that psyche's malaises: Oedipus was the first detective looking for the murderer and the ultimate detective story, the one where the detective turns out to be the criminal. In the case of a detective story, the evidence usually comes in the form of a dead body; in the case of analysis, the evidence is also in the patient's body, or more accurately, in the patient's speech. While the detective has to excavate from death back into life, with the analyst the work of excavation also starts with the body except that the body the analyst is working with is alive; alive, but too often, very sick.

8 The hangover

However enjoyable the party, the morning after has to be negotiated, for hosts who must clean up as well as guests nursing a hangover. In contrast to the celebration of the super-detective of classical detective fiction, in contemporary crime fiction addressed in this collection, there is both an acknowledgement and a critique of the founding violence within the law itself and the corruption at the heart of the system. Further, the detective as super-reasoner uncovering order and meaning is undermined if not denied: often fragments of events don't necessarily add up to a coherent story. In Janet McCabe's analysis of Henning Mankell's *Wallander* series, we see that fragments accumulate but the author is aware (and shares with the reader) that other solutions are possible: far from dissipating the mystery, the anti-detective novelist maintains it. If the arch-detective eliminated the temporary disruption of an ordered universe, the anti-detective abandons its desperate victims to live with it: participants as much as spectators are often left with more mystery, and more misery, and more broken human stories, dead or alive.

The violence at the institution of the legal system and the corruption at the heart of the law means no critical project is possible without interrogating the blurred boundary between law and lawlessness, between legal and illegal. Fiona Macmillan and Chris Boge's chapter in this collection analyses John Hillcoat's adaptation of Matt Bondurant's Prohibition era novel, *The Wettest County in the World*, into the film *Lawless*. As Hillcoat relates, the film depicts

> the next generation of country outlaws – the men and women who gave birth to the big-time urban mobsters like Capone by supplying the Prohibition cities with their illegal liquor . . . [It is] the story of the little guys out back, the foot soldiers and the worker bees who propped up the urban criminal empire.

For Macmillan and Boge, the film's central thesis of lawlessness is based upon the endemic corruption in law enforcement and the general disregard for the law as promulgated by the government and (not) enforced by its agents. The chapter considers whether, in relation to the concept of lawlessness, a meaningful distinction can be drawn between being without law and being in a state of non-compliance with the law.

In the cold light of the morning after, we must also pause and wonder why interdisciplinary studies generally, and law and literature in particular, encountered such little resistance in legal education to the extent that today it not only forms part of mainstream curricula but is enlisted to prove so-called diversity and plurality in legal studies. In the meantime, law's machine, in and out of the academy, in and out of courts and parliaments, and its enforcement at local and global levels, continues unhindered and relentless. My view is that law and literature studies have anything but threatened the legal academy or its investment in the legal profession. If anything, the existence of law and literature courses satiates a desire for exoticism and difference, without fundamentally challenging the tenets of the academy, let alone the profession itself. If literature is in danger of becoming law's alibi, the means by which we can avoid doing justice in and by law, where does a good detective go from here? Does focusing on crime fiction bolster or undermine some of the comfortable ideas that law and literature, initially subversive and challenging, slowly smoothed and domesticated into the legal academy?

Patricia Tuitt's contribution takes us back to the project of critique and interrogates the critic's naive confidence that declaring that there is no such thing as a right answer would deliver effective critique of legal discourse: her provocative contention is that 'the principle that there are no right answers to legal questions undermines and discourages critical thinking'. Tuitt enlists the services of none other than arch-detective Poirot to prove her thesis that critique of law must begin with the conviction that 'the thinking party can (indeed must) determine the moment of closure'. Critics wavering in this faith, Tuitt argues, risk undermining rather than supporting the fragile legal rights of the poor and the dispossessed. It is Tuitt's attention to the changing political and social environment of legal services that makes her call for a different philosophical approach to the 'no right answer' thesis both ethical and urgent.

9 The morning after

Adding and subtracting the joys, humiliations and dangers of law and crime fiction, the modest premise of this collection is that although law and literature serve different functions they are both products and parts of the same social, historical and cultural forces. At most, and this is its modest claim, literature is often quicker and more likely than law to challenge and question those forces. Cultural texts, though unable to escape the dominant ideology, and though part and parcel of the same society that produces laws, are also quicker at challenging that ideology. This is partly because the aesthetic in general is discredited in a capitalist economy with its emphasis on utilitarian calculations and benefits: because they are perceived as being relatively useless, as play rather than work, cultural texts enjoy greater freedom to take risks.

This hope is not without its dangers: one consequence of investing in literature the hope of critiquing law, is the treatment of literature as the fantasy object that will fulfil law. The danger is that we construe literature as the fantasy object which eludes law and which is capable of completing it. Literature becomes the place where law's lack is projected and conversely as the object that can remedy that lack: literature as law's fantasy object guards against law's own uncertainty and incompleteness. This means that the difficulties inherent in law are displaced onto literature. Indeed, culture, art, beauty can mask, repress and domesticate rather than reveal, expose and confront law's limitations. At worst, fictional representations of law appease and make palatable our anxieties about law so we are less, rather than more, likely to challenge and critique our existing rules and systems. Patricia Tuitt takes up the crucial issue of critique in her chapter, excavates the possible contributions crime fiction can bring to existing legal studies and, like a good detective, delivers if not the right answer to the 'no right answer' thesis, certainly a different answer with an unexpected final twist.

In the cold light of morning my suggestion is that we need to tone down our enthusiasm for inter-disciplinarity, and in particular stop using it as an excuse to avoid addressing problems in our own discipline. Treating literature as the fantasy object that will complete law also absolves us of the task of addressing law's own limitations. We should be cautious of the fact that one of the reasons such unions were proposed in the first place was that law saw in literature what was lacking in law, while literature saw in law what was lacking in literature. Unions that treat the other as the fantasy object that will complete the self are destined for disaster for both the lover and the beloved. The plea also involves abandoning the temptation to find in other disciplines (be they literature, religion, economics) what is missing in law. Too often such projects, rather than fundamentally interrogating and challenging legal discourse, unwittingly bolster its foundations by finding, in other disciplines, what is missing in law. Like a lover fantasising that her beloved has that little indefinable quality that is missing in herself and will complete her, the disappointed lawyer imagines she will find in another discipline what is missing in law. But by extolling another discipline's virtues and expecting it to make up for the lack in law, the lawyer does not only 'mutilate' the other discipline, she also exonerates herself from doing anything about the problems in law. My suggestion is that we must de-sublimate both literature and law, acknowledging the lack not only in law but also in literature.

10 Enjoyment within the limits of crime fiction

Borges was not alone in drawing attention to the twin desires for law and crime: 'Death', Dorothy Sayers (1937, p. 11) pointed out, provided 'the minds of the Anglo-Saxon race with a greater fund of innocent enjoyment than any other single subject.' Enjoyment of course is never innocent, whether in literature, or, as in our case, when it is harnessed and invested in legal circles. And as this collection makes clear, it is not only Anglo-Saxons who partake of this illicit enjoyment. Anton Schütz hones in mercilessly on this enjoyment, and compels us to confess our guilt: 'crime fiction humiliates its reader by making her confess her guilty enjoyment', he warns. Nor is this any guilty enjoyment but an enjoyment profoundly invested in radical evil: a death that is an accident, Schütz reminds us, is of no interest to writers or readers of crime fiction – the death has to have been caused by pure, premeditated and cold-blooded agency. Crime fiction therefore diverts from law's normal promise to keep making promises: the irreversibility of the deed means the genre is mired in 'impossibilism'; it is hard-boiled as the deed cannot be undone any more than an egg, once cooked, can be uncooked. This irreversibility, as Schütz calls it, is, I suggest, another name for the crossing of boundaries between the symbolic and the real, a crossing that, once done, affords no prospect of return. The temptation for crossing is the temptation, as Freud would say, of going beyond the pleasure principle: an enjoyment that we think we want and strive after, but run away from when we encounter. Crime fiction, I suggest, enables us to enjoy beyond the pleasure principle, safe in the knowledge that the symbolic law is always there to catch us when we finish watching, reading and, of course, enjoying the gruesome murders and their investigation.

No wonder, as this introduction has tried to show, these twin desires are, far from incompatible, found side by side. How far beyond the pleasure principle can the subject go without provoking the wrath of the symbolic (with its bad enough consequences in the form of penal sentences) but nowhere near as bad as the hell that would break loose were we at the mercy of a jouissance uncontained by the pleasure principle? For the pleasure principle, paradoxically, and contrary to popular myth, is on the side of the law: we can and should have pleasure, but only within the confines of the law; that is, some pleasure, but not too much. Crime fiction and the law studies therefore achieve the conciliation of two far from contradictory, as Borges suggested, desires, but, as Lacan knew, aspects of the same desire: we get to enjoy, a little, but, god forbid, not too much. Proving, as my title claimed, that the introduction, although complicit in and partaking of this enjoyment, by staying on the side of the pleasure principle, must be declared innocent.

References

Aristodemou, M. (2000) *Law and literature: journeys from her to eternity*. Oxford; New York: Oxford University Press.

Borges, J.L. (1999) *Selected non-fictions*. Weinberger, E. (ed.), translated by E. Allen, S.J. Levine and E. Weinberger. New York: Penguin.

Hutchinson, A.C. (1989) 'That's just the way it is: Langille on law', *McGill Law Journal*, 34, pp. 145–59.

Sayers, D. (1937) *Omnibus of crime*. Garden City Publishing.

Todorov, T. (1977) *The poetics of prose*. Translated by R. Howard. Oxford: Basil Blackwell.

White, H. (1978) *Tropics of discourse: essays in cultural criticism*. Baltimore: John Hopkins University.

Žižek, S. (1991) *Looking awry: an introduction to Jacques Lacan through popular culture*. Cambridge: MIT Press.

Chapter 2

Critique, crime fiction and the no right answer thesis

Patricia Tuitt

> 'and I may say that though I have now arrived at what I believe to be the true solution of the case, *I have no material proof of it*. I *know* it is so because it *must* be so, because in *no other way* can every single fact fit into its ordered and recognised place. And that, to my mind, is the most satisfying solution there can be'.
>
> (Agatha Christie 1936, p. 303)

1 Introduction

For the purposes of the argument in this chapter, crime fiction is synonymous with the detective novel. This is not because I necessarily ally myself with those that claim that the genre is the only authentic form of crime fiction but because of the genre's preoccupation with what John Scaggs (2005, p. 19) refers to as 'the analytical and rational deductive ability of a single, isolated individual'. The uses to which crime fiction can be deployed in relation to law are many and varied. Not surprisingly, it is often deployed to demonstrate the intimate relationship between law and violence – in particular the fundamental principle in 'European legislation' that refuses to sanction individual violence (Benjamin 2004, p. 280). Beyond the phenomenon of legal violence, crime fiction is used to explore questions of criminal evidence and process, and questions of moral culpability. As I hope to show, the uses of crime fiction extend well beyond the terrain of what may fall within the notion of sanctioned and unsanctioned violence/state and individual force, but can create the platform for an analysis and critique of the intellectual effort demanded of the legal mind – whether that mind is of the student, academic, lawyer or judge. Nowhere is that effort most clearly expressed than in what has come to be known as the 'no right answer thesis'. Through Agatha Christie's thinking detective, Hercule Poirot, I hope to demonstrate why and how the intellectual fabric within which judgement occurs – as espoused in the no right answer thesis – must alter.

2 Legal theory

Setting the argument in context, the study of crime fiction and the law takes place within the broader interdisciplinary field of law and literature. Founding texts, such as those authored by James Boyd White (1973), Peter Goodrich (1996),

Maria Aristodemou (2000) and Ian Ward (1999) have established law and literature as one of the (foremost) strands of contemporary legal theory. Law and literature propounds a theory of law that lays emphasis on the appearance of law in texts; of the existence of law in the written word and (by logical extension) law and literature is a theory that posits the essentially fictive nature of law. For Aristodemou (2000, p. 1):

> Both law and literature are, in the first instance, signs on a page. Both the legal and literary worlds are constructed by and depend for their definition and existence on words.

Central to the claims of law and literature is not merely that the great works of fiction often hold legal themes at their centre, nor merely that texts, however varied their origin and orientation, are accessed through similar interpretative tools; at its core, the theory of law offered by adherents to the interdisciplinary field of law and literature is that of a force whose potency rests in its capacity to produce material effects in the worlds it imagines.

In short, the principal intervention of law and literature scholarship is (toward) *the* fundamental question of jurisprudence, which is the nature of law *itself*. The law that is produced through the interrogations of law and literature is one which is wrested from a supposedly 'real' world which can be productively contrasted with a 'fictional' realm of which literature is a key instance. Yet, in common with all legal theories, law and literature has a secondary function to that of (elucidating) the nature of law itself. The secondary function is to serve as a teaching aid, engaging in the broader field of legal theory, philosophy or jurisprudence. As a movement, law and literature would undoubtedly have floundered if it had not been able to demonstrate that the study of literature could bring new perspectives on enduring questions of legal theory and philosophy – questions that have exceeded/transcended the movements and traditions of legal scholarship; questions usually posed (originally) by scholars working from perspectives far removed from the disciplinary vantage points from which law and literature scrutinises legal phenomena and the legal instance. For example, Aristodemou (2000) in her seminal work, *Law and Literature: Journeys from Her to Eternity*, is not preoccupied with the textual ordering of law per se. Rather, attention to the textual character of law offers Aristodemou a means through which to (explicate) the feminine in the construction of the social – especially as that social world is conveyed in classical history and philosophy. The literary supplement to feminist legal theory is both recent and still relatively marginal but the question of feminist affect comes prior to law and literature and will foreshadow critical fields as yet unwritten and unimagined.

Turning to the particular preoccupation of the chapters in this volume, scholarship that deploys crime fiction to the study of law carries the tropes of law and literature – specifically the hermeneutic turn in legal studies that the law and literature movement represents. At the risk of overgeneralisation, I would say that crime fiction and the law scholars do not claim to pose new questions to theory or philosophy but rather seek to enter an established field of moral and ethical questioning through a genre of fiction that attracts an ever-growing readership. In doing so, law and literature *invites* greater participation in the exchange of questions and answers to problems of legal theory and philosophy. This statement about the objectives and achievements of crime fiction and the law is not to undermine the potential of the field of study as an engine of invention. By offering different sources/tools with which to contemplate enduring questions of legal theory and philosophy, the field of reasoning is broadened and with the broadening of the field of reasoning comes also (and inevitably) a productive contamination of the original question.

3 The no right answer thesis

As regard the 'original question' on which this essay is based – the 'no right answer thesis' – there is an abundance of descriptions or definitions, and the following from Woozley is as good as any. According to Woozley (1979, p. 25) the thesis holds that:

> In law a question may arise and come up for adjudication to which no answer can be given such that it is the right answer and that any different answer would be wrong.

Put succinctly, a range of reasonable responses to legal questions may present themselves to a judge, legal practitioner, scholar or student but the 'no right answer thesis' would dispute that a choice of one answer over another – even if prompted by the conviction that one answer is more convincing than another – can be construed as a discovery of a right answer in the sense of being 'the one and only answer which the court could give' Woozley (1979, p. 25).

The question of whether right answers to legal questions can be found is a disputed one – with the majority of those involved in the debate holding to the position captured in the quotation, above. However, this chapter does not seek to engage in the dispute about the objective existence or otherwise of right answers. Rather, it interrogates a seeming consensus over the framework in which the 'no right answer thesis' is posed – the framework being the *fact* of legal indeterminacy and the extent of judicial discretion in the face of that indeterminacy. I am prepared to concede that the 'no right answer thesis' originated from the practices of the higher judiciary but what must now be conceded is that the thesis has long strayed from the anchoring framework of the courts and the question of the choices open to judges in the course of adjudicating on 'hard cases'. Central to the argument in this chapter is the claim that the thesis has matured into a way of thinking whenever the question of judgement arises; and judgement is not confined to the courts and other arenas of practice, but permeates the classroom in which aspiring legal professionals are taught and in the wider academy in which jurisprudential questions are posed. The 'no right answer thesis' captures in shorthand a way of thinking that crosses the different strands and levels of the legal apparatus. It is the way of thinking that the 'no right answer thesis' inaugurates that is interrogated in this chapter. The core argument of the chapter is that the thesis signals a way of thinking that *is* being transcended and that *must* be transcended as the legal services market transforms and demands a different philosophical approach to questions of law from those whose intellectual labour underpins the legal services market. It is a way of thinking that is contrasted in this paper with a mode of thinking that I argue is *necessary* to address contemporary legal challenges – especially the challenges of the increasingly fragile legal rights of the poor and dispossessed. The 'no right answer thesis' signals a way of thinking which must and will give way to what, in shorthand, we can call 'legal critique'. To critique the law is to adopt a particular mode of interrogation. It is to engage in what has been very well described as 'a kind of thinking that never finds itself at the end' (Lawlor 2014).

4 Crime fiction and legal critique

What can crime fiction possibly have to say about the necessary modes of thinking in the contemporary legal services market? How can crime fiction be brought to bear upon the 'no right answer thesis'? We can begin to answer these questions only once we accept that crime fiction in all its chronologies and categories (e.g. Scaggs 2005, pp. 7–32) offers to readers rich and varied ways of thinking through the *matter* of law, and by *matter* I mean more than the material physical evidence so integral to the early detective fiction and the police procedure novel. It is the humans caught up in often violent and tragic events who form the primary matter upon which the question of judgement about hard cases is made – in all arenas in which legal actors are required to contemplate 'real' or 'moot' points of law.

In its various expositions upon the matter of law, the work of crime fiction can hold the ingredients of legal critique. The protagonist of this chapter (the critical thinker) is none other than Agatha Christie's famous detective, Hercule Poirot. The quotation with which this chapter opens – taken from the 1936 novel *Murder in Mesopotamia* – exemplifies Poirot's ways of thinking in and against an indeterminate/contingent world. As I hope to show, Poirot (and all critical legal thinkers) must eschew the 'no right answer thesis' but (notwithstanding the coincidence of names) Poirot's way of thinking is unlike Dworkin's (1977) 'ideal' all-knowing and all-seeing judge Hercules.

Although legal education has long since exceeded the purely technical induction into rules and procedures as a result of the gradual emergence of law as an academic discipline, the practice of the courts – especially the practice of the higher appeal courts – has until recently wielded enormous influence over the measures against which law students' intellectual attainments are judged (see e.g. Bartie 2010). No more persuasive example of this claim can be found than in the 'no right answer thesis' which, whilst originating from an acceptance of the contingent nature of law and the consequent challenge to decision makers, has hardened into a core tenet of legal reasoning and analysis in the university law school. Indeed, from the first year of study – almost from first entry into the classroom – every law student will have had drilled into their consciousness the proposition that there are no right answers to legal questions. The belief that in any given instance more than one equally persuasive answer can be given in response to a legal question is (or has been) fundamental to the working life of the law: to how law is taught, how law is practised and how law is analysed and theorised in the vast body of scholarly works spanning the fields of jurisprudence, evidence, process and legal method – to name but a few legal categories. And whilst this chapter anticipates the demise as an (intellectual pre-condition almost) of the 'no right answer thesis' it does not seek to do so by taking issue with the proposition that law is inherently indeterminate. Rather, the chapter suggests that as law and legal systems and services become more networked and complex, the effectiveness of legal professionals in response to the complexities that the law's inherent indeterminacy brings is negatively influenced by adherence to the 'no right answer thesis' – which, contrary to what might be supposed – is a thesis that contends with indeterminacy by *refusing* to acknowledge that legal indeterminacy should be met with a more rigorous form of thinking than the 'no right answer thesis' will ever permit. For the avoidance of early confusion, the intellectual rigour that the thesis denies cannot be achieved by seeking to *discover* right answers – there is thus no succour be found in Dworkin's alternative to the 'no right answer thesis' and this chapter should not then be read as an attempt to engage and revive the marginal side of the jurisprudential debate as it is conventionally framed.

If not by rejecting the search for right answers, nor by engaging in a determined search for the right answer, what should be the lawyer's response to legal indeterminacy? And is the question of the nature of the response contingent on questions that arrive prior to the question of decision or judgment that awaits an answer – whether that answer is seen as the right answer or simply one of a range of potentially appropriate answers? These two questions already point to a reframing of the jurisprudential debate on the 'no right answer thesis' as one not predominantly about the inherent opacity of legal rules but one that is fundamentally about legal *culture* and the *objectives* of legal action. For let it be understood that thought is *the* primary mode of action within a given framework of legal services. As much as it may seem to be a reaction to characteristics inherent to all legal rules and principles – which cannot be other than fluid, the 'no right answer thesis' reveals more about the objectives of the legal services market and the broader legal culture within which it is enunciated than it reveals of the consequences of indeterminate rules and principles – even less does it serve as an adequate weapon against the contingencies inherent in all of law. As regards legal culture, only as long as law and the legal system is conceived of as '[a]n entomology of rules, a guide book to technocratic legalism, a science of what – legally – exists . . . vocational skills training' (Douzinas and Gearey 2005, p. 4) can the 'no right answer thesis' survive as a way of thinking. Only with an approach to legal studies that is 'situated' within the 'judge's reasoning process' (Bartie 2010, pp. 347–9) can the central question of concern in the more prominent of jurisprudential enquiries into the question of the determinate nature of answers to legal questions remain intact. The core task set by commentators on this question has been to affirm or dispute the proposition *itself* – that is, to support or reject the idea that the indeterminate nature of language from which legal rules result and against which legal cases are adjudicated means that there are no right answers to the legal questions posed in relation to these rules and legal disputes.

Notable among the legal scholars engaged in this debate, Ronald Dworkin (1986), Richard Posner (1990) and Matthew Kramer (2007) are prominent protagonists and provide the background against which I will eventually introduce the intellectual activity of Agatha Christie's private detective as presenting not just an alternative way of thinking but an alternative way of thinking that must resituate the debate about right answers to legal questions – even if the thesis survives. For the present, however, Richard Posner and Ronald Dworkin provide essentially the arguments for and against the 'no right answer thesis', respectively. Matthew Kramer (an adherent to the 'no right answer thesis') is of interest here not because he offers different substantive arguments than those to be found in Posner but because his particular way of expressing the thesis demonstrates to me more effectively than does Posner why the thesis more or less adequately served the 'old' legal services market, but is potentially problematic for the legal critique which I argue must be the foundation on which the 'new' legal services market will mature.

This positivist view is disputed by Dworkin who has revisited the question in a number of works. For example, in *Taking Rights Seriously* (Dworkin 1977, p. 54), he argues 'the occasions on which a legal question has no right answer in our own legal system must be much rarer than is generally supposed', and further 'for all practical purposes, there will always be a right answer in the seamless web of our law' (Dworkin 1977, p. 84).

So, against the weight of general opinion, Dworkin has sought to argue that right answers *do* exist to legal questions but what we lack is knowledge of facts or law sufficient to determine what the right answer to a legal question is. Dworkin pursues his argument by positing an 'ideal' judge (Hercules, J.) whose knowledge of law and fidelity to demands of due process would always ensure that he arrives at the right answer – though the process may involve discovery of rules and principles that addresses conflicts between other incommensurable rules and principles. Comparisons between Dworkin's fictional judge and Christie's fictional detective (both named after the hero of classical mythology) is one that I will determinedly resist. The significant divergence resides in the fact that Christie's Hercule (as the opening quotation shows) sets a standard of certainty or conviction in place of the (classic) conception of 'right' or 'truth' on which Dworkin's ideal judge must insist.

In an essay directly in response to Dworkin's analysis, Richard Posner dismisses Dworkin's claims, arguing that Dworkin merely offers the commonsense defence that the material against which one might be able to offer a definitive answer to a legal question may not be accessible. For Posner (1990, p. 198) this defence simply provides evidence in support of the 'no right answer thesis'. Surely, he says, an answer that is '"inaccessible" . . . is as if there were no right answer, or as if . . . the question were meaningless'.

Such debates often ascend to the level of metaphysics without addressing what I believe to be a question of at least equal importance as that concerning the objective existence of a determinate answer to a legal question, and that question concerns the intensity of the intellectual effort that can be legitimately demanded of students, practitioners and scholars in the face of the thesis – a thesis which is a reaction (but not, I suggest, an inevitable one) to law's admittedly indeterminate nature. To foreshadow what follows, the intellectual effort now demanded of professionals in the new legal services market is encapsulated in the notion of *legal critique* and, as I hope to demonstrate, the 'no right answer thesis' is *inimical* to critique.

5 Legal critique

The question of what constitutes legal critique is one about which I cannot hope to do justice here, since it is itself an involved and disputed question of legal scholarship and legal culture. The answer offered here is one that (for reasons that I hope will become apparent) focuses on the concrete appearance of critique in the form of two dominant scholarly movements in the legal academy – socio-legal studies and critical legal theory – and even this approach cannot fully capture the various guises and manifestations of the concerns which these two movements support.

These two movements expressly reject the judge's frame of reasoning as the only legitimate basis on which the other inhabitants of the legal profession can reason. Both take cognisance of a range of methodological frameworks, disciplinary influences and contexts and empirical, sociological, anthropological and scientific methodologies. Feminist, race and postcolonial political and cultural frames – all these and others – have combined to bring about a very different understanding of what is understood by legal indeterminacy than captured in the idea of legal rules and principles that, though sufficient in themselves, can never be fully comprehended and comprehensible. If law is endlessly entwined in literature, politics, and philosophy – if law is always suffused in its context – the question of indeterminacy *itself* far exceeds the concerns of those engrossed in the analysis of the 'no right answer thesis'. Indeed, the question of right answers to legal questions becomes meaningless, since law's contexts make the search for right answers among the various literatures and other 'jurisprudences' (Goodrich 1996) beyond even Dworkin's ideal judge.

6 Legal thinking in/against the new legal services market

To summarise the foregoing, the 'no right answer thesis' authorises a form of thinking that is resolutely situated within the judges' reasoning processes. Critical legal scholars would argue that such an approach was always a deficient one, since law must stray beyond the confines of the concerns that confront the judge. I do not intend here to elaborate on the argument from socio-legal and critical legal studies about the inherent limitations of a 'traditional' legal education. What I argue is that if the approach was ever adequate for legal practice – including legal adjudication – it has ceased to be so and the critical project that began in the universities in the late 1970s is a critical project that the new legal services market now demands. It will come as no surprise to readers to learn that I suggest that it is a critical project that could usefully begin from a *critical* interrogation of the 'no right answer thesis'.

Richard Susskind's (2013) recent monograph on the legal profession propounds that the complex nature of contemporary legal problems has long since demanded lawyers with skills beyond the technical competences that allow them to engage successfully in the conventional legal activity of advice, representation and litigation services. Particularly in the field of social welfare in relation to which citizens reliant on public services have been the subject of swingeing cuts, the possibility of accessing conventional legal assistance is limited and interventions in the form of community legal education and other modes of legal advice increasingly shape the legal services market and its emerging practitioners. University law schools have been drivers of change but have had to respond to external challenges and changes to the legal services market. An important feature of these changes has been the reorientation of legal education in the direction of law in contexts, socio-legal studies and critical legal studies. These changes have brought insight from other disciplines into the frame of legal reasoning – including the literatures underpinning this essay. Inevitably, this form of interdisciplinarity has altered the criteria against which the intellectual strengths and attainments of aspiring practitioners are judged.

More striking is the response to these challenges beyond the legal academy. In 2007, the Legal Services Act (which came into force in 2011) effectively confirmed as appropriate for the twenty-first century legal market the intellectual shift seen in the academy. The 2007 Act inaugurated a legal services market that no longer privileges advice and litigation as the primary activity of working and aspiring professionals. The Act gives an at least equal role to what we might call critical interventions into what Hazel Genn (1999, chap. 4) aptly describes as the 'landscape of justiciable problems'. Practitioners in the new legal services market are by virtue of section 1 required to: 'Protect and promote . . . the public interest', 'to support . . . the constitutional principle of the rule of law', to 'improve' access to justice, to encourage 'an independent, strong, diverse and effective legal profession and to increase public understanding of the citizen's legal rights and duties', among other things.

The present concerns are different. Through the character of Hercule Poirot, Agatha Christie occasionally offers an intimation of the kind of intellectual effort that sits well with 'thinking that does not find itself at the end'. As will become apparent from the quotation from *Murder in Mesopotamia* that commenced this chapter, such thinking must always begin from the conviction that the thinking party can (indeed, must) determine the moment of closure: 'I know it is so because it must be so' (Christie 1936, p. 303).

In this quotation from *Murder in Mesopotamia*, Agatha Christie's Poirot responds to indeterminacy by fashioning for *himself* a form of closure and in doing so refuses to seek the comfort and reassurance contained in the belief that 'every answer is correct in the sense of not being incorrect'. And, as you would have gathered by now, I think such reassurance is inimical to critique. Speaking of a particular form of closure considered typical to golden age fiction – the closed setting – Stephen Knight (2004) acknowledges that 'the enclosure itself carries deep personal threats' (p. 9), a threat that arguably the 'no right answer thesis' removes. Critique is always (to borrow a term from Fitzpatrick) the '*dangerous* supplement' (Fitzpatrick *et al.* 1991). Yet, Poirot is not a simple positivist, for his form of closure is of a kind that entirely transcends what Posner *et al.* could conceive of as a right answer – even if they were to accept any serious assault on the 'no right answer thesis'. For Christie's Poirot, answers are right answers in perhaps the most absolute sense in which the notion of right can be understood: for his answers are understood by him as determinate when they simply fall into place.

The following from *Murder in Mesopotamia* are familiar ways in which, in virtually all the novels in which Poirot appears, Christie (1936, p. 337) describes when, for Poirot, the 'true solution of a case' is found: 'everything falls into place, everything psychologically perfect, but there is no proof'. And again, 'the letter, the roof, the window . . . yes, everything was explained, everything fell into place'. Is there any greater commitment to thought than that offered by someone who refuses to stop thinking until everything within the frame of the question is not only explained, but explained in relation and sequence to other things?

In *The Murder of Roger Ackroyd* (1926), which is considered to be one of the best of the Poirot novels, we see further examples of this intellectual effort. The novel is noteworthy for the many seemingly irrelevant details that Poirot is determined to explain – to fit into its ordered and recognised place – even when he could offer a plausible answer, plausibility being at once both the minimum and maximum standard of intellectual engagement required when so many possible answers are 'correct because . . . not incorrect'.

Critique does not seek to inaugurate a kind of thinking that cannot decide, for no expression of critical thought evades the necessity of decision making. In the Christie novel, the emphasis on place or placing as descriptive of Poirot's thought processes is instructive – especially so when we take note of the equivocal or ambiguous boundaries that the notion of 'place' carries. In the idea of a true solution being a matter of the careful placing of facts, the author conveys a sense of a form of thinking that is decisive but never absolutely fixed or exhausted – the form of thinking that does not find itself at the end.

Whether Poirot is a critical thinker and, if so, whether his ways of thinking could be introduced as useful supplements to analysis of the particular element of legal method known as legal reasoning, are the questions on which the reader must eventually decide. For now, I challenge him or her to find a better expression of the work that a true critique can achieve than is to be found in the words of nurse Amy Letheram, the storyteller in *Murder in Mesopotamia*, who opened Poirot's *denouement* in the following terms (Christie 1936, p. 303): 'and somehow I felt that when M. Poirot had finished we'd all be somewhere quite different'.

References

Aristodemou, M. (2000) *Law and literature: journeys from her to eternity*. Oxford; New York: Oxford University Press.

Bartie, B. (2010) 'The lingering core of legal scholarship', *Legal Studies*, 30(3), pp. 345–69.

Benjamin, W. (2004) 'Critique of violence', translated by E. Jephcott, in Bullock M. and Jennings, N. (eds.) *Walter Benjamin: selected writings, volume 1: 1913–1926*. Cambridge: Harvard University Press, 2004, pp. 236–52. (Original published in 1921)

Christie, A. (1926) *The murder of Roger Ackroyd*. London: Collins.

Christie, A. (1936) *Murder in Mesopotamia*. London: Collins.

Douzinas, C. and Gearey, A. (2005) *Critical jurisprudence: the political philosophy of justice*. Oxford: Hart Publishing.

Dworkin, R. (1977) *Taking rights seriously*. Cambridge: Harvard University Press.

Dworkin, R. (1986) *A matter of principle*. Oxford: Clarendon Press.

Fitzpatrick, P., Carty, A., Goodrich, P., Hachamovitch, Y. and Hunt, A. (eds.) (1991) *Dangerous supplements: resistance and renewal in jurisprudence*. London: Pluto Press.

Genn, H. (1999) *Paths to justice: what people do and think about going to law*. Oxford: Hart Publishing.

Goodrich, P. (1996) *Law in the courts of love: literature and other minor jurisprudences*. London; New York: Routledge.

Knight, S. (2004) *Crime fiction, 1800–2000: detection, death, diversity*. London: Palgrave Macmillan.

Kramer, M. (2007) *Objectivity and the rule of law*. New York: Cambridge University Press.

Lawlor, L. (2014) 'Jacques Derrida', in *The Stanford Encyclopedia of Philosophy* (Fall 2011). Zalta, E.N. (ed.) http://plato.stanford.edu/entries/derrida (Accessed: 19 March 2014).

Legal Services Act 2007 (c. **29***)*

Posner, R.A. (1990) *The problems of jurisprudence*. Cambridge: Harvard University Press.

Scaggs, J. (2005) *Crime fiction*. Abingdon: Routledge.

Susskind, R. (2013) *Tomorrow's lawyers: an introduction to your future*. Oxford: Oxford University Press.

Ward, I. (1999) *Shakespeare and the legal imagination*. London: Butterworths.

White, J.B. (1973) *The legal imagination*. Chicago: Chicago University Press.

Woozley, A. (1979) 'No right answers', Philosophical Quarterly, 29(114), pp. 25–34.

Chapter 3

The rise of crime fiction and the fading of law's empire

Chronicle of a swap foretold

Anton Schütz

I

Crime fiction, a widely successful source of popular passion and mass recreation, and an evergreen topic of academic analysis, one of the few surviving branches of spontaneous – rather than professionalized – literacy, is the effect of a preference for the irreversible one-off event. More than any other type of deeds, crime mesmerizes, captivates, 'thrills'. This is so courtesy of a specific quality of its subject matter: the quality of being beyond repair, the impossibility of undoing the deed. The culture of crime fiction is the use of crime as a theme that allows us to touch this impossibility (= the 'real', in Lacan's (2008) fanciful, yet – moderately – enlightening terminology). The enabling condition to which the crime fiction genre can be traced, the generative principle of the literary dispositive, the 'fact of pure crime fiction reason' (Immanuel Kant shakes his head), is in the fact that it is *now too late*, that nothing can be done to put that which has happened once again back in the state before, that there is no power left that would enable one to re-naturalize the de-naturalized, no way to re-enter the paradise after the expulsion. The inadmissible but undeniable upshot is the enjoyment of one's being expelled. Crime fiction humiliates its reader by way of making her confess her guilty enjoyment.

Its vitality is, however, predicated on its own aerial, uninstitutionable mode of being. Justice plays a role – but he who alone helps it to happen, the personal investigator, does so at his own expense, without any help, not unlike a Jesus Christ persecuted by all, except a vague bunch of pupils not of this world (the readers, mainly). Underlying this is a view of creation and human life and society portrayed not as a set of indifferent surrounding circumstances in the classics Poe, Conan Doyle, Chesterton, but rather as a set of barely commendable pseudo-gifts in the more gnostic than neo-testamentary world view that underlies the hard-boiled detective prose. Impossible to believe that the world in which Dashiell Hammett's novels unfold could have been intentionally created by a generous or caring God, and not by either a pervert adventurer or an experimenting nerd, omnipotent but indifferent. There is the figure of the sleuth, more angelic than divine, and more christic than Christian. He gives himself away, in order to/by means of (the two are difficult to distinguish) finding out what has happened in a particular case. Beyond that, he has nothing to offer – and strictly nothing to 'all'.

The cultural singularity of modern crime fiction, the reason of its greater vitality than that of entire sections of the academically instituted genres of 'knowledge', its unmatched authenticity in comparison with philosophy or 'critique' (let alone law or politics), is that the Private Investigator, while sparing himself nothing until the case at hand has yielded to him its never-admitted dirty secret, remains faithful to his powerless innocence. The narrow, selective beam of light he has succeeded in throwing upon the case at hand, by putting himself at risk, is all; the punctual enlightenment has no general application, gives no rise to any Good News. There is, in the crime fiction universe, no worthy programme or valuable suggestions, no dreams of changing the world, no soft liberal arrangement, no (even less) arid revolutionary calling, no promise that 'yes we can' of any sort. 'Hard-boiled' means just that. (Obviously, on the other hand, the drudgery, the misery, the peril that the detective has to put up with, contribute an equally decisive distance from other, especially socially privileged groups of non-offerers of Good News, such as, for instance, Orson Welles's *Citizen Kane*.) For a reader of earlier twentieth century continental philosophers, the term 'hard-boiled' irresistibly calls up the postcard in which Franz Rosenzweig, then aged 35, having already communicated to his mother that he had been diagnosed with a degenerative muscular disease (amyotrophic lateral sclerosis) that would increasingly paralyse him throughout his remaining years, replied to her first reaction to this news – that there was still hope left, that the doctors were making steady progress etc. – in writing, dear mum, my disease cannot be reversed, any more than an egg, once cooked, can be uncooked. The hard-boiled metaphor is a metaphor of irreversibility.

II

In social life, private and professional, it is indispensable to know how to use a basic stock of social techniques enabling the individual to forge sympathies and get along with his social surrounding. The fact of being no harbinger of Good News, and of having absolutely nothing to promise to 'all', is a serious stricture in this regard for the private investigator – whose spell on the reader is counterbalanced by the lack of sympathy he has to endure in his in-fiction surrounding (where, typically, the sleuth is sympathetic, at best, to one person). It is probable that, with his lack of 'positive beliefs', if not of 'motivation', the hard-boiled PI would do poorly in a job interview, say, to join a law school as a teacher. At the same time, the resemblance with the narrative of Christ's Passion, already mentioned, amounts to a constant and indispensable, yet constantly, and in a sense constitutively, overlooked and sidelined condition of intelligibility of the genre, founding its unmistakable attachment to the Western-Christian dispensation in its modernist-universalist phase of trans-religious self-founding and religious 'nondescriptness', or latency.

In order to locate its site on the Western-Christian, Western-Postchristian map, we must make a further step, now into law, raising the point of a certain missed encounter between the crime fiction approach, and law's own long-standing approach to its dividedness in the twin spheres of private and criminal. On the law side, it should be noted that what might be understood as the *promise* of the legal order consists in the commitment of granting efficient remedies against unlawful conduct. Yet, as it has been hinted at by many observers, enacting a gamut of very diverse vantage points (and which include the Walter Benjamin (2004) of the *Critique of Violence* of 1921 and the Niklas Luhmann (2004) of *Law as a Social System* of 1993), law as an institution, forced to stand the unending ordeal of its sustainability, is primarily confronted with the need to preserve its ability to keep on promising: to provide, by means of ever new instalments and moratoriums, for the uninterrupted flow of serial promises relating to further promises, of never stopping to promise. In order for this routine to continue, law subscribes, as to the ultimate content of its promises, to the idea of *in integrum restitutio*. The term *restitution* looms large, for instance, in the symbol-founding theory of private law of one of the few significant late twentieth century expounders of the law, Peter Birks (1988). Decisively, what interests the private lawyer, is an art of the possible – the restitution of that which can be restituted. What private law can successfully impose, is – at least in the large majority of cases – the restitution of something in the place of something else, the restitution of a *quidproquo*, money (with money *counted* as a restitution, everything can be restituted). Still, this restitution is obviously not a restitution of (or 'in', as the Latin formula has) the 'whole' (*integrum*). Its promise is unlimited – its possibilities are limited.

One of the factors separating the realm of crime fiction from the province of jurisprudence is that, while on a level, it includes the private law horizon of restitution, this ultimately fails to define its ultimate exposure. The architecture of the literary real of the murder mystery is the fact that it is constituted by the impossibility of retrieving the irretrievable. Law is subject to the fact of being an art, at least a production site, of the possible. Statutes, contracts, judgments are literary forms of the possible, of 'non-fiction' as it is often, and rather misleadingly, called. From crime fiction we expect more and less at once, more in the way of experience (with the impossible), less in the way of satisfaction (by the possible). In referring to these matters, and in borrowing the terminological distinction of Austin's (1995) *Province of Jurisprudence* the crime fiction approach can be said to operate with '*restitutio in integrum* properly so-called', posing the return to the state of things before the crime – which is *always* (at least in all murder cases) *impossible*. The private law approach to restitution, on the other hand, appears as predicated upon an *always possible* '*restitutio in integrum* improperly so-called' – improperly, because involving a *quidproquo*, which, rigorously speaking, defeats the purpose of restitution, as epitomized in the prefix 're-' – considering that there is no return; instead, something else is only *counted* as being a restitution. This diminution does not, however, prevent the law from forming a legal 'order', even a legal 'system', two forms which, most resolutely, summarize an exclusive focus on the law's positive contributions – its 'potential'.

If crime fiction is in its essence sparked off from the impossible task of restitution, it is not original to suggest that the factor that produces the craving for the suspended solution, and thus underlies the addiction which makes, to its subjects, a piece of fiction worth reading, is precisely this inherent 'impossibilism'. The sweet slavery to which the crime fiction reader typically gives in, the shadowy site of the encounter between crime fiction reader and crime fiction writer, the enjoyment predicated upon the lastingly intact virginity of the un-'spoilt' enigma, the resulting resistance against knowledge and the celebration of ignorance, each of these presents a separate piece of evidence in favour of a clear-cut case of an addictive relationship. Here, the merest appearance of knowledge breaks the desired spell, threatening to destroy the reader's precious motivation. It could make sense, however, to extend the question from modern crime fiction to fiction at large – and to the grounds of its distinction from non-fiction. 'Undeniably, that which has happened up to now' affects, in the name of its irreversible given-ness, every page of every novel, while nothing of the sort can be asserted in relation not only to law, but to non-fictional, non-addictive genres generally, such as, pell-mell, philosophical treatises, scientific monographes and textbooks, legal pleadings and judgments, but also diverse sorts of political speeches, poems, letters, even prayers.

More specific to the case of crime fiction in relation to other types of fiction writing or, more exactly, reading, is the amount of 'suspension of disbelief' that is required from the generous reader. It falls close to its lower limit, to the minimum commitment necessary to cover the fact that a crime, most especially the uniquely original constellation in the area of being and time that knots together intention, intervention, and irreversibility, and that we call a murder – has effectively taken place. This, however, is sufficient; apart from this, no further strings are attached, or instalments of suspended disbelief, required. Except one of course, which will occupy us on most of the remaining pages, because of its wide-ranging ramifications and kinships within the underworldly *arché* of Western-Postchristian literacy: that the happening that has caused the irretrievable loss is located in a deed, and more precisely, a deed that executes an intention or, ultimately, a will.

The will question touches the distinctive fictionality of the fiction element in 'crime fiction'. In the supposed non-fiction of what is called real life, the roots even of decisive, dramatic outcomes often enough turn out to have been accidents effectively. Rather than a wilful deed, what has happened has been the collateral consequence of some other happening, and so on – notwithstanding of course the application of the usual nuances, the usual gradation-casuistry in-between the two poles, which the legal cutlery has the duty of fine-cutting. Life is now closer to a slalom between systemic threats and anonymous chain reactions. In the 1980s, one US sociologist even became famous for the alarming claim expressed in his title: *Normal Accidents* (Perrow 1984). We almost don't get the joke here any longer, considering that, in our own times, the transition from normalcy to accident has become, to a rather uncanny extent, a conspicuously smooth, familiar, indeed expected one. But other distinctions still hold good. Crime fiction facts are different from real life facts in precisely this respect: for the reader, or should we say the user, of crime fiction, if it is an accident, then there is no story. And this is why crime fiction, its writers and its readers, are biased in favour of premeditated, cold-blooded agency. Crime fiction readers, being hooked on their pleasure, don't believe in innocence; as soon as an accident appears on the horizon, they get impatient to know what intention the accident serves to cover.

III

'Crime' – this means, first of all, agency, not accident: the enjoyment that imparts its specific attraction upon the whole genre, finds its effective resource in a partiality in favour of human intervention, human expertise, and human will. Each of these three elements is essential. The first element, the action, the deed, the crime, triggers, if not, as in real life, a legalized responsibility, at least an intersubjectively warranted response; the action, the crime, being first in a rhythm of two steps, entails the expectation of some return of the pendulum, some reply, payment, or revenge, some *Abarbeiten* (drudgery imposed as punishment) or some *Durcharbeiten* (working through, as in psychoanalysis), in short, some second act that replies to, corrects, annihilates, accomplishes etc. the criminal deed that has provided the first act. The expectation of the second act is, however, invariably delayed by various manoeuvres, occasionally *sine fine*. Most of this delay is due to the presence of a second element, which we might define as a technical maestria or know-how, a positivist skill, a geekish adroitness. The architecture of crime, which the detective (both words derive from Greek or, respectively, Latin forms of an identical Indo-European root) ventures to deprive of its *tegos* or *tectum*, its 'roof', its perfection or structure, provides the constitutive elements of a competition in the pursuit of which the most characteristic resources are offered by technological prowess and instrumental brilliancy. The modernist-instrumentalist slant of the thriller finds its most characteristic dimensions both in this merely technical, instrumental virtuosity, and in the vocabulary required to adequately handle it. Looking closely enough, one discerns that these attitudes and competitive prowesses are mostly made of markers of masculinity turned into themes of crime fiction (the 'cold-blooded'; the 'hard-boiled').

I have already suggested a first approach of the downright preference for guilty agency over innocent 'bad luck' that singles out modern crime fiction. A second, cognate preference relates to instrumental, technologized bravura. Taken together, both give rise to modern masculinity (any reader of Gadamer, whose gaze might peradventure fall onto these lines, can identify here a 'melting of horizons', in the case at hand between pre-modern theological and modern – albeit definitely 'pre-post-modern' – masculine attributions). A further ingredient of no lesser importance, indeed superior to both others in its actuality and its mystery, is integrally owed to the faculty known as the will, and the doctrine called voluntarism, in relation especially to the members of the voluntarist camp in the long war of theological doctrines that rages, in lecture theatres, on pages (first manuscript, later printed) and only rather exceptionally also on burning stakes, between the latest years of the thirteenth century and the first decades of the eighteenth. Voluntarism is best described by saying that it allocates the will as a universal stopgap, grounding anything by means of a wilful, authoritarian act of the will's self-positing. '*Quare illud voluntas volet? Nulla est alia causa nisi quia est voluntas*' (Why does the will will this? Because it is the will – there is no other reason) (Scotus 1956, p. 797). On the other hand, Schopenhauer's saying that one can of course always do what one wills, yet not will what one wills, shows the hollow, crumbling, 'garbage' nature of the will, owing to which the voluntarist is led to an act, either of ultimate self-submission (Schopenhauer's unwilled, only incurred will), or to an ultimate positing or self-positing (cf. the all-powerful divine will of a Scotus-type theology and, closer to us, the political or military will abundantly exemplified by modern political history). As a spin-off, voluntarism remains controversial, both in theology, where the leading camp of the self-referential 'will-totallers' following John Duns and William of Ockham and the modist and nominalist schools that will continue their ideas, have coexisted all along with a large minority of opponents who placed their bets safely in an intellectualist base.

What needs to be investigated here are the genealogical connections linking the best authors of modern crime fiction to the most uncompromisingly God-absolutist theologians of a much earlier age. To start with, let me present my main conjecture. What links both groups together is the shadowy category of the will, indispensable for law (a gaze into Kelsen's *Pure Theory* is sufficient to gauge the absolutely central role embodied in it by the notion of the will), yet eerily empty of any content that would precede its purely conventional or if one prefers, engineerial use as a shorthand for 'contingent causality' (Sylwanowicz 1996).[1] The cunning move consists, here as there, in allocating the sovereign irresponsibility of the willing agent or subject, or – with Hegel – the position of the Master, as far away as possible from the investigating agent (even if mastery is ultimately held, here by the criminal, there by God). The business of the detective is far more than a fact-finding one. It has nothing to do with the simple use or application of available objective information waiting out there; instead, it refers to the need to make sense of the a priori meaningless chaos constituted by the available atoms

1 There is no such thing as the will before the advent of institutionalized Christianity. We need to get used to the fact that the term, commonly decisive for all movements our contemporaries like to identify with, liberal and anti-liberal, revolutionary and anti-revolutionary, is but the most discreet, yet also most capital product of modern meaning-engineering. Greek terminology had the semantic content, strategically condensed by legalized modernity in order to create a compact, 'reasonable' burden of responsibility to be shouldered by the individual, distributed between four or five different words; worse in Latin, where the one overwhelmingly quoted (by Kant, among others) occurrence of the word 'voluntas' is in the Sixth Satire by Juvenal (1st–2nd century AD). The poet, at the pinnacle of his frivolousness, stages injustice embodied by a rich Roman lady imposing her will (to have one of her slaves killed) upon her husband, who asks 'why?'. She replies: 'Because this is what I want and how I command: Take my will for a reason!' (*Hoc volo, sic iubeo: Sit pro ratione voluntas*).

and undecipherable shards or traces of information left inadvertently as part of a hairball of wilful, often whimsical actions, by means of transforming them (again nearly inadvertently, namely in the way of Picasso's saying: 'I do not search, I find') into fitting clues. The great Franciscan theologians, for whom any action – any action set by God, but equally, by any other free agent,[2] has its roots, not in that which is (or in modern parlance: in that which is the case), nor in God's (etc.) understanding or cognition thereof (which, to the observer, the theologian would alone open the access to any question relating to the adequacy of action), but in the (ultimately mysterious) soil of the will. In both cases, the situation we are confronted with has little in common with the self-assurance provided by some normatively codified method of how to behave in front of objective facts. It favours not sovereign theoretical understanding, but submission and humility. Human agency, as in modern crime fiction, divine agency, as in the theology of the power of God during the first half of the second millennium AD (which however dominates important areas of old-European thought still in the centuries of early modernity and modernity) both confront us with a common set of phenomena and duties arising from them, which are all rooted in what we might refer to as the quest for some method, some discipline, in dealing with the undisciplinable and the chaotic.

IV

God's will and the criminal's involuntary inclination have an important feature in common: they are equally unaccountable/irresponsible.[3] Moreover, the possibility of drawing lessons from the criminal's conduct is equally decisive for its detection

2 An important proviso! It enables Scotism to make the claim of providing, in addition to the absolutist theological conception that results from its privileging of power over goodness and will over intellect in God, a sharply immanent philosophical doctrine at the level of – if in dispute with – Aristotle. Doing so it programmes modern philosophers including Descartes, Kant, Husserl (de Muralt 1991) and triggers the take-off of decisive later social innovations such as subjective rights (Grossi 1972; Schütz 2012). It points the legacy that Dupin, Holmes and their entire problem-solving, clue-deciphering offspring – down to what we might refer to as the 'software of the hard-boiled' – has received from the *doctor subtilis* (=Scotus), no less than that, already noticed by Umberto Eco, of the *venerabilis inceptor* (=Ockham).

3 An obvious nightmare for the scholastics, and most especially for the power-pious Franciscans, who never tired of looking for avenues of escape from it. The doctrine of two coextensive yet distinct powers in God was one of those. They were, (a) *potentia absoluta*, an 'anything goes', limitless type of power, enabling its incumbent to any deed *whatsoever* (which includes, for Ockham, God's power of commanding not to love, but instead to *hate* one's neighbour, and God himself), (b) orderly, disciplined power (*potentia ordinata*) – but *nota bene*, God, more exactly God's will, 'willing in a most reasonable way', *rationabilissime volens* (Scotus 1893, p. 433, [Distinctio 32, *quaestio unica*]), is the unique source of any order. Eminently ordered, if only subject to His own ordering, God is supremely responsible, if only to Himself. These were arguable, even nearly undisputable, points around 1300. They are not now. What has happened? My suggestion: if an academic in a forlorn discipline like legal history is looking for a way to show how *Verrechtlichung* ('legalization', 'juridification') could have

and prosecution, as the art of competently conjecturing God's motives used to be/is for the understanding of the Christian bipolarity of the divine creation and the no less divine redemption. That the abductive epistemic mode, which, cutting through the well-educated partnership between mutually respectful inductive and deductive modes, offers a way of avoiding their common blind spot, and which is followed by the detectives of classical modern crime fiction,[4] or the conjectural one – for those whose claim to be practitioners of 'abduction' has not been allowed[5] – spectacularly coincide with a believer's quest for God, *fides quaerens intellectum,* in the words of a French-born English bishop of the eleventh century, Anselm of Canterbury, has been observed many times. The detectival genius of a cleric, Chesterton's 'Father Brown', can be seen as forming part and parcel, as intimately as enigmatically, of the unfolding of a genuinely religious potential.

The next conjecture here suggested posits that the referent which, if any, deserves, or would deserve, the name 'God', has been a source or resource for the writing and reading practice of modern crime fiction throughout. This does not include, to be sure, the academic or critical practice of that same literature – induced as it is, by the very form of its intervention, to transform this source or resource – a 'wind that blows wherever it pleases', according to the logion of John 3:8 – into a neutered and subordinate, fungible and amphibious mere 'topic'. The role of crime fiction on a general map is defined by the anomaly crime constitutes with respect to the normal flow of normal life; crime forms a void in the fabric of the whole. Contrary to law, described as an 'integrity' by Ronald Dworkin (who undoubtedly considered just this as being the clearest claim law has to the lawyer's full self-commitment as a humble servant and minor Hercules-substitute of its empire), crime is an interruption in the smooth fabric made up by the happily uneventful lives that most people wish to live. The truth is that the same people do not wish, most usually, to read about the type of lives they wish to live. This is also the limit, the one element that definitely prevents detective fiction from being 'catholic': whoever has committed a crime, his wish is *not*

come about, this is the point where she should start. If simple divine self-reference is now out, this is owing to the ever mounting tide of law, legal remedies, legal procedures etc. that has been allowed to take hold of the world and life of an ever-growing part of humankind, transforming it as deeply as capillarily, over many centuries. In the world that results from this process, ours, the basic issue boils down to whether one has legal standing. For the subtle doctor, only God has legal standing to move a question as to whether God's power has been used in a well-ordered fashion. An instance of exclusive self-responsibility, which today would in all likelihood be assimilated to irresponsibility. (Patients are certified for less than this).

4 Cf. the characteristic claim of a French Benedictine monk's more mundane brother, according to whom 'psychoanalysis is a conjectural science' (Lacan 1988, lecture of 22nd of June, 1955). The decisive contribution to the twentieth century take on 'abduction' is Charles S. Peirce (1929).

5 Especially Sherlock Holmes does not seem to succeed in mustering unanimity of professorial juries, about his mastery of the skill of 'abduction' (cf. Giovannoli 2007; Ginzburg 1994; Eco and Sebeok 1983).

to be found out; the detectival mission of finding out who it was cannot count, therefore, upon universal agreement,[6] or rely upon everyone's favour. There exists, however, another side to this limit of intrinsic catholicity. Considering the anti-social genius boys' club of the Dupin and Lupin, the Holmes, Brown and Maigret, the Marlowe and Spade etc., the one thing that appears as immediately obvious is the fact that nothing is more remote from the mind of its members than the ambition of being taken seriously, being correctly valued, by the members of the opposite, the rather non-genius, rather consensus-based, the more socially minded and community-committed boys' club, embodied either by people interested in politics or – mostly – police officers. This is where Hegel's dialectic of recognition has its limits. The paradigm of a confrontation between the inconsistent but infallible detectival hero, who lets himself fall unreservedly into the hole that the crime creates in the integrity of the social fabric, and the strictly methodically, thus consistently proceeding policeman, who unsuccessfully attempts to heal the imperilled whole, is what constitutes the unabated power of modern crime fiction. The ambivalence of the meaning of 'integrity' is such that the reader of hard-boiled detective fiction is not always safe against the temptation of identifying the detective, equally as or even more than the culprit, as the site of the disturbance and peril of 'disintegration'. The continuous confrontation with this limit – which is, as we have seen, but an enacted, atheoretical form of the unsustainable universal theorized by Lacan (Milner 2014) – gives rise to a cluttered, intransparent situation, characterized by an uneasy atmosphere of morose moral undecidability and unsustainable adiaphoria; the suck for simplification will rise (or, in many respects, descend) from a single case level to a universal level (i.e. properly speaking a pseudo-universal level, once one stops repressing the inherent inconsistency haunting the claim to universality). It will find a certain stability in the figure of the common geo-political enemy, capable of re-endowing the mediatized imaginary with a clear bipartite situation, by means of an unambiguous, glamorous morality. It will result, after the end of WWII, in the geo-choreographic mode known as the Cold War, the successful replacement candidate of the intra-Western conflict with Germany – which will soon appear as an unnatural, anomalous and short-lived mere 'accident of history', incapable of generating a sustainable world-structuring motion – by a stability-promising reshuffled version of the Western-Eastern conflict, able to build on a pattern rehearsed throughout a millennium and more of history of Western self-profiling in reference to, and at the expense of, the 'East'.[7]

6 What is called 'catholic', according to earlier fifth century champion of the 'orthodox' fringe of the Western church, Vincentius of Lérins (a monastery on an island near Cannes), is any doctrine that has been believed 'always', 'everywhere', as well as – here decisive – 'by all'.

7 Current evolutions show the immense energy of the East-West divide, which has easily survived the fall of communism and of the Soviet Union. The signifiers 'Western', 'West' 'occidental', 'abendländisch' pose a prickly problem. Think for instance of the celebrated *History of Western Philosophy*, published in 1945 by an otherwise courageous non-conformist author, who, nonetheless, at a certain

In matters of crime fiction, the advent of the Cold War involves the restorative advent of the immemorial Western morally 'bonded' fabric in the subjective make of the post WWII secret agent. He is essentially a warrior and a crusader. In the service of majesty that is nominal yet ubiquitous, absent yet glamorous, he will simultaneously announce, in the big image, the final victory of the Good, self-controlled Westerners over the corrupt collectivists in the East, and, in the smaller image, a sharp decline of critical distinction in the readership: an unprecedented loss of complexity from the respectable level of the hard-boiled detective genre, into literary nullity, mended by technocratic gadgets.

In several letters written by Wittgenstein to Norman Malcolm, the philosopher compares the articles of the prestigious journal of scientific psychology and analytic philosophy, *Mind*, to the detective stories of the Pulp magazine *Street&Smith*. In the letter dated 30 October 1945 he says: 'If I read your mags I often wonder how anyone could read "Mind", with all its impotence and bankruptcy, when they could read Street&Smith mags. Well, everyone to his taste.' (Hoffmann 2013, p. 196) Apparently, Wittgenstein was neither deprived of some familiarity with the intrinsic reasons of this superiority nor, even less, interested in offering an explanation for it. Effectively, Wittgenstein also says this: 'If I were told something that is a *theory*, I would say: No, no! I am not interested. Even if the theory were true, it would not interest me. It would never be what I am looking for.' (McGuinness 1979; Giovannoli 2007).

V

In this conflict between the whole and its police protection on the one hand, and the injury inflicted upon it by the Don Quichote-Sancho Pansa (or Don Giovanni-Leporello) -like complicity between the criminal and the detective, on the other hand, it is important to see that a relationship to religion is involved on *both* sides. On the one hand, without theological foundations, or some close substitute for them, no institution can be sustained, neither Church nor Army, and least of all probably a police force. Religion, however, at least as far as

moment around 1950, famously was more than tempted to recommend the nuclear bombing of the Soviet Union. These are *fighting concepts*, schmittian *Kampfbegriffe*. The reason people feel awkward about them – and why most feel under the duty of either putting them in custody inside safe quotation marks, or pushing the universalist bet to its neutralized extreme, replacing 'Western' with the more peaceful 'global', or finally replacing 'Western' by 'we', a construction in the neutral third person by the eminently military/militant first person of the plural – is not to be found in philological, historical or genealogical niceties, but in the history of the anti-Eastern campaign, which is the constituent power to which 'the West' owes its constituted existence. As e.g. 'monotheism' has been a secondary, derivative notion forged – around 1800 – after the earlier (late sixteenth century) coinage 'polytheism', to designate 'the others': in the same way 'West', 'Western' etc. are mere derivatives of the ostracizing 'East', 'Eastern', 'oriental', etc. 'Worstward Ho!', one of Samuel Beckett's late prose fragments, has equally its Western-relevant message.

Christianity is concerned,[8] has both its saintly and its sustainable aspects. What is the religious element that is close to those detectives? The work of the definite non-church-goer Raymond Chandler (2000) leaves no doubt about this: God is involved in their dealings in the same way in which God is involved in the dealing of the Saint, the sick, the poor, the rejected and the expelled, the early martyrs. It is not the God of Churches and States, of dignitaries and predications, institutions and accreditations, political justice and social justice, not even the God of argument or moral commitment, or of the appropriate theological reasons for endorsing, or opposing, this or that. It is not the God of theology, of knowledge, of the collective creative effort of theologians or other sustainable agents of sustainable regimes.

It is decisive in this context to avoid certain recurrent and common misidentifications. In order to take the most obvious case, that of Father Brown: Father Brown is not a cardinal, of course, but Father Brown is arguably even less a theologian, a critical lawyer, a legal theorist, or the like, let alone a legal philosopher (at least, as long as scepticism is not counted as a philosophy, rather than as an anti-philosophy). Theologians are, by dint of their professional title, not only practitioners of a (highly text-dependent and speculative) science. They also carry the claim of a knowledge about God. Indeed, the claim that such a knowledge exists, or could exist, is a claim upon which, by the fact of being its salaried depositaries, they are suspended.

Also, while it is a question whether theo-knowledge fits the image of the modern, productive and proliferating beehive, of which Foucault (1972) supplied the archaeology, the one thing that is obvious is that, offering the very paradigm of an access-controlling knowledge-power, theology does function as what is called a 'capital'. This capital of which theologians certainly no longer are, but of course used to be, the depositaries, is no other than 'the-name-in-which' of power – of power exercised, according to the prevailing politico-theological mode, either (for a long time) gloriously in its own name, or (now) without glory, without power even, in the name of powerlessness, as the power used in the name of there being no power, 'no alternative', as it is said with a perfectly equivalent formula (Agamben 2011). This knowable God, who 'provides' – in the sense of supplying legitimacy, precisely via those in charge of theological knowledge, this eminently constructive God, who might be able to help any attempt at building consensus and achieving credibility, impressing colleagues and bolstering one's lobbying action or

8 The relationship between 'religion' – used, as in Marx's overly quoted 'opium' phrase, as a delicate euphemism to avoid 'Christianity' (Milner 2015, pp. 83 ff.) – and 'Christianity' – used as the Aristotelian-style indicator of the relevant '*to ti en einai*' ('that which, for and within the Western European tradition, is [called] "a religion"') – and the energetic give and take between their respective specialities and attributions, gives a sense of the state of mystery and perplexity in which the Western-Christian and, even more so, Western- 'no-longer-Christian', Western-secularized, humankind remains with respect to a common horizon for itself and in-itself.

institutional career, this universal provider, does not interest Father Brown. The detective's favourite is the God who ever-already knows what has happened, first in this singular case, then in that singular case; never universally and 'for all'.

VI

In order to allow for a representative *tour d'horizon* of the relationships at work between crime fiction and religion, we should immediately add that a divide closely similar to that just hinted at, applies to 'No-God' as fittingly as it does to 'God'. In Western history, during a small number of centuries, most of the best exploring minds fared better without invoking God, a 'hypothesis [which] I do not need' (as reportedly God was referred to by one of them, a mathematician, in conversation with Napoléon Bonaparte). It is absolutely out of the question that he could have agreed, but in hindsight one might guess that Laplace's saying makes more sense understood as an appeal, a prayer almost, directed to 'No-God', rather than merely a statement of 'no need of this hypothesis', which, in today's ears, does sound a bit jejune. Be that as it may, the fact that should not be overlooked is that during this era, the 'in-the-name-in-which' of power, of government, of management, was provided, in turn, by 'No-God', rather than by God. In summary, the problem of which the detectives of modern crime fiction are the indicator as well as the symptom, seems to have a somehow more complicated structure than that suggested by the well known divide between the 'religious' and the 'non-religious'. There is one great line on the 'universalist' side, which connects the powerful political and consensus-building God of the earlier second millennium, the God of the resonant and efficient argument wielded by those who also hold the relevant knowledge-power, to the entire field of non-theological variants and schools of consensus-inducing, institution-sustaining, occasionally 'critical' argument, such as utilitarianism, in the modern age; and there is, in front of it, on the singularity side, another great line, connecting a large fraction of No-God people, amongst them a large majority of unambiguous and passionate atheists of recent and even current times, on the one hand, to their non-lukewarm, or anti-lukewarm correspondents in earlier centuries, amongst whom we find an inordinate percentage of the most arduous and uncompromising confessors of the Christian faith.[9]

In this sense, Chesterton's anti-utilitarian Christianism should be deciphered as a paradigm rather than as an exception; clearly, he is an unrepenting elitist, to

9 The account entails severe simplifications. The most urgent correction concerns the anti-utilitarianism tendency, which is, in fact, in no way limited to Edgar Poe and his fellow nineteenth–twentieth century English-writing crime fiction authors, but equally definitely present far outside the literature that glorifies the detective and the grace of his clue-deciphering bravura, in the vast literature of nineteenth century German romantics and later nineteenth century French poets and novelists including Baudelaire and Huysmans.

be counted entirely among the 'few and rare'[10] – even if in his case the elitism is dimmed by the fused filters of personal understatement, consummate literary style, and the catholic mode of putting oneself last rather than first. Yet, precisely by dint of being an exception, Chesterton should be understood as a paradigm – not because the exceptions should be considered as being, really, the rules (although this seems to be a fair rendering of some current schmittian beliefs!) or because there is some common element that would link the case of the detective either to that of the sovereign as a decider over the state of exception, or to that of God as a worker of miracles, but precisely as a correction of these views. The detectival agent is eminently *not* an actor – detecting is less of a deed or an act, than a passion, an 'experience'.[11] Exceptional he is by dint of his powerlessness – by the utter distance that separates him from either miracle-worker or sovereign. But this goes far beyond the sole case of Father Brown. The inherent exceptionalism of modern crime fiction is, notwithstanding its definitely dated or 'period' appearance, epitomized in the uncanny, marginal, decentred embodiment of the inconsistent detective, who authorizes himself to know, or more precisely to find out, and to nothing else – and this, importantly, not by means of a recourse to a 'master', but to God, or 'No-God', alone. A zero value of power is in this way combined with an infinite value of intelligence.

The will remains a philosophical mystery. Everything looks as if the voluntarists needed, at some point of their reasoning, to recur to some sort of – 'voluntary' – cut-off, some groundless, wilful, self-submission. The classics of the detective novel, Edgar A. Poe, Arthur Conan Doyle, Gilbert K. Chesterton, as well as their heroes are, in their common epistemo-theological genius, hard-boiled voluntarists. They are working in the shadow of the world-wide leadership of a form of intellectualism; under the sheer despair about the boredom of this anonymous and procedural horizon, they redevelop a voluntarism, but an *alter-voluntarism*, a 'voluntarism of the will of the other' which has effectively a most obvious historical example in late medieval voluntarist theology. The near blasphemic element in the theological take they practise consists in the fact that the investigation leads them to secularize voluntarist theology in voluntarist criminology.

Around the Mediterranean, one way of exploring the character of locals is by asking them about the proportion according to which they would distribute the origin of the forest fires that destroy important parts of the region every summer, to accidental causes or wilful human agency. There are the responsible ones: their choice takes place within in a mindset of possibilities, they are well-meaning,

10 Different from the philosopher Heidegger (1999), whose formulation '*[f]ür die Wenigen, [f]ür die Seltenen*' ('for the few, for the rare') (p. 11), I am borrowing here, it is meant to single out the public that the philosopher wishes to address.

11 For Chesterton (1927), this is programmatic, cf. the empathy, the becoming-similar-to-the-criminal, indeed the becoming-the-criminal, which Father Brown confesses to the reader allows him to solve his cases.

and they have good, utilitarian reasons to be. They opt for accidents. There are, on the other hand, the more fragile characters who cannot help suspecting: for them the answer is agency. Writers and readers of crime fiction are much of their mind. Accounts of murder and, respectively, of murder-investigation, are arts of the limit-impossible (leading to the discovery or re- or retro-discovery, in certain types of crime fiction, of unusual paradigms such as the indicial or the abductive). That which is inductively or deductively unaccountable, becomes abductively or conjecturally approachable. In real life, it is clear that a well-educated, non-sociopathic professional individual is expected, not perhaps to love their neighbour (that would be far too ambitious a task, more than looks credible), but to behave in a collegial, unpreconceived, professionally correct way. This often entails the effort of silencing the hunches and inklings the ego might have – in fact always and forcefully has, even over-abundantly so – about the alter's motivations, in favour of a non-descript neutrality.

VII

One of the more striking success stories of the history of popular culture (Priestman 1998), crime fiction has given rise to numberless interpretative visions of literature, law, the mass media, and other fundamental and fundamentally distinct topics.[12] It has been repeatedly celebrated as one of the most prolific and liberal venues where the resource 'normative meaning' undergoes the work in progress of its unending self-undoing and self-substitution through repair and replacement work.[13] Courtesy of the many fingers and even more numerous eyes of crime fiction writers and, respectively, readers, there has thus emerged a new dispositive, best described as an advertisement panel, permanent but quickly reprogrammable and perfect as a venue to lodge a continuous mirror-stage encounter in which the law,

12 Instructive in this context is the spectacular miscalculation of an author to whom, a century ago, it seemed 'unlikely' that the 'subsidiary genre [sic!], [namely: of crime fiction] will attain to the rank or to the influence of its picaresque parent'. See the classical study of F.W. Chandler (1907, pp. 547 ff.) – no relation to Raymond. If Chandler's implicit claim, of a genealogical bond linking late twentieth/twenty-first century crime fiction to the early modern genre of the picaresque novel remains defensible, this is so owing precisely to the apocryphal or acanonic status that had singled out, each at its time of flourishing, *both* picaro and crime fiction, which share the fate of entering the stage of successful fiction as nameless, undignified, merely curiosity-provoking 'home productions' of popular culture. As it happens, crime fiction has become, *pace* Chandler, one of the few global successes of the post WWII era and the twentieth century at large. Yet, both despite and because of his puzzlingly delusive bet about historic tendency, Chandler's claim can still be read as a precious hint, (a) that crime fiction's distinctive feature is – or used to be, until recently – that of an asylum-genre or, if one prefers, an outcast of the literary canon, (b) that canons are a short-lived, swiftly outdated matter.

13 For a theory of the self, conceived as the site of ongoing self-substitution rather than the result of experiences: Luhmann (1981).

by cunningly entrusting its fundamental dilemmas and irresolvable aporias to the external mooting practice known as 'literature' – thus: by the detour of replacing real by artificial/fictional crime (or, if one prefers, of outsourcing its confrontation with itself, eminently democratically and redeemingly, to a wider constituency) – succeeds in compensating, by an increased share of public attention, for a decline in integrity and intrinsic coherence. The focus on professional competence in decision making is replaced by a focus on the suggestive and atmospheric potentials in the experience of a consumer, giving rise to a justice seen to be done, as the immemorial common law maxim had it, yet now stripped of the doing of justice itself.

A certain 'de-verticalization' or 'flattening' of the traditional key dimension of legal subjectivity – the dimension that unfolds, in two floors, between the law, its greatness and its highness, its always victorious majesty and its unmistakeable sublimity, and its transgression, the 'pits', the pitfalls that characterize those who have proven to be *not* 'up' to law's requests – characterizes the recent evolution of society. Yet, alongside this evolution of a levelling of the vertical order, and of the latter's gradual replacement by a map charting, in an analytical and somehow 'egalitarian' way, both law-conformity and law-transgression, emerges another tendency in the evolution of crime fiction – or rather, I should probably say, in the evolution of both crime fiction and what I would call *crime non-fiction*, namely the totality of factual evolutions touching the legal correctness, and its absence, in effective, expectable, and general everyday conduct. By enshrining the sphere of modern crime within the bottomlessly unlimitedly domain developed, in Scotus's theology, in connection with the will, crime fiction offers crime non-fiction a chance of intelligibility that contradicts control and suspends discipline.

References

Agamben, G. (2011) *The kingdom and the glory: for a theological genealogy of economy and government.* Stanford: Stanford University Press.

Austin, J. (1995) *The province of jurisprudence determined.* Rumble, W. (ed.). Cambridge: Cambridge University Press. (Original work published in 1832, London)

Benjamin, W. (2004) 'Critique of violence', translated by E. Jephcott, in Bullock M. and Jennings, N. (eds.) *Walter Benjamin: selected writings, volume 1: 1913–1926.* Cambridge: Harvard University Press, 2004, pp. 236–52. (Original published in 1921)

Birks, P. (1988) *An introduction to the law of restitution.* Oxford: Oxford University Press.

Chandler, F.W. (1907) *The literature of roguery. Vol. 2.* New York: Burt Franklin.

Chandler, R. (2000) *The Raymond Chandler papers: selected letters and nonfiction, 1909–1959.* Hiney, T. and MacShane, F. (eds.) New York: Atlantic.

Chesterton, G.K. (1927) *The secret of Father Brown.* London: Cassel.

Eco, U. and Sebeok, T.E. (eds.) (1983) *The sign of three: Dupin, Holmes, Peirce.* Bloomington: Gaslight.

Foucault, M. (1972) *The archaeology of knowledge.* Translated by A.M. Sheridan Smith. London: Routledge. (Original work published in 1969, Paris: Gallimard)

Ginzburg, C. (1994) *Clues, myths and the historical method.* Baltimore: Johns Hopkins' University Press.

Giovannoli, R. (2007) *Elementare, Wittgenstein! Filosofia del racconto poliezesco*. Milano: Medusa.

Grossi, P. (1972) 'Usus facti: la nozione di proprietà nell'inaugurazione dell éta nuova', *Quaderni Fiorentini*, 1, pp. 287–355.

Heidegger, M. (1999) *Contributions to philosophy: from enowning*. Translated by P. Emad and K. Maly. Bloomington: Indiana University Press. (Original work published in 1989, *Beiträge zur philosophie: vom ereignis*. GA vol. 65, Frankfurt: Vittorio Klostermann)

Hoffmann, J. (2013) *Philosophies of crime fiction*. Harpenden: No Exit Press.

Lacan, J. (1988) *The ego in Freud's theory and in the technique of psychoanalysis: the seminar of Jacques Lacan, 1954–55, vol.II*. Translated by S. Tomaselli. New York: W.W. Norton. (Original work published in 1977, *Le moi dans la théorie de Freud et dans la technique de la psychanalyse, Le séminaire, vol.II*. Paris: Seuil)

Luhmann, N. (1981) 'Identitätsgebrauch in selbstsubstitutiven Ordnungen, besonders Gesellschaften', in *Soziologische Aufklärung, vol. 3: Soziales System, Gesellschaft, Organisation*. Opladen:Westdeutscher Verlag, pp. 198–227.

Luhmann, N. (2004) *Law as a social system*. Translated by K.A. Ziegert. Oxford: Oxford University Press. (Original work published in 1993, *Das Recht der Gesellschaft*. Frankfurt: Suhrkamp)

McGuinness, B. (ed.) (1979) *Wittgenstein and the Vienna Circle: Conversations recorded by Friedrich Waismann*. Oxford: Basil Blackwell.

Milner, J-C. (2014) L'universel en éclats: court traité politique 3. Paris: Verdier.

Milner, J-C. (2015) *La puissances du détail: phrases célèbres et fragments en philosophie*. Paris: Grasset.

Muralt, A. de (1991) *L'enjeu de la philosophie médiévale*. Leyden: Brill.

Peirce, C.S. (1929) 'Guessing', *The Hound and Horn*, 2, pp. 267–82.

Perrow, C. (1984) *Normal accidents*. Princeton: Princeton University Press.

Priestman, M. (1998) *Crime Fiction from Poe to the Present*. Plymouth: Northcote House.

Schütz, A. (2012) 'Epigenesis, law, and the *medium aevum* as a medium', in Schütz, A. and Traversino, M. (eds.) *The theology of 'potentia Dei' and the history of european normativity*. (=115 *Divus Thomas*, 2012), pp. 418–52.

Scotus, J.D. (1956) *Quaestiones in metaphysicam, IX, q.5, n.5*. (ed. Vat., vol. IV, p. 797).

Scotus, J.D. (1893) *Ordinatio vol. III, d.32, q.un*. (ed. Louis Vives, vol. XV, Paris: Vives).

Sylwanowicz, M. (1996) *Contingent causality and the foundations of Duns Scotus' metaphysics*. Leiden: Brill.

Chapter 4

French television crime fictions

The case of *Spiral* (*Engrenages*) – coming out of the confusion

Barbara Villez

1 Introduction

If you asked a French policeman to name some of the things that annoy him when making an arrest, he would probably answer: being sneered at for neglecting to read the detainee his Miranda rights. These rights, which come from a landmark United States Supreme Court decision in 1966, have nothing to do with what the French can expect. For a long time, the police have also complained that people ask to make a phone call immediately upon arrest. This is yet another expectation coming from American police series on television. A phone call is made for the detainee in France, but the timing and the caller differ from what happens in the United States. The police in France have attributed such confusion to 'too much television'. Indeed, a huge number of police and courtroom dramas coming from the United States can be seen on French television, nearly every day on nearly every channel, once if not several times a day.

Still today, French television channels consider it cheaper to buy a licence to broadcast foreign dramas than to produce their own. Consequently, over the past 20 years, French television viewers have acquired a legal culture through imported American television series like *Law & Order* (1990–2010),[1] *Ally McBeal* (1997–2002),[2] *Damages* (2007–2012)[3] or *Suits* (2011).[4] This has led to major confusion as to how justice works in their own country and what the corresponding legal professions are like. Although things have slightly improved with more French productions on the air, judges have also complained of being addressed as '*Votre honneur*', the literal translation of 'Your honor' which is not what one calls a French judge in court.[5] In 2005 the then Minister of Justice, Dominique Perben, encour-

1 In France on TF1, 13è Rue, TMC among others at various times.
2 In France on Téva and M6.
3 In France on Canal+.
4 In France on Série Club.
5 '*Monsieur (ou Madame) le juge*' if a single judge panel and '*Monsieur le président (Madame la présidente)*' if a three judge panel, like in the *Cour d'assises* (indictable criminal cases).

aged French television channels and producers to create national procedural dramas which would rectify the public's '*imaginaire*' of French justice.

The first attempts to produce national programmes on the subject of law and justice did not remedy this problem, however. Many documentaries were made, but in general they were broadcast late at night. In addition, the cases filmed often involved petty crimes committed by people living in marginal situations. French law prohibits filming trials except in cases with an 'historical dimension', for example, trials concerning crimes against humanity. One of the reasons for this refusal was to preserve the right of people involved in proceedings to turn the page (*le droit à l'oubli* – literally, the right to be forgotten). The right to be forgotten of those who figured in the documentaries apparently gave way to the herculean efforts to obtain authorisation to film in court. In March 2009, Channel France 2 devoted five minutes each day of one week, during the midday news, to segments of a murder trial. The accused admitted killing another man but the court had to determine whether this was a hate crime (as two different ethnic groups were involved) or an ordinary homicide. The sentences imposed under French law in racist cases are far more severe. Allotting 25 minutes to a complex legal issue at the rhythm of five minutes a day did very little to help French viewers put the pieces together to understand how the trial was organised and to notice important elements of French legal culture.

At about the same time, television fictions also increased, either one shot films or film series revolving around a recurrent character like Judge Ferrare (*L'Affaire Valéra* 2004, *Président Ferrare: L'Affaire Denise Chabrier* 2004; *Président Ferrare: L'Affaire Gilles d'Aubert* 2006).[6] Contrary to the organisation of French criminal courtrooms, Judge Ferrare sat alone on the bench and 12 jurors sat in a jury box to the side of the court rather than on the bench on either side of the three presiding judges. Why was misinformation of this sort planted in such films? For the simple reason that channels considered audiences had expectations corresponding to American trials and that the public should be given what they 'expected to see'. *Femmes de loi* (2000) is a French series,[7] combining both police and law genres. The main characters are two women working together in each episode: an assistant prosecutor and a police detective. The organisation of courtroom space is again full of American trial characteristics (the jury sits in a box, the lawyers and the prosecutor move around the courtroom and question witnesses directly).[8] The necessities of dramatic tension had the police detective breaking all the rules of her profession and breaking many laws as well. Her unlikely tactics were inspired by American

6 All directed by Alain Nahum.

7 Although identified as a series, this fiction, with recurring principal characters, has not run weekly but 46 episodes have been produced and broadcast on TF1 between 2000 and 2009.

8 A French trial is not lawyer-led but judge-led. Judges do the questioning and lawyers can ask questions through the judge. Other than that, as in English trials, lawyers stay at their places and do not move freely around the courtroom.

police dramas and thus, again, considered familiar entertainment for the public. Television in France has never been considered high on the cultural ladder, while cinema has always occupied a privileged position. Television viewers have not been taken seriously either, not even by the industry itself (if the public were cultured they would go to the cinema).

2 *Engrenages*: awareness of the foreign markets

In 2005, Canal+, the pay television channel, often wishfully compared to HBO, decided to launch a new series, partially in answer to Perben's call for a fiction capable of giving the French a true image of their own legal institutions. Canal+ was more in a position to do this than other stations at the time because of their reputation, their financial independence and a relatively loyal public (having started with the exclusive right to broadcast French football matches, the channel enjoyed a stable audience). The channel was not only concerned with the minister's request however; they had also noticed the popularity of police and courtroom dramas exported from the United States and had understood that the future of the industry depended on producing series capable of appealing to foreign markets. Their first effort to meet these objectives, in 2005, was *Engrenages* (2005). The series sold well to other countries, although at first it had a lukewarm reaction from French audiences. BBC4 bought the series and broadcast it under the title of *Spiral* in 2006. Whatever British television critics saw in the show, the first two seasons failed at providing a viable alternative to the erroneous representation of the French criminal justice system. Realism revealed itself to be found less in procedural details than in the expression of French attitudes towards their institutions of justice. Indeed, dialogue, camera shots and facial expressions relayed these attitudes. The French legal professions saw certain elements of realism in the show whereas it is not sure that the French audiences were aware of what was communicated. Nevertheless, it is unlikely that foreign viewers were able to decode such clues and even less probable that they understood anything about French justice from watching the show.

3 The more things change, the more they remain the same

The first season of scriptwriting went to a member of a television dynasty, which is a frequent occurrence in the French entertainment business. The participation of a legal consultant was announced in the title credits, but whether that person was actually on the set or at all vigilant is a legitimate question. The first two seasons written by the original team were composed of eight episodes, each loaded with not only erroneous information, but also ridiculous narrative developments. Whether this came from a lack of information about the law and legal professions or naïve efforts to privilege drama over realism matters little; the result was clumsy and confusing. Mistake or negligence, or perhaps once again disdain for the television viewer, the judges and prosecutors were made to look like whimpering bunglers and the police so overwhelmed by work that they were constantly out of breath and apparently in need of a good shower. The stereotype of the plainclothesman on watch in his car, sniffing coke and missing the passage, right before his nose, of the person he was on the lookout for, was too predictable and a lame narrative code. The young prosecutor, Pierre Clément (Grégory Fitoussi), transferring to Paris from a provincial town (both a promotion in his civil service career and a move away from the pain of a failed marriage) is called to the crime scene that opens the pilot. Upon discovering the extent of mutilation of the victim's face and body, he remarks 'She must have been very beautiful'. How he could figure that out from what was left of her aimed perhaps at revealing his acute investigatory talent despite his young age. A later scene has him move into a splendid apartment that his close friend, a very successful young businessman, is able to procure for him. No young prosecutor would otherwise be able to afford the rent of such a place and the audience will learn that this same friend is implicated in the murder of the young woman found at the outset of the show, which causes Clément considerable ethical problems. The friend is, in fact, placed high on the crime ring that led to this horrible murder and several others. France may be a small country, but such a narrative coincidence is annoying. When Pierre Clément finds out about his friend's involvement in the girl's death, he is faced with a major dilemma, but happily only for an instant. He overcomes this emotional weakness although other moments reinforce his fragility, for example when, still in the first episode, his wife drives up to Paris to return some of his things in order to help him get settled in his new life. The scene that follows unloading the car puts them in bed together. After such passion, the audience never sees her again, either in the rest of season one or in the seasons that follow. For a series that identified itself as a police *and* courtroom drama, more moments in court than in bed might have been useful.

Credit must, nevertheless, be given to the producers and writers of *Spiral* for their conscious effort to create a different show from the rest of the genre on the French television landscape, and press reviews at home and abroad generally did recognise its innovative features. A chorus of regular actors has allowed for multiple story lines. The different institutional departments dealing with criminal justice do interact with each other and give the public, if not insight into how their work is articulated in the judicial process, at least some awareness of their existence and sometimes their animosity towards each other. Despite the initial efforts to portray French criminal justice, the influence of American crime shows was still very present at first. Autopsy scenes were marked by the CSI-type blood and gore. The coroner exhibited the same ironic humour and, as he demonstrated his findings on the corpse, the detectives became a bit weak in the knees. The police team led by Captain Laure Berthaud (Caroline Proust) already, in season one, seemed like family with all the fragility and emotional injuries of *NYPD Blue* tradition. The multiple creaky corridors that detectives and prosecutors cross, delivering documents from one office to another or obtaining authorisations, do give an impression of the dilapidation of the *Palais de Justice*. Piles of documents on every desk sent a signal translating the strong emphasis on the written word in French procedure.

An important figure in French criminal justice has always been the *juge d'instruction* and naturally one of the main characters of *Engrenages* is *Juge d'instruction* François Roban (Philippe Duclos). Although a judge, the *juge d'instruction* does not preside over trials. He conducts investigations to collect evidence that can prove as well as disprove a suspect's guilt ('des preuves *à charge et à décharge*'). Once he has examined all the evidence he has been able to gather, he will decide whether that person should be brought to trial or not. This *juge* works independently and his investigation is conducted in secrecy (*le secret de l'instruction*). He cannot initiate an investigation, but is called upon to do so by either a member of the prosecutor's office or by the victim or the victim's family who has chosen to take part in the proceedings.[9] If he finds that there is more condemning evidence than evidence to the contrary, he will transfer the case back to the prosecutor for trial; if not, he will dismiss the case (issue a *non-lieu*), which in some cases only means putting it on hold for an indefinite period. The *juge d'instruction* has traditionally been a popular figure in French culture, despite a relatively small number of highly mediatised investigatory scandals in the past that tarnished the reputation of the profession.

Although the police and Clément show him respect, Judge Roban does not really benefit from the consideration usually accorded to these '*petits juges*',[10] neither from his judicial hierarchy in the series, nor from the writers of the show, at least not in the first two seasons. Indeed, in season one, he is portrayed as a sad grey evasive figure, at times even totally inept and unprofessional. A significant example occurs several episodes into season one when a taxi driver brings to the police the diary of the young victim discovered at the beginning of the pilot. It turns out she was a call girl and her diary, forgotten in the taxi, contains a client list that would embarrass several important men, among them, several government officials. As is customary, the police bring this evidence to Roban. He, in turn, most unprofessionally brings the diary home to study in the evening. To make himself a cup of tea, or for some other reason, he leaves the room, the diary still on his desk before an open window. When he returns the diary is gone. His surprise is only slightly greater than that of the television viewer to see that the scriptwriters actually stoop so low as to have someone swipe the diary off his desk through the window.

9 Another particularity of the French criminal justice system is that victims or their survivors can be represented in a criminal trial as a third party (*la partie civile*).

10 A frequent way of referring to these judges reflecting their independence, solitude, and integrity (many of them have conducted investigations against big business, political corruption etc.).

4 A new team of writers, the effect of research

The first season was composed of eight episodes and ran between December 2005 and January 2006 drawing 720,000 viewers or 13.2% of the general audience, which are good ratings considering that not everyone is willing to pay for Canal+. It may have been curiosity that brought viewers to the show at first. Sales to England were quite successful; the English apparently loved the French exoticism (Mazdon 2012), but remained mostly in the dark as to how French criminal justice worked. Season two fared less well with another eight episodes between May and June 2008, drawing only 600,000 viewers, 9.6% of the market share. Could this be because audiences were disappointed to find more unhappy policemen and women, more lawyers disdainful of pathetic clients or more disabused *magistrats*[11] in the throes of political intrigue, outweighing dramatic intrigue?

As of season three however viewers noted a surprising change. Twelve episodes per season, rather than eight, gave more time to the development of different stories including more time for short discussions shedding light on the responsibilities of the various services participating in an investigation, or the rivalry between them. More time was taken to develop a problem of strategy or the consequences of political pressure; in fact, a lot of time was given to political pressure. If the crimes of season three were still typical of police series (a serial killer mutilating his female victims), the investigation offered several twists that would carry over into season four. Seasons four and five, however, dealt with current issues of French society, bringing the series closer to reality and to actual concerns of the viewing audience. Indeed, French left-wing terrorism, illegal aliens and teenage girl gangs were linked to the different crimes. The narrative was still complex, but carried elements of realism: the different professionals who deal with crimes and misdemeanours and their difficulties in carrying out criminal justice. The characters' moods changed as did their attitudes: Roban could be severe, understanding and ironic, and the disdainful lawyer Karlssen took chances to warn the squatters of an imminent police raid.

Once past the initial surprise, it became clear that the writing team had changed. Although still not former lawyers or *magistrats*, which is the case for many law series in the United States or Great Britain, the writers nevertheless had more experience with the law than the previous team. Anne Landois was hired as the principal scriptwriter. She was known for her work on a docudrama directed by Denys Granier-Deferre in 2007, *Rendez-moi justice* (2007)[12] about the horrible murder of a little girl in south-eastern France in 1988. It has been forbidden to film or

11 In France both judges and prosecutors are *magistrats*, neither are lawyers. *Magistrats* and lawyers have the same initial university training but as of the fifth year students either prepare for the Bar or go to the *Ecole Nationale de la Magistrature*.

12 Written by Anne Landois, directed by Denys Granier-Deferre, co-produced by Maha Productions and France 3.

photograph trials in France since 1954 and consequently there were no film archives available for this docufiction. For her research, Anne Landois only had recourse to the notes of the court secretary, to help her create a reconstitution of the trial at the centre of the docudrama. Her rendering of the trial and its complex elements was an important part of the film and began a particular interest on her part in law and justice. Her arrival at *Engrenages* (2005) led to clearer roles and a more faithful articulation between the various services involved in the administration of criminal justice.

Fully aware that not having formal training in the law, she would need the collaboration of justice professionals, she began to construct a circle of consultants with whom she met regularly before and during writing. In addition to this, she co-authored seasons three and four with a police commander writing under a pen name because still in active service. Season five was written with a different co-author but still in consultation with a team of lawyers and *magistrats*. However, it took time to attenuate the traditional power of French television stations and it was not until the end of 2013, at the outset of writing season five, that Anne Landois became the showrunner of *Spiral* (*Engrenages* 2005). This was a major event in French television history, a showrunner meant that Canal+ would deal with one interlocutor who had control over all the rest of the production of the show. The fact that the first showrunner was a woman is not to be neglected either, as the television industry is not yet a model of gender equality.

The popularity of seasons three to five attest to these changes producing the improved quality of the show: season three (May–June 2010)[13] raised the number of viewers to 871,000 or 15.2% of the market share, and season four (November–December 2012) to 960,000 or 15.6% of the potential audience. Season five was broadcast between November and December 2014 and although, as of this writing, total statistics for the year are not yet available, it has been established that the viewing audience of *Spiral* was up 34% with respect to season four. This success can suggest, especially to the main channels, that the public is interested in quality and, especially in light of these statistics and the continued television consumption of imported police and law series, that they may also be interested in justice material. As viewers become more familiar with the legal professions in France, the aspect that *Spiral* has done the most to make clear so far, they are more competent to follow current issues covered in the media as well. Far from transforming viewers into specialists, *Spiral* can nevertheless help viewers understand media reports of a two-day interrogation (implying detention) of a former minister by a *juge*

13 Unlike US productions, seasons do not follow each other closely; in some cases, a year or more can separate two seasons. French television policies make it impossible to begin broadcasting a series until the whole season has been written and presented to the station. This results in longer intervals between production periods and thus also between broadcasts. Finally, when a series is composed of six or eight episodes only, they may be aired two at a time, covering only three or four weeks of programming and consequently ending more rapidly within the season.

d'instruction, the possible reform of the status of the *juge d'instruction*, a case of fraud going to a particular court rather than another and so on. These are the issues French viewers live with, but media reports do not explain the judicial aspects of these cases which comforts the public's perception of justice as a political institution, a point we will develop below.

5 Rome was not built in a day either

Of course justice can be messy and in terms of cinematic tradition, the French have perfected the art of representing messy, or to say the least they have not produced their own version of 'American slick'. French realism as a filmic style is known for the fast-moving, jumpy effect of the camera on the shoulder and street sounds that parasitise the conversations of characters as they walk outside. The few scenes taking place in court are sometimes hard to follow because of the shuffling of feet or bad acoustics masking ritual judicial phrases. Many outside scenes in *Spiral* are shot at night, on dark wet pavements. A truck passing in front of two characters talking in the street as they walk, will momentarily block out not only their words, but the sight of them as well. When viewers *are* able to hear them, and especially in the case of police characters, their use of slang and '*verlan*', a French form of pig Latin composed most often of inverted syllables, further complicates the task. One can become used to the slang, but to understand the myriad of acronyms the French use to talk about most anything will often necessitate a lot of fact checking on the internet. For example, the *police judiciaire* is the *PJ*, the *Inspection générale de l'éducation nationale* is the *IGEN*, the *judge des affaires familiales* is the *JAF*, the *Brigade de répression du banditisme* (a police service for particular types of crimes) is the *BRB*. The dialogues of *Spiral* are sprayed with these initials throughout and the terms they represent are rarely, if ever, pronounced in full. There are numerous police forces in France and several types of judges with different responsibilities; several *catégories* of judges do not preside over trials. Thus unless one is already familiar with the administration of justice, these conversations can cultivate confusion, which may well correspond to the French idea of justice as more confused than effective.

The fast-moving camera work, almost dizzying at times, corresponds well to another cultivated image acquired through television and cinema fictions, that of plain-clothed police inspectors. They are portrayed in frequent danger which makes them often lose control, yelling at each other, banging doors, constantly using foul language. *Spiral* reinforces this image of rough and tough crime fighters, angry, tired, unpolished. Their family lives are a shambles, when there is a family life; most of them are alone, and scenes of sudden sex are anything but subtle. For example, Captain Laure Berthaud leaves the police station in the first episode of season five and rather than going home, picks up a stranger in a bar, then throws him out of her car when she notices she is bleeding. This is not a miscarriage, but her pregnancy will be part of her back story for the whole season.

Representations of the police thus remain traditional, even if more crude. It must be understood that 'coming out of the confusion' is really an act in progress;

there is still much confusion concerning the administration of justice. French fictions have always centred on social and psychological issues rather than legal or judicial. People making bad choices however can lead to good courtroom fictions, but there are few writers who have the experience to tell good courtroom stories, or who even care to do so. Traditional representations of French justice in *Spiral* therefore remain dark, negative and, to some, depressing.

Lawyers are usually shown as not concerned by their clients' problems, especially in cases of legal aid. All justice professionals, except perhaps Roban, are career motivated and play a political game. Recognition is vital. Clément, who leaves the magistracy after a demotion in season three to become a lawyer, is the only one in the following seasons who tries to play by the rules but his devotion to clients and idealism will get him shot and killed. Roban sometimes goes against the hierarchy to get to the bottom of an investigation, but at other times, curiously when an insignificant individual is involved, he will jump to conclusions, separate a child from his father, incarcerate a psychologically fragile suspect. His non-linear evolution is a particularly interesting aspect of the five seasons permitting unexpected developments and more realism of character.

People who come before justice in the series usually belong to one of three groups: influential businessmen or diplomats, pathetic members of the lower classes, evil serial killers or drug dealers. Young girls get themselves in trouble for love or lack of self-confidence, often both. Wiretapping is rampant and cell phones lead to localising everyone, but frequently when the law arrives, the suspects are gone. The police often act on bad leads, raids wither without results. Berthaud's team seems to run here and there and get nowhere. They cannot get to the bottom of cases and sometimes have to resort to illegal means to make arrests possible. This of course often backfires in their faces. An allusion can be detected here to the pressure many institutions were under to show their efficiency during the Sarkozy presidency. For the police, the motivation to show statistics resulted in more arrests than proof of decreasing crime.

In keeping with the reluctance to represent justice as 'neat', even if some of the seasons end with the identification of perpetrators leading in certain cases to their arrest, there will always be some form of chaos. The police station is bombed by one of the terrorists in the finale of season four. Season five ends with the probable drowning of a youth gang leader who stabs pregnant Berthaud before falling into the water. The last scene has Berthaud's colleagues listening to the doctor suggest they contact the father (who may have been one of the victims in the bombing at the end of season four) because she is out of danger but not the baby.

6 The beret, the baguette, and anti-legalism

Landois intended for season five to be the end of the show; however pressure came to do a sixth season, which at the time of this writing, is going into production. Since season four the themes and crimes dealt with in the narrative have been closer to current issues in French society. As mentioned above, illegal aliens and questions of immigration have plagued French politicians. The older issue of left-wing terrorism and street riots, as well as political corruption, were among the themes handled in seasons three and four. To begin season five, Landois was inspired by a newspaper story in which a police officer was killed in a car accident. Evidence pointed to his being run over by a police car. In the first episodes, a simple citizen, simple in mind as well as status, is arrested for causing the accident. His legal aid lawyer, who clearly only handles important cases unlike this one, advises him to confess, but Roban is not convinced. He pursues the investigation and brings two of the deceased's colleagues to trial. They are acquitted. At the same time Berthaud and her men have been investigating the murder of a young woman, killed and dumped in the Seine. What makes this crime even worse is that her body was tied to that of her little girl, who apparently was not dead before being thrown in the water. The investigation leads to a group of very violent teenage girls who commit a series of terrible acts until the police, at the end of the final episode, apprehend them. The question of young girls engaging in violent crime, as part of a gang and sometimes putting the films of these acts on YouTube, has been reported in the papers. The choice to use ripped-from-headlines stories as inspiration has been used before in France but in general the narratives reproduced the exact details of the news stories, right up to the names of those involved. To use back page stories as a starting point for a televisual creation is an innovation.

The representation of the administration of justice, even if considerably simplified, has brought satisfaction to a number of police agents. Anne Landois has received feedback that they are pleased with the more realistic view that *Spiral* gives of their dedication, despite the hard lives they lead and the pressure of their work, both in dealing with crime and with their hierarchy. Reactions from French *magistrats* are more divided. The series can be appreciated for its treatment of current news issues and the representation of different services, which work together.[14] It is true that some of the characters are seen to occupy functions that are rarely represented in film or television: the *juge d'instruction*'s assistant, *une greffière*, or the chief prosecutor (*le président du parquet*) for example. On the other hand, the negative view of French justice is perceived by some *magistrats* as unfair, and even dangerous. The writing team may not see the messages that come through the narrative as negative; at least they do not deliberately encode them. However, traces of French anti-legalism (Quinet 2002) can be clearly found in the show as in nearly all programmes dealing with justice on French television. Anti-legalism does not mean the French are 'against' justice, but they do not see it as a real institution because its power comes from the State which is, for them, the legitimate seat of authority. Justice is not considered as truly independent of political power and it is not the

14 Judge Sylvie Perdriolle (former justice of the Court of Appeals of Paris, former chief judge of the *Cour d'assises* [criminal justice] of Paris, former directrice of the Ministry of Justice Agency for the judicial protection of youths [Jan 1998–Sept 2002]), Paris.

source of resolution of social conflict: the State is. Thus, in *Spiral*, season five, the charges against an important Libyan businessman for domestic violence and illegal servitude are dropped under the influence of the head of the prosecution service because of a contract for a huge purchase of French cars by his government. The interest of the State overrides that of justice. In the corridors of the *Palais de Justice*, a *juge d'instruction* informs a very surprised lawyer Karlsson that her client (the Libyan businessman) would not be brought to trial; a *non-lieu* was pronounced in his favour. The *juge* then adds: 'Let's just keep pretending that justice is independent'. In the same season, inspector Escoffier is accused of using stolen goods to arrange an arrest. Karlsson defends him and explains that if he defends himself by implicating his superiors who put pressure on him to use any means to get this arrest, there would be many heads rolling. The charges against Escoffier are also dropped. Clément in season four remarks bitterly that in the corridors of justice, tennis matches and social dinners are essential to get ahead with a case.

Justice in France is a network of different departments intervening at various moments in a case. Their role is not necessarily over when a dossier goes to the next person. For example, the police give the results of their investigation to a prosecutor, who may call a *juge d'instruction* in on a case and the *juge* can call the police back in at any moment to carry out a particular act. The *juge*'s decision will lead to an accusation which brings the prosecutor back or a *non-lieu*, suspending or abandoning the investigation. This back and forth movement of the different agents can be confusing to a viewer because it *is* confusing. It is all the more confusing because French viewers are familiar with American procedure rather than their own. In American series, the various services are depicted to have a set and limited role in the criminal process, when their action is completed, they step out of the narrative.

It is important to note that in seasons three to five,[15] criminals who are either identified, apprehended or officially accused, either escape, die or find their charges dropped. Thus rarely does punishment enter the picture. There are scenes in which lawyers give an argument in court, but these are soundbites of justice, not portrayals of trial proceedings. The main dealings of justice are in the streets, the police bureaux, judges' offices, the corridors of the *Palais de Justice*. Courtroom procedure (argument, pleading, decision making and sentencing) are rarely, if ever, the point where a person's case will end. The message is not really that disorder triumphs over order, but that justice is not represented as the place where such problems are resolved. For a country that holds a trial even if the accused confesses to the charge, it is curious that courtroom activity is so unrepresented in this series. *Spiral* does not bring crime to punishment, at least not punishment

15 This article does not concentrate on seasons one and two because pre-2005 the writing of *Spiral* showed no evidence of concern to portray the administration of justice in France with any accuracy or any respect.

decided by the court. Can it be said then that in *Spiral*, it is not of 'fundamental importance that justice be seen to be done'?[16]

References

Ally McBeal (1997–2002) FOX.
Damages (2007–2012) FX.
Engrenages (2005) Canal+.
Femmes de loi (2000) TF1.
Law & Order (1990–2010) NBC.
Mazdon, L. (2012) 'Spiral on BBC4: putting quality first?' *Critical Studies in Television*, 7(2), p. 114. (McCabe, J. and Villez, B., issue eds.)
Président Ferrare: L'Affaire Denise Chabrier (2004) JNP, France 2, RTBF.
Président Ferrare: L'Affaire Gilles d'Aubert (2006) JNP, France 2, RTBF.
Quinet, E. (2002) *Philosophie de l'histoire de France.* Paris: Payot. (Original work published in 1857)
Rendez-moi justice (2007) Maha Productions, France 3.
Suits (2011) USA Network.

16 Lord Chief Justice Hewart in *R v. Sussex Justices, Ex parte McCarthy* [1924] 1 KB 256, [1923] All ER Rep 233.

Chapter 5

Locating justice in *Wallander*

Trading TV stories, local jurisdictions and global injustice in the Swedish and UK *Wallanders*

Janet McCabe

There are no less than three distinct televised versions based on *The Kurt Wallander Mysteries*, written by best-selling Swedish author Henning Mankell, in existence. Each interpretation of the titular detective is different, but remains relatively faithful to the weary dishevelment – both in dress and demeanour – of the fictional original. Rolf Lassgård was the first to play Kurt Wallander, in a set of Swedish TV-films that span the mid-1990s to 2007, starting with *Mördare utan ansikte* (*Faceless Killers*) in 1995. Krister Henriksson was next to take the role. His tenure lasted from 2005 until 2013, with his final performance in *Sorgfågeln* (2014, *Grief Bird*), after he decided to quit the role, saying, 'I thought: "We don't have anything more to say to each other," because it would be too complicated. So in a way I was relieved' (Frost, 2014). Next came Kenneth Branagh, who played the character as a deeply troubled soul, profoundly affected by the crimes he has witnessed, in the UK primetime BBC One adaptation, *Wallander* (2008–16). The British actor describes Wallander as 'living in a raw world . . . perceptive and intelligent about human behaviour' (Hoggart 2008, p. 20). Still, and as this chapter will explore, how exactly does 'living in a raw world' shape the interpretation of global crime and local justice in the Swedish and UK versions? How is the law embodied in the different interpretations of Kurt Wallander? And how do these various creative endeavours designed to travel circulate within a broader, more globalised, broadcasting ecology, as each series, individually and collectively, stage a vibrant dialogue concerned with crimes that routinely spill across territorial borders; and how, in turn, does the nation-specific dimension of justice concerned primarily with *representation*, in terms of *social* belonging and *who* is represented in the community alter as a consequence?

The TV detective has long proved a potent national symbol, with a vivid sense of belonging. They are emblems of an individual bounded territorial state, differentiating countries around the world in terms of how the sleuth tracks down corrupt officials and brings to justice swindlers and child murderers. *Maigret* (1959–63; 1964–8; 1992–3) focuses attention on the *commissaire* of the Paris *Brigade Criminelle* chasing criminals through Montmartre and in the remote French countryside; while Miss Jane Marple demonstrates her considerable crime-solving acumen to crack the most baffling of murder cases in the quaint village of St Mary Mead, located somewhere in the English home counties (*Agatha Christie's Miss Marple* 1986–9; *Agatha Christie's Marple* 2004–7/2008–13). More recently, there has been the Sicilian-based detective stories featuring Inspector Salvo Montalbano (Luca Zingaretti) (*Il commissario Montalbano* 1999–2013) set in the ancient rural landscape of gnarled olive trees and drystone walls, situated between the fictional town of Vigàta, with its honey-coloured sandstone buildings and Baroque palazzos, and the azure of the Mediterranean. Others include Mma Precious Ramotswe (Jill Scott) (*The No. 1 Ladies' Detective Agency* 2008–9) and her adventures solving crimes and misdemeanours in the expansive land-locked country of Botswana, from its vast areas of wilderness and the parched scrublands of the Kalahari to the bustling capital of Gaborone. A sense of place and social belonging profoundly define these characters, the landscape mapping jurisdiction and entangled with the practice of the law and its relation to the local community.

Wallander is no different. In each series, all of which were filmed on location in and around the southern Swedish coastal town of Ystad, the mood remains inherently *noir*, thanks largely to the bucolic emptiness of the Skåne landscape with its unending, open fields and wide, flat horizons, darkened furthered by human depravity and compromised justice. This acute sense of place speaks directly to the modern social democratic nation state – with its distinctive claims to protect its citizens equitably *under* the law, but also at the same time declaring everyone formally equal *before* it. At the core is a claim of liberalism and the liberal polity, in which institutional frameworks and the social order seek, in principle at least, to ensure that everyone participates in society with an equality of opportunity, in spite of individual differences and plural values. As that sense of a clearly defined, bordered nation state increasingly recedes, and as individual countries encounter transnationalising forces and the rise of neoliberalism, with its market-based solutions and consumer-oriented thinking, an almost nostalgic sense of place that features so prominently in these different TV shows has taken on added significance within a dynamic *mise-en-scène*.

Witnessed also in how the world has been consuming Scandinavian crime fiction of late, *Wallander* is a story that travels widely. In the wake of the phenomenal international success of Stieg Larsson's *Millennium* trilogy – *The Girl with the Dragon Tattoo (Män som hatar kvinnor*, 2005), *The Girl Who Played With Fire* (*Flickan som lekte med elden*, 2006) and *The Girl Who Kicked the Hornets' Nest* (*Luftslottet som sprängdes*, 2007) – and boosted by worldwide sales of what has become known as 'Nordic noir', Mankell has also found a global readership for his shambolic, deeply troubled detective. Wallander made his first appearance in the novel, *Mördare utan ansikte*, in 1991 (translated as *Faceless Killers*, Mankell 2000). Nine titles followed and the series concluded in 2009 with *Den orolige mannen* (*The Troubled Man*, Mankell 2011). More than 30 million copies of the *Wallander* stories have been sold around the world and the novels translated into more than 40 different languages. So successful are the *Wallander* books in translation that it led Barry Forshaw (2012, p. 21) to say, 'In the past, various non-English-speaking crime writers have achieved classic status, but if there's one modern writer who is the market leader for foreign crime in translation, it is Sweden's Henning Mankell.'

This remarkable global literary success created an ideal opportunity for television, first with the TV miniseries (1995–2007) made by Sveriges Television and Tre Vänner Produktion AD, and later as a franchise for international export. Yellow Bird Productions, a joint collaboration between Mankell and producer/director Ole Søndberg, was set up according to Erik Hultkvist 'with the sole focus of one project, which was to turn the Wallander character into a franchise, making films based on the character' (Peacock 2014, p. 147). Now the property of one of the world's largest media conglomerates, Zodiak media group, Yellow Bird (also responsible for the films based on Larsson's *Millennium* trilogy) produced the first 13 Swedish *Wallander* movies (2005–6), starring Henriksson. These original Swedish TV adaptations were made possible because of co-international partners, based on investments made by various European TV broadcasters, including: Canal+ (France), Danmark Radio (Denmark), Degeto Film (Germany) and TV2 Norge (Norway). Financial arrangements were set up in such a way as to satisfy individual TV stakeholders and tailored to specific territorial requirements. As Mikael Wallén, Executive Producer of the Swedish *Wallander* at Yellow Bird, put it:

> The whole *Wallander* concept was based on the investment made by TV broadcasters in Sweden and Germany. The whole project has been designed such that the broadcasters are satisfied . . . giving the German broadcaster rights for Germany, and in Scandinavia the rights to release the first [film in the] cinema to market the new series of films, especially for the DVD sales.
>
> (Peacock 2014, p. 151)

What the various business arrangements and financial agreements illustrate is how transnational media networks are coming into being centred around the production of particular types of stories, and ones that hold strong within the primetime schedules of individual nations, namely: crime. As Hultkvist from Yellow Bird explains, regarding the scheduling of *Wallander* on Swedish television:

> *Wallander* had been very strong on TV and DVD ever since we started making them. Every time we . . . put up a *Wallander*, even if it is pay-TV and DVD before going to free-to-air TV, they have a 50 per cent share [of the audience]; it's a habit to watch a *Wallander* or Beck movie on a Saturday or Sunday night on TV4 in the 'crime slot'.
>
> (Peacock 2014, pp. 148–9)

The Swedish *Wallander* is a primetime show in Sweden, but also in the UK, where it holds strong in its Saturday night 9pm BBC Four slot, as it defines the cultural value and critical import of the minority digital channel. This globally produced cultural TV product offers new opportunities for representing the law differently and with new stories for a national TV audience defined in terms of what Benedict Anderson (1991) called the 'imagined community'. With changes in the imagined nature of belonging, in forms of participation and cultural production, film-TV shows like *Wallander* are making visible, as well as defining, shifts in the relationship between nations, regions and television markets (e.g. main and minority channels, DVD sales).

The popularity of these Scandinavian-based crime stories has contributed to a surge of traffic from the periphery to older, more established metropolitan centres of television production. In addition to the Swedish versions, Yellow Bird was involved in the adaptation of *Wallander* for the British market, in partnership with Left Bank Pictures. 'Left Bank was set up with a very clear intent of making quality, top-end television with an international dimension,' says CEO Andy Harries. 'In this way, *Wallander* was a natural project for us' (Peacock 2014, p. 157). The British-based production company entered into a business alliance with Yellow Bird, after Søndberg approached Harries with the UK rights to the Henning Mankell novels (Peacock 2014, p. 157). Next Harries went to the BBC and Jane Tranter, the then Controller of Fiction, and in January 2008, she and BBC Scotland's Anne Mensah commissioned *Wallander*, starring Branagh, at a cost of £6 million for the initial three 90 minute episodes. Each one cost £2 million, with the initial financial outlay coming from a variety of sources. As budgets tighten, and the BBC as a public service broadcaster becomes increasingly accountable to its stakeholders, multiple co-investor partners represent a new way of financing high-end TV drama. Half of the money raised to produce *Wallander* came from the BBC and international presales. Previously Harries had sold a 25 per cent stake in Left Bank to BBC Worldwide (formally known as BBC Enterprises), giving the more market-oriented BBC subsidiary an exclusive five-year distribution deal on all his subsequent productions (Peacock 2014, p. 158; Armstrong 2008). Co-production funding also came from presales to WGBH Boston (US) and the German ARD Degeto, with a tax break for filming in Sweden (Armstrong 2008), involving Film i Skåne (Clarke 2008), which is a regional (rather than nation-focused) film centre based in the Øresund Region of southern Sweden and Greater Copenhagen that actively encourages domestic and foreign investment to film in the local area, itself a relatively newly formed transnational geographical territory made possible by the construction of the Øresund Bridge (featured in *Bron/Broen* 2011–present, *The Bridge*). Such transnational-oriented conditions of co-production and distribution, based on new global networks of ideas, capital transfer and forms of co-operation, are thus creating new creative opportunities and new ways of conceptualising and thinking about how we produce culture and give representation to the world around us.

What emerges from these various financial agreements, transnational negotiations and global-regional-national interactions is how the 'glocal' profoundly shapes the making of *Wallander* as a TV product. It is tailored for specific cultural consumption, with reference to a particular national culture (more of which later), but also as a profit-oriented necessity within that market. 'Glocalisation' is produced in and through these cross-border business collaborations, epitomising how the global embraces both the transnational and geo-cultural as it taps directly into local broadcasting jurisdictions and production territories. In so doing, this glocalisation strategy allows media corporations to flow across media borders with stories shaped by a television grammar able to tell truly global stories about criminal activities, human rights and (social) injustice perpetuated in a globalised world of interdependence. What gets revealed is a television product fit for global purpose, where we witness a convergence between a worldliness embedded in the formal properties of the original stories and the global-regional-national impulses underlying what is involved in their transnational movement and cultural exchange.

No discussion of the global appetite of what goes under the umbrella title of *The Kurt Wallander Mysteries* would be complete without recognising how these crime stories have struck a universal narrative chord. This subgenre of crime has been particularly amenable to exchange, confirming what Joseph Strauhbaar (2007, p. 201) writes about shareability, which 'refers to common values, images, archetypes and themes across cultures programs to flow across cultural boundaries'. Such a conceptualisation of cultural shareability takes on added meaning when we consider how these crime stories from Sweden often deal with states of statelessness – stateless individuals (itinerant workers, asylum seekers, refugees), cyberterrorism and transnational corporations. What lurches in the shadows of neoliberal global ambition for a 'world without borders' – between humanitarian progress and human rights violation, between consumption (and the rhetoric of choice) and the movement of labour (both voluntary and involuntary) – is what Homi K. Bhabha (2008, p. 39) describes as 'a complex and contradictory mode of being or surviving somewhere in between legality and incivility'. These 'no-man's-land' stories of crime and the power to punish (or not) are ones routinely shared across territorial borders. These tales deal with the inbetweenness of identities, affiliations and experiences *behind* and *beyond* borders as a condition of our globalised, often cosmopolitan, world, but nonetheless are told and negotiated at specific national levels. It thus seems possible to speak of international, perhaps global, stories based on widely shared beliefs and experiences like migration and immigration. But where the contestation of those experiences in terms of social belonging and those denied the possibility of justice are being played out in definitive territories and among nation-specific social and cultural groupings.

The *Wallander* novels set in the commercial seaport of Ystad, on the southernmost tip of Sweden, directly tackle pervasive social anxieties and the new challenges made salient by globalisation, transnationalising forces and cross-border activities for individual nation states and supposedly stable democracies around the world (see Held 2008; Beck 2003; Robertson 1992, pp. 8–30). It is well known that Mankell started writing the *Kurt Wallander Mysteries* after an extended period of living in Africa during the 1980s, where he worked in the theatre, mostly in the Mozambique capital of Maputo. He returned to Sweden to find a different country, a more xenophobic, troubled society. Mankell thus offers his readers a disorientating sense of the world, viewing the West from a different perspective, or as he himself put it, 'I stand with one foot in the snow and one foot in the sand.'

> I am like an artist who has to stand close to the canvas in order to paint, and afterwards take a step back to be able to see what I have painted. Africa has

> enriched my life with that movement. Some things can only be perceived from a certain distance.
>
> (Mankell 2014)

The unsettling disquiet created through the migratory prism of distance translates further into the ways we think about justice and society where so-called globalisation has altered the grammar of what is meant by democratic participation, social belonging and public accountability. Put another way, Mankell's stories explore questions of *who* belongs and *who* counts in matters of the law and justice. His novels are preoccupied with the themes of immigration and racism, inequality and hierarchies, the breakdown of communities and divisions in social obligations and loyalties, as well as questions of inclusion and exclusion; and four of the six stories first chosen for adaptation in the UK openly address issues of broken borders and border crossings in staging and resolving conflicts over injustice: *Sidetracked* (sex trafficking and sexual enslavement of teenage girls from abroad), *Firewall* (cyberterrorism and the international financial system), *Faceless Killers* (refugees, migrant labour and racial hatred) and *The Man Who Smiled* (transnational corporations and the trade in human organs from the Third World). These stories – *Villospår*, *Brandvägg*, *Mördare utan ansikte* and *Mannen som log* – were also made into TV-films in Sweden, starring Lassgård.

These stories are given added piquancy from the fact that such monstrous crimes are perpetrated in a country for so long regarded as a bastion for enlightened Western liberal democracy. Of this social liberalism, Francis Sejersted (2011, p. 6) writes:

> The Scandinavian model is marked – to cite just a few of its characteristic traits – by comprehensiveness of social security systems, institutionalised universal social rights, a high level of public support, and a high level of equality, which grew out of a combination of public commitment to the principle of universalism and equality of income distribution, which in turn, is partly a tribute to the strength of the trade unions.

This emphasis on the integrated principled and social character of modern governance is particularly revealing if we consider the Swedish welfare state – or 'People's Home' (*Folkhemmet*), as the embodiment of that project. Maintaining the social welfare and individual freedom of Swedish citizens speaks directly to a moral and political commitment to a common humanity that unites us all. Difference and diversity are less important than an intrinsic belief in the idea that all human beings are fundamentally the same and as such deserve to be treated equally. This treatment based on equality of care and consideration, irrespective of background, is embedded deep into the very fabric of Sweden's institutions of tolerance and social inclusiveness. Such principles of social equality and human rights, civil liberties and individual freedom have, in turn, long proved a strong mobilising force behind Swedish national identity. So strong in fact that Francis

Hopkinson at Left Bank Pictures reported how 'it was a deliberate choice to go for the [UK *Wallander's*] 1960s and 1970s look because that was when . . . the Swedish welfare state dream entered British consciousness' (Forshaw 2012, p. 184).

'Sweden has laid itself out as a very open society where the ideal of the common good is something to be cherished,' Branagh said in an interview. 'When that is abused and spoilt by the loss of human life, it's particularly poignant' (Rampton 2008, p. 16). This 'poignancy' is especially appropriate, and telling in relation to Sweden, where confidence in the universal codes and ethics related to the welfare of citizens, so central to Swedish statehood, have long been in tension, often contradiction, with the countervailing values of protectionist policies and extreme racist strands lurking in the collective psyche since the Second World War (Peacock 2014, pp. 29–35; Gilmour 2010). Yet today, the challenge to these universal liberal principles goes much deeper than charges of simple hypocrisy or double standards. Such unease in the ways in which Sweden thinks about its civil society in part reflects the long shadow cast by the unsolved murder of Prime Minister Olof Palme (shot dead in 1986 while walking home with his wife on Sveavägen, one of Stockholm's busiest streets) and later the murder of the Social Democratic politician and Minister of Foreign Affairs, Anna Lindh (who died after being stabbed by Mijailo Mijailović in 2003). More profound still, and in the wake of Sweden's 1995 entry into the European Union, has been the impact of globalisation, the flow of international capital and economic migrant labour across borders in this period of neoliberal hegemony. The unanticipated, often unplanned social consequences frustrate the idea of the nation state and a national society and security, but instead 'create new transnational forms of living and communities . . . new ways in which groups and individuals see themselves and others' (Beck 2008, p. 60). Such side effects, unintended or otherwise, have provided fresh opportunities but also new instabilities, reawakening old insecurities and deep-rooted bigotry. As a result, the very foundations of this liberal order are once again being questioned internally, as a result of failures in assimilation and multicultural policies.

It is a malaise that has translated into the ideological and political critique embedded right into the distinctive forms and narrative style of modern Scandinavian crime fiction. Starting with the Martin Beck series, created in 1965 by two Swedes from the political left, Maj Sjöwall and Per Wahlöö, who seized on the police procedural as a form, the emergence of the socially committed crime novel interwove realism with a radical political agenda, 'as a scalpel cutting open the belly of an ideologically pauperized and morally debatable so-called welfare state of the bourgeois type' (Winston and Mellerski 1992, p. 16). Writers like Mankell continue in that tradition of using fiction as social critique; 'The *Wallander* novels are a sort of requiem for a lost utopia, for the lost innocence of Sweden,' said Branagh (Stasio 2009). Mankell has gone as far as to suggest a subtitle for his *Wallander* cycle, 'Novels about the Swedish Anxiety' (Stasio 2009); and it is that intense sense of social disquiet, which is embodied in the downbeat insomniac Wallander, troubled and disillusioned by how fallible and intolerant his society has become.

Global crime, the question of jurisdiction and how to police imaginary, often borderless, spaces feature in *Wallander* as a way of exploring how so-called social democratic nations like Sweden often simply pursue Western (imperialist) policies, as well as how national economies are often subject to transnational corporations and supranational agencies like the European Central Bank beyond the reach of constitutional democracies. Some acts of injustice carried out in a globalised world are inherently non-territorial in nature. Examples include international currency regimes and the supranational governance of global markets determining patterns of employment and economic migration, which, in turn, regulate *who* is rich and *who* is poor ('Firewall' 2009), *who* gets paid a living wage and *who* does not ('Täckmanteln' 2009, 'The Container Lorry'; 'Faceless Killers' 2010); global communications, networks of information and cyber-technology, which dictate *who* can access systems of power and knowledge and who cannot ('Firewall' 2009); and the bio-political power of health and medical ethics ('The Man Who Smiled' 2010), drugs ('Kuriren' 2010, 'The Courier'), sex ('Sidetracked' 2010, 'Vittnet' 2010, 'The Witness'), which govern *who* lives and *who* dies, often young, violently and in poverty. In these matters of justice in relation to networks of global interdependence and movement of goods, capital and bodies, Nancy Fraser (2013, p. 201) puts it best when she said, 'so fundamental to human well being, the forces that perpetrate injustice belong not to the "the space of places," but to "the space of flows"'.

A demonstration of how *Wallander* explores this 'space of flows' in relation to how globalisation is changing the ways we determine justice may be illustrated in a comparison of the Swedish and British adaptations of Mankell's 1994 novel *Mannen som log* (*The Man Who Smiled*, Mankell 2006), which concerns the illegal trade in human organs and forced donors from the Third World. *Who* is judged, *who* gets justice and *who* can claim the moral right to intervene and adjudicate on such matters in the first place emerge as central themes within the original story. But how these matters are translated in the nation-specific adaptations offers different approaches to thinking about questions of morality and responsibility, justice and democracy in a world of global interdependence. The story begins with Sten Torstensson, a lawyer and old acquaintance, who approaches Wallander for help. Torstensson's father, Gustaf, recently died in what looks like nothing more than a tragic car accident along a deserted road. But his lawyer son isn't so sure. Suspicion shrouds the circumstances of his father's death and Sten wants the Inspector to make further inquiries. Initially Wallander turns Torstensson away. When the son also turns up dead, Wallander is drawn into the investigation. It is not long before his inquiries lead him to the home of billionaire businessman, Alfred Harderberg, famed for his charitable support of humanitarian causes and the arts. The philanthropic tycoon presides over a vast international trading empire, but Wallander soon uncovers a hidden, more sinister side to Harderberg's business dealings, namely, a diabolical trade involving the importation of human body parts from the Third World – South America in the Swedish version, Africa in the UK adaption. In exposing heinous crimes perpetrated by those with extraordinary wealth and political clout to violate the human rights of those denied the possibility of participating equally in society offers a more deep-rooted inquiry into justice and the law, in terms of the evil that men (and in the Swedish version a woman) do, both as individuals and as members of a new amoral global imperialist order. Decisions taken in one territorial state that impact on the lives of those outside it may be conditioned by the actions of transnational corporations and subject to the global interdependence of capital and investment, but what happens in the murky shadows of those global movements, including the infringement of human rights? In the Swedish film-TV version, *Mannen som log* (2003), featuring Lassgård, the clinical organisation TLL (Tools for a Longer Life) reaches into 123 countries around the world and is owned by the enigmatic, but rather charming billionaire businessman, Harderberg (Claes Månsson). His global business empire is entwined with the Swedish establishment, an interrelationship between international commerce and humanitarianism that allows for an unimpeded flow of trade with little regard for national borders. Behind the respectable company that handles 'voluntary' organ donations, supposedly helping two million people worldwide desperate for a transplant, is the exploitation of those in the Third World with a limited capacity to defend themselves. Human organs are harvested from otherwise healthy bodies. If consent is not granted body parts are taken anyway, with vulnerable individuals, mostly children, left to die without access to proper medical treatment and their bodies quite literally discarded as rubbish. TLL may acknowledge the universal value of human life, talking eloquently of a shared humanity through the 'value of giving' and donors 'making' choices with their power to improve and save the lives of others beyond territorial states, but *only* certain bodies truly matter. What emerges is the question of how to define and even defend the 'human' in human rights of those involved in the trafficking of body parts, when the good of a common humanity is valued over the individual. The team uncover stories of street children in Brazil, with a 15-year-old boy from Hamburg receiving a kidney from Claudio Ramirez, aged 17 and from São Paulo. She was found murdered and dumped in a skip three days before the transplant operation in Germany. Her organs presumably were removed without consent. And given that hers is an undocumented life, and besides she is beyond the jurisdiction of both Sweden and Germany, nothing can be proved. Being poor and homeless means no post mortem. What has happened to her is quite literally hidden from the law.

Wallander works through the night trying to build a case against Harderberg. He imagines the fate of another child, Loisa Jorgez from Rio de Janeiro, registered as dead five days after the transplant operation. Grainy, black and white images re-imagine Loisa's grisly fate on the operation table, her body dumped, before cutting to the stillness of the gentle rolling fields of Skåne. Rooting this speculative nightmare within a bucolic landscape of social democracy reminds us of what Hannah Arendt (1973, p. 302) said:

> Deadly danger to any civilisation is no longer likely to come from without. The danger is that a global universally interrelated civilisation may produce

> barbarians from its own midst by forcing millions of people into conditions, which despite all appearances, are the conditions of savages.

What is at stake when 'barbarians' of a new corporate internationalism emerge from supposedly stable, civilised centres of democratic civility and champions of universal human values? Under what jurisdiction do victims fall if what happens to them is *internal* to the global, rather than national, condition? Especially if these Brazilian children have left behind few visible documented traces of their existence within their own territorial state?

Trying to secure a warrant to search Harderberg's property proves the next hurdle. Wallander presents his evidence to Chief of Police Lisa Holgersson (Kerstin Andersson). 'It's complicated,' she says. 'TLL's owners are in Holland, it has offices everywhere.' Wallander replies that the company is registered in Brösarp. 'It's the Harderbergs' home.' Wallander gets his warrant. Still, at the moment the police convoy arrives at Harderbergs' Wallander receives a call from Holgersson telling him that authorisation has been revoked. The Prosecutor General intervened; there isn't sufficient evidence and without any physical proof there is no case to answer. Harderberg is immune from prosecution – literally above the law, visually represented by him looking down at the police driving away from an upstairs window of his fortified property. No wonder he smiles. So 'inside' power is Harderberg, so advantaged by wealth and resources – his company providing jobs for the region and contributing wealth to the Swedish economy, that his legal rights matter most as someone who belongs completely inside the system. Framed by the territorial state apparatus as a *representative* of the community, he is insulated from the reach of justice. What is legal and what is (un)just almost becomes invisible in the experience of the quotidian, as society turns a blind eye to the source of the economic power and political influence that it requires to prosper.

News reaches Wallander that Harderberg is leaving Skåne. He is relocating to São Paulo, not necessarily to evade capture, but to escape the disciplinary gaze of the Ystad police: the case is 'officially' closed. Wallander visits Harderberg late at night, following a call from his Head of Security, Kurt Ström (Peter Sundberg), after the grisly discovery of the putrefying corpses of the Latvians who tried to kill Wallander earlier. Wallander arrives to find Harderberg presiding over a 'family' meal. Represented in the gloomy opulence of the baroque interior, the extravagance of the electronic monster truck gifted to Ström's son and the awkwardness of Ström and his wife is an uneasy sense of vulnerability and moral ambivalence. This *mise-en-scène* of the domestic reveals how the chance for a comfortable life is dependent on trespassing the borders of what is right and wrong and destabilising definitions in the process. Faced with the true depravity of Harderberg's crimes, including the insemination of his adopted daughter, Kristina (Melinda Kinnaman), now carrying his child, Wallander is paralysed in his inability to act. 'There's hope for mankind,' Harderberg tells him, referring to his unborn child. 'You murder children for money,' comes the Inspector's reply.

Harderberg: We murder no children. We are testing the system. Some suppliers got a bit too eager.
Wallander: But innocent children have been killed. That's enough for me.
Harderberg: In 10 years TLL will be saving lives round the clock. No one will care.

Harderberg rationalises that he has committed no crime. Believing instead that these deaths are permissible in pursuit of a higher humanitarian purpose.

Harderberg: People see moral principles as something good . . . And they are, if you're arresting a thief or a wife-beater. But . . . in my case, this more noble cause . . . such attributes are restrictive. This is why, Inspector Wallander, you'll never touch me.

Wallander pulls his weapon. He aims it straight at Harderberg's face. 'You won't shoot me, because you respect the law. That's your restriction,' Harderberg calmly informs the Inspector. Wallander, of course, doesn't shoot; and besides, his position to judge is severely compromised after inadvertently sleeping with a prostitute, which has escalated into a full-blown media scandal. Harderberg returns to the table. Wallander appeals to Ström, but to no avail. For he, too, as well as his family are so mired in compromise. Wallander can do nothing but walk away in silence, revealing deepening corruption where justice may not prevail.

The story does not end with Wallander unable to secure a conviction. Instead he leaks the case files to a female journalist, as he stubbornly pursues justice and seeks to make the facts as widely known as possible. Such a gesture is conceived of as an ethical one, where a moral resolution for victims excluded from active Swedish citizenship is found in the court of public opinion where universal standards, human rights and democratic values hold strong. With the crimes exposed in this way there is a sense that Wallander sees the value in the public (service television) as judge and jury. Despite the salacious media coverage of his sexual indiscretions, there is a narrative acknowledgment of the role played by global communications and information networks like the press in disseminating testimony and defending human rights. The Swedish *Wallander* engages directly with an idea of the State as an exceedingly significant agent in *producing* and sustaining the delivery of effective civic regulation, social equality and public justice in and through stories that explore how far the judiciary system makes good on those ideals and how far it fails to do so.

Whereas the Swedish Harderberg is positioned as an establishment figure, someone of political influence and social importance to and for the Swedish nation state, the UK version of Harderberg (Rupert Graves) is far more of a stateless, possibly transcendent individual. When the illegal trafficking from the Sudan links directly back to Gustaf Torstensson, by way of orders placed for the organ transplant cases and end-user certificates, Wallander guarantees that nothing will lead directly to Harderberg. It is almost as if he doesn't exist, certainly not within the legal structures of specific nation states. Unlike his Swedish counterpart, Harderberg lives alone in his castle, outside of Ystad, with its cool interiors and minimal design. In the background is a bustling coterie of staff, often out of focus; and Harderberg is always preparing to depart for somewhere else. He is thus positioned as a more eccentric, maverick figure, lacking political influence, and not quite belonging to the territorial state in quite the same way as his Swedish counterpart. Instead he embodies a more stateless sense of being, someone neither at the centre nor at the social margins, but nonetheless in the midst of a new internationalism where the boundaries defining legality and incivility are not always entirely clear.

Central to the UK adaptation is the question of *who* is judged and not, and *who* is punished and not. Kurt Ström translates into Anders Ekman (Vincent Regan), and the story of the ex-policeman turned security assistant for Harderberg takes more of a centre stage. Ekman's career in the Malmö police ended ignominiously after he accidently killed a teenage girl while driving an unmarked police car. His crime is not only pitched against the one Wallander thinks he committed in shooting dead a racist killer ('Faceless Killers' 2010), but against Harderberg and his trafficking in human body parts from Africa. When Wallander confronts Harderberg with the allegations, the detective knows full well he does not have a shred of physical proof to convict the tycoon. Their conversation soon takes an existential turn, where the nihilism of *Crime and Punishment* meets Michel Foucault's discourse of discipline and power, as Harderberg delivers his thoughts on the morality of murder.

Harderberg: Look, you killed a man, a racist killer. Killed in self-defence, in the line of duty. A perfectly reasonable cause of action. But then you ran away into the wilderness for six months, sweating and shaking. One big question: does your pain make you a good man, or a weak man?

Wallander: I took a life.

Harderberg: Exactly, life or death. Who lives, who dies? Who decides? Was a racist killer's life worth as much as yours? You know it wasn't. You know in your heart.

Wallander: No one has the right to make those kinds of decisions.

Harderberg: It's my strength. Who lives or dies. My family, my children.

He smiles. Wallander walks away. The sparseness of the bleached-out *mise-en-scène*, slightly shaky camera and obtuse angles draw the viewer into uneasy ethical territory. It pulls them into the *midst* of the ambivalent, *internal* logic of the new global condition – of the universal worth of human life related to the commercial value of the corporeal body, calculated at £125,000, and *who* has the moral right to decide the worth of either.

Wallander returns home to find Ekman with proof – incriminating Harderberg's henchman Sjølander (Kimmo Rajala), but not, unsurprisingly, the tycoon. In exchange Ekman wants back into the police force. Wallander takes the evidence to Lisa Holgersson (Sadie Shimmin), but she will not broker any deal in exchange for information.

Wallander: [Ekman] broke the rules, an accident. Nothing that Harderberg does is an accident. It's murder hundreds of times over. People are dying because he decides that they are worth no more than their body parts. And you're talking to me of Ekman and rules.

What distinguishes the UK *Wallander* is how its distinctive visual style allows for the depiction of the emotional effect of crime etched in the performances about the crime itself. *Wallander* was the first BBC project to shoot using the Red Camera, which records four times the resolution of high definition as raw data, allowing more detail in the image for the colourist to work with in post-production. Seeing the moral contours of despairing faces emerges as a visceral experience through the dazzling visual clarity of the image. It translates matters of justice into questions of personal integrity and ethical choices scored in the faces of those captured on camera. The final confrontation over justice and punishment pitches Ekman and Wallander against Harderberg and Sjølander in a series of close-ups, some extremely tight, in which the action takes place away from the public gaze on private property. It is an almost hidden, twilight world of bruised pastel shades and ambiguous jurisdiction. Ekman is fatally shot, not before he saves Wallander from Sjølander's bullet; while Wallander decides to wound rather than kill Harderberg, he is giving Ekman his personal benediction that his dying colleague is now back 'inside' the law.

If the 'no-man's-land' of Harderberg's property suggests a frontiers territory policed by mavericks and personal actions, the Swedish *Wallanders* are often staged in locations where the team (rather than the individual) must perform that law locally in areas inadequately policed or protected from those with affiliations to international cartels and criminal organisations operating in a regional (rather than national) geographical spaces. One such episode is 'Cellisten' (2010, 'The Cellist'), featuring Henriksson. Following a recital, Wallander rescues Russian cellist Irina Konsalevska (Sandra Stojiljkovic), who is targeted in a car bomb attack. Wallander and the team soon discover that Irina is in witness protection, because she is the chief witness in a murder investigation, involving none other than Russian Mafioso Yuri Rina, son of the notorious boss Leb Munchin (Baard Owe) (who incidentally has no criminal record and is nicknamed the 'Phantom'). Wallander and the Ystad police, along with special agent Jens Riis (Magnus Roosmann) from Malmö, find themselves drawn into a vortex of cross-border warfare involving narcotics (smuggled in Irina's cello), kidnapping and murder (executions, shootings) and pitched against a powerful cross-border adversary whose methods are nothing less than ruthless. After another attempt made on her life while recovering in hospital Irina is moved for her own safety onto a houseboat, guarded by Svartman (Fredrik Gunnarsson). Soon tracked down by her assassins, Svartman is tortured and Jens' daughter Ella (Mimmi Benckert-Claesson) is taken hostage. Irina, however, proves her mettle as she shoots one of her pursuers in cold-blood within this frontiers land of international territorial waters and transit sites.

While Irina has no ethical problem in shooting dead her assailant, Wallander, Jens and Katarina Ahlsell (Lena Endre) have more ethical scruples about the legality of discharging firearms. Wallander enquires about the legitimacy of putting a gun into the hands of Katarina, the Ystad prosecutor, and compromising her authority. When the second assailant tries to escape in a motorised dinghy it is left to Katarina, alone on deck, to stop him. She has no other choice but to shoot, missing him, but instead hitting the boat – with more luck than judgement. What follows next is a linguistically complex interrogation, with Wallander speaking in English, the assailant understanding English, but speaking only in Russian, leaving it to Irina to translate the Russian into Swedish for the others. (More than the UK version, the Swedish *Wallanders* recognise the lived experience of this multilingual region.) Shifting dimensions of the inside/outside status of peripatetic villains travelling across national borders to commit crime reveal how much the very definition of the border and territorial limits is changing. Wallander finally tracks down the mafia boss to a Russian Orthodox church in Ystad, before father and son are brought to justice and sentenced in Sweden. What this Swedish TV adaptation, based on stories inspired by Mankell rather than the original novels, acknowledges, as do the other versions, is how the law is constituted within a complex variety of legal zones.

Cross-border crime based on longer histories, diasporas and territorial claims within the Baltic region further explore questions of individual nation states and its role in the violation of human rights. None more so than in *Dogs of Riga* (Mankell 2001), where the action is set in Latvia, a democratic republic emancipated from Soviet rule in 1987, and where *Wallander* experiences an almost lawless territory. In the UK version ('Dogs of Riga' 2012) Søren Malling (known to British audiences from the first series of Danish crime drama, *The Killing* [*Forbrydelsen*, DR/Denmark, 2007]) turns up as hard-drinking Latvian detective Karlis Liepa, arriving in Ystad to help Wallander identify two corpses washed ashore on the remote Swedish coastline in a rubber dinghy (later discovered with a hidden stash of cocaine). Liepa recognises the men as his informants, telling Wallander that they were part of an internal mafia dispute involving a drug-smuggling cartel. Liepa returns home, but shortly afterwards a communication arrives from Riga that Liepa has been murdered. Wallander travels to the Latvian capital and learns from former colleagues Colonels Putnis (Arturs Skrastins) and Murnieks (Zoltan Butuc) that Liepa worked undercover in the drugs squad, mostly on the new heroin and cocaine routes, but never shared his case notes with anyone. Wallander becomes involved with Liepa's widow, Baiba (Ingeborga Dapkunaite) and, thrown into a forbidding, sinister post-Cold War world of police surveillance and deception, finds himself entangled in a web of corruption where no one is safe and no one can be trusted, before finally unmasking Putnis as a double agent. Justice prevails, but inherent unresolved contradictions and older political allegiances in the shadow of the collapse of the Soviet Union compromise the new European principles of integration and tolerance in terms of defining what is legal and what isn't.

'If there is a subtext to my novels,' Mankell has said, 'it is that the cornerstone of a functional democracy is a working system of justice' (Stasio 2009). What this chapter has aimed to do is explore how series like *Wallander* provide narratives in ethical thinking in what determine the *who* and *what* matters in questions of (social) justice. Each provides a space of contemplation where we, like Wallander, must reflect on questions of collective responsibility, inequalities and injustice in our world of neoliberal economic markets, global interdependence and transnational movements. If, as David Held (2004, p. 172) says, 'To think of people as having equal moral value is to make a general claim about the basic unit of the world as comprising persons as free and equal beings', then these new hybrid stories explore what exactly that might mean, both the advantages and disadvantages. Penal responsibility may fall to individual perpetrators – Harderberg, Yuri Rina, Leb Munchin – the authors of the atrocities against others, but there is also a sense of shared collective responsibility. What *Wallander* offers, and it may help explain why these stories travel so widely, is how these narratives provide a developing vocabulary for exploring our collective role and responsibilities in matters of justice beyond local jurisdictions.

References

Agatha Christie's Marple (2004–7/2008–13) Granada.

Agatha Christie's Miss Marple (1986–9) BBC.

Anderson, B. (1991) *Imagined communities: reflections on the origin and spread of nationalism*. London: Verso.

Arendt, H. (1973) *The origins of totalitarianism*. New York: Harcourt Brace Jovanovitch.

Armstrong, S. (2008) 'Making mischief is a good thing', *The Guardian*, 27 October. www.theguardian.com/media/2008/oct/27/bbc (Accessed: 1 July 2014).

Beck, U. (2003) 'Toward a new critical theory with a cosmopolitan intent', *Constellations: An International Journal of Critical and Democratic Theory*, 10(4), pp. 453–68.

Beck, U. (2008) 'Realistic cosmopolitanism: how do societies handle otherness?', in Held, D. and Moore, H.L. (eds.) *Cultural politics in a global age: uncertainty, solidarity, and innovation*. Oxford: Oneworld Publications, pp. 60–7.

Bhabha, H.K. (2008) 'Notes on globalisation and ambivalence', in Held, D. and Moore, H.L. (eds.) *Cultural politics in a global age: uncertainty, solidarity, and innovation*. Oxford: Oneworld Publications, pp. 36–47.

Bron/Broen (2011-present) Filmlance International AB; Nimbus Film Productions; Sveriges Television (SVT); Film i Väst; Zweites Deutsches Fernsehen (ZDF); Danmarks Radio (DR); Film i Skåne; ZDF Enterprises; Norsk Rikskringkasting (NRK).

'Cellisten' (2010) *Wallander*, Series 2, episode 5. *Swedish TV*, 24 April.

Clarke, S. (2008) 'Brit drama in rewrite', *Variety*, 14 December, p. 23.

'Dogs of Riga' (2012) *Wallander*, Series 2, episode 3. BBC One, 6 September.

'Faceless Killers' (2010) *Wallander*, Series 2, episode 1. BBC One, 3 October.

'Firewall' (2009) *Wallander*, Series 1, episode 2. BBC One, 17 May.

Forshaw, B. (2012) *Death in a cold climate: a guide to Scandinavian crime fiction*. Basingstoke: Palgrave Macmillan.

Fraser, N. (2013) *Fortunes of feminism: from state-managed capitalism to neoliberal crisis*. London: Verso.

Frost, V. (2014), 'Krister Henriksson: why I'm leaving Wallander', *The Guardian*, 20 June. www.theguardian.com/tv-and-radio/2014/jun/20/krister-henriksson-on-leaving-wallander (Accessed: 2 December 2015).

Gilmour, J. (2010) *Sweden, the swastika and Stalin: the Swedish experience in the second world war*. Edinburgh: Edinburgh University Press.
Held, D. (2004) *Global covenant: the social democratic alternative to the Washington consensus*. Cambridge, Polity.
Held, D. (2008) 'Cultural diversity, cosmopolitan principles and the limits of sovereignty', in Held, D. and Moore, H.L. (eds.) *Cultural politics in a global age: uncertainty, solidarity, and innovation*. Oxford: Oneworld Publications, pp. 157–64.
Hoggart, P. (2008) *The Times (Magazine)*, 5 December, pp. 40–1.
Il Commissario Montalbano (1999–2013) Palomar; RAI fiction.
'Kuriren' (2010) *Wallander*, Series 2, episode 3. *Swedish TV*, 10 April.
Maigret (1959–63) BBC.
Maigret (1964–8) Belgische Radio en Televisie.
Maigret (1992–3) Granada.
Mankell, H. (2000) *Faceless killers*. Translated by S.T. Murray. London: Vintage Books. (Original work published in 1999, *Mördare utan ansikte*)
Mankell, H. (2001) *Dogs of Riga*. Translated by L. Thompson. London: Vintage Books. (Original work published in 1992, *Hundarna i Riga*)
Mankell, H. (2006), *The man who smiled*. Translated by L. Thompson. London: Vintage Books. (Original work published in 1994, *Mannen som log*)
Mankell, H. (2011) *The troubled man*. Translated by L. Thompson. London: Vintage Books. (Original work published in 2009, *Den orolige mannen*)
Mankell, H. (2014) *Africa*. http://henningmankell.com/africa (Accessed: 06 August 2014).
Mannen som log (2003) Tre Vänner Produktion AB; Sveriges Television; ZDF Enterprises; Danmarks Radio; Norsk Rikskringkasting; Nordiska TV-Samarbetsfonden.
Peacock, S. (2014) *Swedish crime fiction: novel, film, television*. Manchester: Manchester University Press.
Rampton, J. (2008) 'The stunning, troubled world of the Norse Morse', *Daily Telegraph*, 1 November, p. 16.
Robertson, R. (1992) *Globalisation: social theory and global culture*. London: Sage.
Sejersted, F. (2011) *The age of social democracy: Norway and Sweden in the twentieth century*. New York: Princeton University Press.
'Sidetracked' (2010) *Wallander*, Series 1, episode 1. BBC One, 10 May.
'Sorgfågeln' (2014) *Wallander*, Series 3, episode 6. *Swedish TV*, 21 June.
Stasio, M. (2009) 'A Swedish cop, not a Danish prince, but still melancholy', *The New York Times*, 10 May. www.nytimes.com/2009/05/10/arts/television/10stas.html?_r=0 (Accessed: 2 December 2015).
Strauhbaar, J. (2007) *World television: from global to local*. London: Sage.
'Täckmanteln' (2009) *Wallander*, Series 1, episode 19. *Swedish TV*, 24 August.
'The Man Who Smiled' (2010) *Wallander*, Series 2, episode 2. BBC One, 10 October.
The No. 1 Ladies' Detective Agency (2008–9) HBO; BBC.
'Vittnet' (2010) *Wallander*, Series 2, episode 13. *Swedish TV*, 19 June.
Wallander (2008–16) BBC One.
Winston, R. and Mellerski, N. (1992) *The public eye: ideology and the police procedural*. Basingstoke: Macmillan.

Chapter 6

Attainable utopias

Oscar Guardiola-Rivera

1 Introduction

In the wake of the coup d'état that unseated the democratically elected socialist president of Chile Salvador Allende in 1973, writers Gabriel García Márquez and Julio Cortázar collaborated with the Second Russell Tribunal (Russell II, hereafter). The citizens' tribunal considered testimonial evidence and passed judgment on the intervention of big powers in Latin America, which the writers concluded to be a direct consequence of the one-dimensional globalization of multinational capital's interests. Their insight was that traumatic events such as those in Chile had a continuous effect on social practices and institutions. Specifically, in the form of unjust gains by multinationals that continue to appreciate in time and would continue to do so even after the evil of direct perpetrators such as dictators were recognized in verdicts of tribunals such as Russell II. Radicalizing the critique of permanent colonialism and genocide initiated by Jean-Paul Sartre, Bertrand Russell and the members of Russell I, Cortázar and others at Russell II focused on multinationals' plundering and violence, corruption, and the geopolitics of 'our fingers everywhere, our fingerprints nowhere' inaugurated by the Nixon-Kissinger duet in the Americas. The latter aimed at making radical politics and ethics historically impossible. On the one hand by considering them as separate spheres. On the other by alleging that the passage of time confined losses to the past and the backward regions of the world in a way that made the radical political claims of the latter non-negotiable and unethical (or vindictive). Separating politics from ethics and declaring radical claims non-negotiable and unethical would be the key to establishing a 'One World' form of globally integrated capitalism, whose disastrous consequences we witness today. In their writings and interviews during and after their experience at Russell II, writers like Cortázar defended the opposite thesis: the inseparability of ethics and politics, exemplified by the performance of witnesses in and out of the tribunal. They engaged the ethical and the political-normative critically, via a mixture of radical denunciation and utopia that made the latter attainable. This chapter presents and elaborates Julio Cortázar's defence of this thesis in the wake of Russell II in relation to other critical voices emerging at the time, more relevant today than ever insofar as they may provide a 'speculative' outline for radical movements and governments that in Europe and the Americas try to reconnect the normative and the political.

2 Latin American inspiration and a speculative proposal: how to reconnect law, politics and ethics through literature

'My standpoint is that politics and ethics are inseparable', said the Argentinean writer Julio Cortázar in response to a question posited by journalist Jorge Raventos about the political and normative function of activism in general, and of writers' activism in particular, in the face of oppression and violence (Cortázar 1974). Cortázar's stance was an example of the radical investment in law and politics characteristic among Latin American cultural, philosophical-theological and literary circles in the 1970s. That investment was radical, critical and creative. The criticism of one-dimensional law was voiced at the time by the likes of Cortázar and Gabriel García Márquez, himself a former law student (García Márquez n.d.). Although such criticism was contextual, their creative radicalism broke with the given context and may be more relevant now than ever. To recover and elaborate upon it is the aim of this chapter.

Their criticisms were contextual insofar as they coincided with attempts to build in practice independent state and legal institutions in the 1960s and 1970s, to liberate or decolonize them and make them work in a non-statal mode. By far the most influential of them was the transformative use of legal and state institutions that took place after the election of socialist Salvador Allende and the Popular Coalition to the government of Chile in 1971, known since then as the Chilean Revolution.

However, such criticisms became much more significant when these radical attempts to transform state institutions were violently interrupted, as was the case with Allende's Chilean Revolution after the coup d'état of 11 September, 1973. In the wake of the coup, Cortázar, García Márquez and others joined Russell II. A citizens' tribunal, its task was to denounce the 'true criminals' behind the 'cultural genocide' initiated in Chile, enquire about workable ways to remedy their injustices, and communicating them to 'all sectors of the continent' so as to decisively change public opinion in an ethical manner (Cortázar 2009, pp. 463–5). Almost forgotten for more than three decades, the example and ultimate fate of Allende's Popular Coalition, as well as that of Russell II, has returned to the public imagination in the wake of the electoral triumph of Syriza in Greece, the potential of Spain's Podemos in 2015, and their 'Latin American inspiration' (Guardiola-Rivera 2010).[1]

In March 2015 during a 'first report' on the fate of Greece's radical government at Birkbeck College, London, reporter Paul Mason, cultural critic Slavoj Žižek, and legal philosopher Costas Douzinas warned against the likelihood of a 'very European coup' against Syriza in the style of the Chilean coup 40 years ago. Mason spoke of Greece's leader, Alexis Tsipras, as a 'postmodern Allende'. Douzinas, in turn, suggested a moral-legal 'guerrilla tactic' to counter the likelihood

1 For the Chilean legal and political Revolution, see Guardiola-Rivera (2013).

of such a coup. It would include influencing public opinion in Europe to turn Greece's very real humanitarian crisis into a moral indictment against austerity measures, in a way that could also touch upon issues of legal liability.

Douzinas' suggestion raises at least two questions: the first one, more philosophical, concerns the proper relationship between the ethical and the variety of political-normative orders available. This question is similar to the one raised by Cortázar in his 1974 answer to Raventos. The second one, more strictly juridical, concerns the kind of legal order that would respond best to the political aims of Greece's Syriza or Spain's Podemos: not only to contain the coup, but to remedy the injustices committed in southern Europe.

In a nutshell, I believe that the best strategy is not the one that insists upon moral or legal liability (personal harm or loss-based compensation), as Douzinas suggested, but one that views the injustices committed against southern peoples as historical and as such (as transactions forced upon generations of people unjustly, whether legally or not) a suitable object for property-creating remedies. Successors in interest could then lay claims to such rights in rem, more so when dramatic changes in the political landscape or the rate of heightened inequality increase risks exponentially. The latter is, precisely, the situation in which southern European peoples are at present and successive generations will be. Which is why the right time to lay such claims is now. It is also the reason why the right people to make those claims are those who bear witness to the situation of humanitarian crisis taking place in southern Europe, and seek to stop that situation becoming permanent in the future. Raising their collective voice in denouncing that situation they get ready to name, denounce and struggle in the streets as well as in more or less formal tribunals, thereby becoming the political subjects of an attainable utopia: an 'uncontainable multitude', as Cortázar (1975, p. 66) put it, radically invested in justice as a realizable option.

My inspiration for this proposal – that southern peoples constitute themselves as 'uncontainable multitudes' bearing witness and forcing a restitution-transaction as a property-creating remedy in a (global) tribunal, convened to that effect by their radical governments – takes stock of the application of modern finance option theory to the liquidation of historical grievances, recently developed by legal theorists like Ian Ayres and Bob Meister. To go into the detail of their work would be beyond the limits of this chapter, so I will use some of their insights and direct the reader towards the appropriate sources.[2] Rather, for the purposes of this chapter it is more important to emphasize that Cortázar's law-and-literature experiment

2 Meister (2011, especially pp. 232–59); and Meister (2015), I thank Bob Meister for sharing his yet unpublished draft with me. See also, Ayres (2005) and for a summary of legal restitution American Law Institute (1937) by W. Seavey and A. Scott. See also Ackerman and Alscott (2001). For endowment-based remedies, Lear (2006); Saul (2014). Escobar (2014) for community-based and contingency-facing conceptions of attainable justice in the face of catastrophe. For the legal-economic basics see, Alchian (2006).

(his 1975 graphic novel *Fantomas Versus the Multinational Vampires. An Attainable Utopia*, (Cortázar 1975) as well as his posthumously published *Papeles Inesperados* (Cortázar 2009)), the arguments made at Russell II in which Cortázar and García Márquez played a crucial role, and the legal tactics and strategies developed in Allende's Chile, resonate very strongly with Douzinas' suggestion and constitute the best inspiration to develop it.

I refer especially to the so-called excess profits doctrine, which arguably construed historical injustices in connection with the ongoing benefits of foreign investors in Chile as a property-creating remedy that could be claimed by and against successors in interest. It can be argued that Allende's doctrine interpreted the normative order of property rules in a radical manner (as a property-creating remedy rather than as personal liability) and in doing so came up with an ethically worthy way of reversing a historical injustice, one that is compatible with the idea that to approximate the political-normative and the ethical requires a radical investment on the part of disadvantaged groups, but also a cap on remedial justice. Moreover, the resultant creation of legal states in property for disadvantaged groups to counteract the ongoing wealth effects of historical injustice gave the order of property rules an *ordering* function.

This is an instance of how the political-normative can be reimagined in an ethically radical manner, different from the more ubiquitous and not always effective recourse to revolutionary constitutional change. Viewed from this perspective, Allende's 'excess profits', as well as Frantz Fanon's reflections on restitutional justice vis-à-vis (financial) violence at the international level, liberation philosophy's intertwining of denunciation and utopia, as well as Cortázar's experimental law-and-literature shift towards the performative role of the witnesses at Russell II, are compatible with more and less recent efforts to provide the legal-political with a decisive critical momentum (Marcuse, Neumann and Kirchheimer 1945, and Marcuse 1978, p. 131, quoted in Neumann, Marcuse and Kirchheimer, 2013).[3]

3 No justice without speculation: from 'excess profits' to 'an attainable utopia'

Put simply, the 'excess profits' doctrine was elaborated as an answer to the question of the present valuation of past injustice. The core idea was to come up with an explicit accounting that connects the gains of foreign investors (in this case copper multinationals Kennecott and Anaconda) to the losses of Chileans in a way that would supplement the separate accounts maintained by each. Importantly, the ability of law to trace assets in such a way (historically) means that restitutional remedies that do not simply return property 'can, instead, create a

3 For a more recent attempt, which I believe is part of the constellation put together in this paper, see Laclau (2014).

beneficial interest in an asset or fund that has grown in value owing to the original injustice or in close correlation with it' (Meister 2011, p. 239), in the shape of a constructive trust arising from said injustice.[4] When interpreted through the lens of the constructive trust formula of property law theory, it becomes apparent that at stake in the particular example of Allende's excess profits doctrine is the more general issue of the proper valuation of the present claims that can be made by history's apparent losers.

Mainstream (liberal) legal theorists and practitioners often dismiss such arguments for restitution on the basis that the passage of time – decades, even centuries – makes it impossible to calculate the compounded value of such claims. There is a kernel of truth in the liberal warning against reversing a particular moment in the entire history of injustice, since such a prospect would raise impossible questions concerning when to begin the count, why not to continue tracing it back ad infinitum, and so on. But as Bob Meister has argued, there are good reasons to conclude this is the wrong perspective. For the value of settling unjust past history changes over time rather than compounding.

Arguably, an unexpected and dramatic change in political volatility, as was the case in Chile in the 1970s, and a dramatic variation in the rate at which socio-economic inequality changes, as in the case of Greece or Spain today, raise the present value of an otherwise latent historical claim 'and thus create a new opportunity to mitigate or profit from political risk' (Meister 2011, p. 248). Such dramatic changes actually affect the value of settling colonial history (Chile 1973) or the history of Europe's self-colonization (Greece, Spain 2015). Once we recognize that injustice, as well as its correction, is not just interpersonal and intratemporal but also intertemporal and intergenerational, the question becomes one of what kind of asset would better incorporate the constructive trust such that it can be continuously valued over time. That question is political as well as normative and economic: for instance, are historical grievances a kind of 'national debt' that could be swapped by bonds? If they're not a kind of debt, then what would be the just starting point to calculate ill-gotten gains? Would it be to calculate how well off would indigenous peoples have been if conquest never happened? Or, what about Africa without slavery?

This already confirms that justice and practical reasoning cannot be properly undertaken without taking recourse to speculation, or as Hegel would say in relation to Kantian formalism, that we must move from the transcendental to the speculative. Critical theorists of the first Frankfurt School spoke thus of the utopian and against one-dimensionality in this sense. Chief among them, were the critical

4 'Excess profits' considered a case of compensation after takings – the nationalization of the copper industry in 1970s Chile. As such, it pertains to the legal distinction between liability and property rules. Though often understood in terms of the former, here I'm arguing that it may be better conceived in relation to the latter.

theorists who contributed with their reports on the responsibility of industrialists as beneficiaries of the injustices committed during WWII to the efforts of the US team at the Nuremberg Trials. And so did Cortázar (1975), who following in their footsteps wrote a novel subtitled *An Attainable Utopia* in the wake of his experiences at Russell II, as well as the critical liberation philosophers and theologians that were reinventing notions of utopia and 'prophetism' or witnessing more or less at the same time in the Americas.

Notice however that the speculative and utopian can be counterfactual, and in fact this is the way most people conceive of and are dismissive of speculation and utopian thinking. Ditto, there is a kernel of truth in the dismissal of this form of the speculative, as Hegel suggested and as can be seen in the case of the questions asked above concerning how well off indigenous or African peoples would be without conquest or slavery. In answering such questions, we run against unresolvable conceptual and practical paradoxes.

Warning against such kinds of speculation in a Hegelian manner, liberation philosopher and critical theorist Ignacio Ellacuría pointed out that when 'utopia lacks the dimension of the witnessing and denunciation of actual historical reality' it is 'practically unworkable; moreover, it avoids real investment' (quoted by Alvarenga 2014, p. 95).[5] His point was that utopia as counterfactual history provides us with moral images that would not move us to real commitment and investment, making utopia practically and conceptually unattainable. Thus, for instance, we cannot conceive of modern liberty without slavery, or liberation without modern coloniality, or capitalism without labour and its exploitation. To imagine a world in which such things never happened might leave us content, but confused in theory and unmoved in practice

However, in order to remedy injustice, we do not have to imagine a world in which colonialism, dispossession, slavery or exploitation never happened. For it is the actual history of unjust inequality denounced by those who bear witness to it which makes its remediation an option, as Ellacuría and Cortázar contended in their separate but related efforts. 'Utopia requires the prophetic to inspire it . . . just as prophetism requires being animated by utopia', Ellacuría (1991, p. 397) observed. Cortázar spoke of an *attainable* utopia in precisely this sense.

Crucially, what makes the ethical and the political-normative inseparable in this case is an *investment*. First, in the sense of an investment of the ethical into the political-normative; a passionate investment on the part of the witness that transforms the role of the political-normative as merely an order (by becoming an activist and giving to an available order a new and radical ordering function). But also in the sense of a new asset that can appreciate in value and be claimed by and against successors in interest.

5 Also, Ellacuría (2011; 1991).

And if the action takes the shape of a radical investment, what then of its actor? Our focus should be on those who seek to invest given laws and normative orders with a superior ethical worth, those who behave as activists or, as I prefer, radical investors. These subjects denounce unjust situations and institutions affected by traumatic events (conquest, displacement, dispossession, austerity-related precariousness) more or less in the same way in which prophets raise their voice in the wilderness so as to not let us off the hook. Their denunciation (prophecy) acts as a moral image calling us all to act against the perceived injustice. The point here is to shift our focus from the importance of the result and the verdict to the performative role of (prophetic, radically invested) witnesses. I argue this is precisely the point made by Cortázar's law-and-literature experiment.

4 Cortázar's *Fantomas* versus the Multinational Vampires: a law-and-literature experiment

Throughout *Fantomas* (Cortázar 1975) we the readers are led to believe that the main protagonists are heroic Fantomas and his Blofeld-like arch-enemy Steiner. This is the structure of the comic book upon which Cortázar based his novel. This Manichean ethical structure (good versus evil, us versus them) is well known to us from popular culture, from dramas, movies and comic books to news narratives and increasingly political debates. Crucially, these examples of more or less popular culture share something in common with more formal confrontation that takes place in institutions such as the legal trial in a tribunal or in parliamentarian debates. What they have in common is not only their confrontational spectacle but more importantly their organizational dual structure.

Organizational dual structures are in fact quite basic and foundational, as anthropologists suggest when they speak of them as the 'zero-degree' of institutionality (Lévi-Strauss 1963). This helps explain their endurance as well as their hold on our imagination. We do indeed tend to focus more often than not on the battle between good and evil and its resolution. In law, this proverbial point of resolution (in time and space) is the moment of trial adjudication: the verdict. Law students are told more or less explicitly to focus on the verdict and the performance of judges, past and present. This is also what most lawyers do in practice.

In general, the verdict is supposed to be both a resolution and a new unity, insofar as it reflects a non-neutral judgment on the history that preceded it. Each case is a new beginning, but one that reconnects the present with a long line of precedents, past and present. Furthermore, precedents add up projecting the unity of the political community from the past and into the future that is thus conceived as more or less repeating a natural or established order.

This is particularly evident in human rights cases involving political transitions after historical injustices, such as the South African Truth & Reconciliation Commission or the Argentinian post-dictatorship trials, which were not just new beginnings but also produced 'survivor stories'. In this respect 'they are always about what the past will have been now that "we" have changed, and what it would have been had "we" changed sooner. Merely by occurring, political transitions thus instantiate a temporal reconstitution of the "we"' (Meister 2011, viii). This 'we' is reconstituted as a collective subject already forgiven for the past evils we remember to confess. And thus, a 'converted' subject who repudiates past violence by endorsing the exceptional violence of rescue and occupation (as in the 'Responsibility to Protect' Doctrine) against all claims by previous victims or their successors in interest (seen as vindictive), which could threaten the continuing gains of born-again beneficiaries of past injustice. Verdicts in 'transitional' justice cases and the survivor stories told at Truth & Reconciliation tribunals have thus the same effect of a confession/conversion experience. They produce a caesura in time and space that separates good from evil and the present from the past. In the good present there are no longer victims and perpetrators, but a 'rainbow' unity. And those who continue to benefit from past injustices become bystanders, who by not identifying with perpetrators perpetually agonize over whether it is already too late or still too soon to act so as to stop the past repeating ever again (the *nunca jamás* slogan of transitions). The conversion model of transitional justice serves as a poor substitute for prophetic denunciation, leaving beneficiaries off the hook and most of us quite content as bystanders.

However, the more interesting fact about dual organizations is that the relation between the two terms involved cannot be properly described as Manichean – as two opposites out of which a unity is obtained – or as a conversion experience involving the complementarity of two halves. Rather, 'dualism is 'resolved' into a triangularity in which the terms (the legs) and the relation (the hypotenuse) are 'incommensurable". This means that their relation is not an addition but a multiplication, an inversion, 'a repetition of itself by the other' turning each term into a function of the other. Also, the relation between the terms is 'a continuous and involute entity, inward growing and properly interminable'. Neither unity nor mere duality, but, properly speaking, radicality.

Applied to the additive property of verdicts and judges' opinions in general, and to the repudiation/conversion model of transitional justice in particular, this entails a shift in perspective. From the contentment of converts and bystanders let off the hook as a 'rainbow' unity by 'truth and reconciliation' verdicts, to the radical investment of witnesses who prophetically name beneficiaries and denounce that beneficiaries cannot be let off the hook, here and now, in the streets as well as in more or less formal tribunals. The naming entails the isolation of a set of key terms or names as signifiers of a situation experienced as deficient being, lack, or historical injustice. But this lack or deficiency with which we are dealing is not simply an absence of content. It is itself a content. To announce that the named beneficiaries cannot be let off the hook in the present is to point towards 'a fullness that shows itself through its very absence', emptiness or lack, as Ernesto Laclau (2014, p. 130) explains in relation to the connection between a given order and ethical action.

Notice that, as Laclau points out, we have left behind the positivity of a given legal order but not in order to arrive at some sort of (Kantian) ethical formalism. For as he says a formal determination is still a determination and, moreover, 'abstraction and generality are inherent to any formalism' (p. 130), including the ethical formalism of the repudiation/conversion model of transitional justice and human rights culture. In contrast, the experience of the witness at a place such as the Russell II is absolutely subjective and concrete. It can be called 'prophetic' in the sense given to that term by liberation philosophers like Ellacuría before or Cornel West today. What Laclau (2014) says of mystics can also be said of more contemporary cases of prophetic witnessing in places like Russell II. The important point is that the experience 'leads those who have passed through it not to live the recluse life of an anchorite, but to engage themselves in the world in a more militant way, and with an ethical density other people lack' (p. 130). Utopia is, in this sense, the inverse of the opposite situation experienced in which such a fullness is denied, and of the name that signifies the multiplicity of factors and actors complicit in producing that situation. Not a subtracting negative, but the inverse. That utopia becomes attainable through the radical investment of prophetic witnesses, who engage themselves in the world in a more militant, ethically dense way.

Put otherwise, in a properly dialectical manner, this means to emphasize the impotence of verdicts as a function of their allegedly epoch-changing character in mainstream law, and to invert the position of witnesses as a function of their mainstream role as mere evidence gatherers and informants. But also to contrast the impotence of the verdict against the multiplied potency of witnesses as radically invested activists rather than content bystanders.

I believe this is exactly what Cortázar does at the end of his law-and-literature experiment: while reflecting upon his own experience at Russell II, and recovering the radicality of the Chilean example (including the 'excess profits' doctrine) he turns the tables on those let off the hook in the present by the historical consequences of the Chilean coup as well as the so-called transition. Indeed, the initially dual structure of the novel, setting Fantomas versus Steiner in a properly pop-cultural Manichean manner, gives way at the end of it not to some new beginning, but rather, to a triangular relation in which multinationals are revealed as the real culprit whose 'absence' has deceived the great hero himself. And that is actually not the end, but just the beginning of a story that the novel calls for but ought to happen outside of its pages, in real life.

'Julio, Julio, who's the real Steiner? Whom did the Russell Tribunal just condemn in Brussels?', asks a fictional Susan Sontag to Julio Cortázar (1975, p. 42) in the novel. 'They have a thousand, ten thousand, a hundred thousand names' (p. 42), replies Cortázar, the narrator.

> But above all they're called ITT, they're called Nixon and Ford, Henry Kissinger or CIA or DIA, they're called Pinochet or Banzer or López Rega, they're called General or Colonel or Technocrat or Fleury or Stroessner, they have those special names where every name means thousands of names, the way the word ant means a multitude of ants even though the dictionary defines it in the singular.
>
> (p. 42)

The real culprit is revealed in the verdict as multitudinous, and given a name that in its singular emptiness stands for the many fault lines of society. But that is not the end, the verdict is not the end. For what about the opposite term? 'The problem is elsewhere' (p. 59), says Sontag to Cortázar at the end of the novel,

> because our real adversary isn't Steiner or some lose gang of criminals, as you well know. And until many other people understand this, and do their part in their way, we're going to keep getting fried alive like the miserable tadpoles we are.
>
> (p. 60)

The inverse, not the negative, of the culprit named in the Russell II sentence, are the 'many other people'. This is no Negri and Hardt-like 'multitude' (Negri *et al.* 2010). In principle, it alludes merely to those who need to understand, to learn the truth and do their part: the people outside of the novel, the addressees of the novel, its readers. But it also refers to the witnesses of Russell II and those who, like Cortázar himself, undertook the work of the tribunal and in doing so went through an experience that cannot be properly described as conversion. As I have suggested before, it would be best to describe it as prophecy and becoming a prophet, or as I prefer, as radical investment.

What is the role of prophets or activists as radical investors? Is it to lead and unify the people, the usual sense of the vanguard-intellectual or the vanguard-party? No, at least according to Cortázar. When the fictional Cortázar of the novel, the narrator, attempts a further unification of opposites, Sontag stops him.

> Of course I agree with you, Susan, if we could only unite and confront the vampires and the octopuses that are killing us, if we had a chief, a . . . No, Julio, don't say 'Fantomas' or any other name that pops into your head. Of course we need leaders. It's only natural that they rise up and assert themselves, but the mistake [. . .]
>
> (Cortázar 1975, p. 60)

At this point in the final dialogue something stranger happens. Cortázar, the writer, introduces a device by means of which the singularity of the character Susan Sontag begins to transform into a multiplicity – like the Amerindian shamans and the jaguar of the myths about zero-degree institutions studied by anthropologists.

> [W]as it really Susan talking? Other voices were mixing with hers now on the telephone, phrases in different languages and accents, men and women speaking from close by and far away – the mistake is to think we need a leader, to refuse to lift a finger until we have one, to sit waiting for this leader to appear and unite us and give us our slogans and get us moving. The mistake is to be content to let realities stare us in the face, realities like the Russell Tribunal's

> verdict (you were there, you know what I mean) and still to keep waiting until somebody else – always somebody else – raises the first cry.
>
> (Cortázar 1975, p. 60)

This should not be confused with a paean for horizontality. Rather, it is yet another result of the radical dualism at the heart of the novel. The triangulation, revealing a third party where there were two at the outset, results not in a new unity but in multiplication. A fourth party is revealed that is the inverse of the third, each a function of the other. Just as the multinational vampire-squid stands in its emptiness for all the ills of society, its lack, now Susan-the Many stands in its emptiness for the positive reverse of the lack at the heart of society, that is, justice.

But Cortázar takes a further step here. He seems to acknowledge that there is no logical transition from (Unjust) Multinational Vampires to (Just) Susan-the Many. Which is why the paragraph shifts our focus from the verdict at Russell II to the activation of otherwise agonizing bystanders through close contact, a fusion with, in fact, invested, prophetic witnesses. Put simply, it calls for radical investment of the ethical into the political-normative, their inseparability. Or as I prefer, it makes justice an option for us, here and now, not because the harsh realities stated as facts in the verdict stare us in the face (this is not an objective situation) but because activism is a risky business (the subjective transformation of a quiet situation into a volatile one that heightens the value of dormant claims).

Triangulation results thus not in a new unity or singularity but in multiplication. The singular names stand for multitudinous entities: behind Steiner the 'Multinational Vampires' of the title, vampire-squids, in fact. And instead of the deluded Fantomas, are the radically invested who connect the ethical with the political-normative through a few simple images capable of galvanizing the imagination of the many. That is, in my opinion, the function of the visual part of Cortázar's graphic novel. If the first name stands for the experience of injustice (ethical) but also connects such an experience of emptiness with an available legal order, as I have argued, the order of reparative justice and contingent claims triggered by significantly risky events, the latter stands for what is necessary in the absence of any logical transition from injustice to justice: moral images, in the sense given to the term by Drucilla Cornell, a few simple images as well as the investors ready to mobilize them against all odds. A proposal such as the Douzinas-Meister-Guardiola model for remedying historical grievances would be null without the tactics and the strategy of radical investment needed to galvanize our collective imagination.

My contention has been that Cortázar's law-and-literature experiment *An Attainable Utopia*, as a vehicle for the Russell II experience, shows how this can be done. The radical governments of southern Europe and the global south could convene such a tribunal, which would be more effective than Russell II because of its quasi-formal character. It could be an event similar in significance to the Bandung Conference. They can also follow Cortázar's example, conceptual as well as formal, in fashioning a new language-and-simple-images for law to recapture the imagination of the masses instead of contributing to numb them.

5 Conclusion: inseparability and radical investment

This chapter focused on the inseparability of politics and ethics, or the 'inseparability thesis' for short, put forward by Cortázar. It presented the 'inseparability thesis' as characteristic of a specific form of speech and writing that originated in practical instances of people's activism such as the Russell Tribunals during the late 1960s and early 1970s, but one that holds true ever since. It is in fact truer in the sense of having overcome its original context and demonstrating more explanatory and speculative power than its competitors nowadays. Not only in relation to such phenomena as the political comeback made by peoples subjected to the one-dimensionality of law and economics in Latin America and southern Europe, as they try to subvert and transform both law and economics from positions of state power. But also in relation to the fact that the multinational extraction and finance industry, which was the main addressee of the judgment issued by Russell II as well as the protagonist of Cortázar's innovative writing of the period, continues to demonstrate how 'the nexus of politics and capitalism leads invariably to violence and death' (Vulliamy 2015, p. 31) – nowadays threatening not only the lives of those deselected from humanity for genocide and epistemicide but the planet itself.

Historically speaking, this new form of speech and writing emerged against the backdrop of revolutionary attempts like the Cuban Revolution, the student mobilizations of the late 1960s, the Chilean Revolution, and the renewal of armed struggle that followed the events of 11 September 1973. It can be opposed to the merging of counterrevolutionary violence, law and order and 'free' market culture that became the norm throughout the continent and elsewhere after the coup d'état in Chile in 1973, particularly in the 1980s and 1990s.

Philosophically speaking, this new and truer form of speech and writing moves in the speculative direction suggested by the distinction between 'traditional', unilateral and one-dimensional theory, and 'critical' or pluri-dimensional theory, made popular by the first Frankfurt School. Whereas the former views reality as consisting of a series of disperse elements lacking connectivity or relation, the 'world without others' described by existential and structuralist anthropologists working in dialogue with Amerindian cosmologies in the 1970s, the latter appeals to the plurality of grammars and scripts that account for reality – a world with others – not in order to organize them hierarchically but to articulate a transcending or 'liberatory' path to knowledge, dialectically as well as speculatively. That is to say, from the perspective of the totality in its concreteness.

This link between Frankfurt style criticism and Latin American innovative forms of thought and writing has been noticed already, specifically in relation to the use of notions that entail the transcendence of the given and the posited, such as hope or utopia, and the idea of a new departure from a zero-degree (*partir de cero*, in Spanish). These notions were central to a series of interconnected attempts to break new ground, aesthetical as well as philosophical, legal and political in the

Americas, starting in the 1960s and 1970s: for instance, liberation theology and Cortázar's utopian novels. Whereas a concept of hope mediated by Frankfurt-style criticism became central to the former, notions of utopia and practices of negation are notoriously apparent in the architecture of the latter.

Héctor Schmucler's (2014) now classical essay on Julio Cortázar's main novel *Rayuela*, the aptly titled *Rayuela, or Literature on Trial*, focuses precisely on the author's usage of negation and the speculative mode of thinking and writing.[6] Crucially, a notion of utopia very close to the one being elaborated by liberation philosophers and theologians in the Americas at the time, appears in the subtitle of the novella that Cortázar wrote as a means to reflect upon and communicate his experiences in the Second Russell Tribunal, *An Attainable Utopia* (Cortázar 1975).

Cortázar composed this aesthetic artefact in 1975, more or less a decade after the publication of *Rayuela* and Schmucler's essay. In spite of the fame of its author, *Fantomas* went almost unnoticed and was not translated into English until 2014. The fact of *Fantomas'* late comeback may have had something to do with the publication in Spanish of a series of as yet unpublished papers in 2009, under the title *Papeles Inesperados* (*Untimely Papers*). Among such papers, his reflections on the violation of rights in the wake of Russell II and the Chilean coup of 1973 and the 'heterodox, amphibian, and illustrated' character of his *Fantomas* creation take centre stage (Cortázar 2009, p. 460).

But it is perhaps more elegant to explain it as a result of the spirit of the times. It is only now that we can appreciate the full significance and prescience of the work done by Cortázar and others at Russell II, as we enter into the highest and to some terminal phase of extractive-finance capitalism, 'the age of shared austerity', to use the terminology adopted by Salvadorean liberation philosopher and legal theorist Héctor Samour (2014). Similarly, only now can we see the point of the unconventional form of writing exemplified by *Fantomas*: not just its genre-bursting format, but more importantly, its attempt to merge law and literature so as to integrate them dialectically and speculatively. If so, then *Fantomas* can be seen as a critical object rather than merely an object of critique. That is, a composition that transcends posited law as well as conventional literature in the direction of a renewed critical perspective: one running ahead of its time, more or less in the same sense in which liberation philosophy and theology would in time give way to the decolonial turn and the epistemologies of the south, as well as the ethnographic critique of twenty-first century plurinational constitutionalism applied to such novel phenomena as the emergence of Syriza and Podemos

6 At p. 42, pp. 53–8, especially p. 57 and p. 58 on Cortázar's direct references to dialectics, 'broken dialectics', and to 'holes' in the dialectical architecture of reality in relation to the dimension of the unconditioned future. For hope and utopia in the work of liberation theologians and philosophers and the link with Frankfurt criticism, see Tamayo and Alvarenga (2014).

in Europe from the viewpoint of permanent decolonization (Guardiola-Rivera 2014a; 2014b; 2015).[7]

The crucial point to isolate here is the relationship between denunciation (or witnessing) and utopia, dialectical as well as speculative, which is common to the new form of writing emerging in Cortázar's Russell II/*Fantomas* and liberation philosophy and theology, but also to our more recent explorations precisely in the terrain of human rights and contemporary substantive politics. The point is made by liberation philosopher Ignacio Ellacuría: 'Denunciation without utopia is, to a certain extent, blind, just as utopia without witnessing and denunciation is practically unattainable; moreover, it disavows real commitment and engagement' (quoted in Alvarenga 2014, p. 85).[8] This formulation uncovers the link between critical theory and a radically materialist anthropology encompassing and surpassing theological-political notions of political spirituality and representation: the historical (not historicist) incarnation of the moral image, as well as the concept, the passion, and the force that animates bystanders, spectators and consumers to perform and act in a transformative manner. This is also the key to unlock the central image in Cortázar's *Fantomas*, that of an *attainable* utopia. It is the performative act of the witness, who in speaking before the tribunal or taking to the streets, makes utopia attainable.

References

Ackerman, B. and Alscott, A. (2001) *The stakeholder society*. New Haven: Yale University Press.

Alchian, A.A. (2006) *The collected works of Armen A. Alchian, vol. 2: property rights and economic behaviour*. Benjamin, D.K. (ed.), Indianapolis: Liberty Fund.

Alvarenga, L. (2014) 'Una teoría crítica para El Salvador: negatividad, historización y praxis libertadora en Ignacio Ellacuría', in Tamayo, J.J. and Alvarenga, L. (eds.) *Ignacio Ellacuría: utopía y teoría crítica*. Valencia: Tirant Humanidades, pp. 71–101.

American Law Institute (1937) *Restatement of the Law of restitution: quasi-contracts and constructive trusts, as adopted and promulgated by the American Law Institute at Washington D.C., May 8, 1936* (3 vols). St. Paul: American Law Institute.

Ayres, I. (2005) *Optional law: the structure of legal entitlements*. Chicago: The University of Chicago Press.

Castro, E.V. de (2010) 'The untimely again', in Clastres, P. *The archeology of violence*. Los Angeles: Semiotext(e), pp. 9–51.

Cortázar, J. (1974) 'Entrevista a Julio Cortázar'. Interview with Julio Cortázar. Interviewed by Jorge Raventos for *Revista Redacción*, June, 1974. www.elhistoriador.com.ar/entrevistas/c/cortazar2.php (Accessed: 18 November 2015).

7 On southern epistemologies see Santos (2014), Schavelzon (2015). For Amerindian perspectivism see Castro (2010), especially his distinction between phenomenological-socialist and radical-materialist readings of 'zero-degree' institutions (pp. 32–3).

8 See also Ellacuría (2011, pp. 435–7) for the connection between the use of negation and Hegel via Frankfurt theorists like Ernst Bloch.

Cortázar, J. (1975) *Fantomas contra los vampiros multinacionales: una utopía realizable.* México: Excelsior. (Translated as: *Fantomas versus the multinational vampires: an attainable utopia.* Translated by D. Kurnick. Los Angeles: Semiotext(e), 2014)

Cortázar, J. (2009) *Julio Cortázar: papeles inesperados.* Buenos Aires: Alfaguara.

Ellacuría, I. (1991) 'Utopía y profetismo', in Ellacuría, I. and Sobrino, J. (eds.) *Mysterium liberationis I.* San Salvador: UCA Editores, pp. 393–423. (Translated as: *Mysterium liberationis. fundamental concepts in liberation theology.* Maryknoll: Orbis Books, 289–328)

Ellacuría, I. (2011) 'Historización de los derechos humanos desde los pueblos oprimidos y las mayorías populares', in *Escritos filosóficos III.* San Salvador: UCA Editores, pp. 433–40.

Escobar, A. (2014) *Sentipensar con la tierra: nuevas lecturas sobre desarrollo, territorio y diferencia.* Medellín: Ediciones Unaula.

García Márquez, G. (n.d.) 'Gabriel García Márquez habla sobre Allende y Chile'. www.lanacion.cl/noticias/cultura-y-entretencion/cultura/en-video-gabriel-garcia-marquez-habla-sobre-chile-y-allende/2014-04-17/173413.html (Accessed: 3 May 2015).

Guardiola-Rivera, O. (2010) *What if Latin America ruled the world?* London: Bloomsbury. 2010. (Spanish version: *Si Latinoamérica gobernase el mundo.* Barcelona: RBA, 2012)

Guardiola-Rivera, O. (2013) *A story of death foretold: the coup against Allende, 11 September 1973.* London: Bloomsbury.

Guardiola-Rivera, O. (2014a) *Can there be religions without belief? Why only Amerindians can save our modern soul* [Presentation at *The Actuality of the Theologico-Political Conference*] Birkbeck College, University of London. 23 May.

Guardiola-Rivera, O. (2014b) *For perspectivism: law and myth in Argentina* [Presentation at the *Comparative Legal Theory Workshop: Legal Critique From Argentina*] Birkbeck College, University of London. 5 April.

Guardiola-Rivera, O. (2015) 'Law's catastrophe and the greatness of Syriza', *Critical Legal Thinking*, 26 February. http://criticallegalthinking.com/2015/02/26/laws-catastrophe-and-the-greatness-of-syriza/ (Accessed: 26 June 2015).

Laclau, E. (2014) 'Ethics, normativity and the heteronomy of the law', in *The rhetorical foundations of society.* London: Verso, pp. 127–137.

Lear, J. (2006) *Radical hope: ethics in the face of cultural devastation.* Cambridge: Harvard University Press.

Lévi-Strauss (1963) 'Do dual organizations exist?', in *Structural Anthropology.* Translated by C. Jacobson and B.G. Schoepf. New York: Basic Books, pp. 132–63.

Marcuse, H. (1978) 'Theory and politics: a discussion with Herbert Marcuse, Jürgen Habermas, Heinz Lubasz and Tilman Spengler', *Telos*, 38, pp. 124–53.

Marcuse, H., Neumann, F., and Kirchheimer, O. (1945) *Sixty-five leading German businessmen.* 28 June, R&A 3020, USNA, RG 153, entry 135, box 14.

Meister, R. (2011) *After evil: a politics of human rights.* New York: Columbia University Press.

Meister, R. (2015) 'Liquidity'. Unpublished. On file with the author.

Negri, T., Hardt, M., Cocco, G., Revel, J., García Linera, Á. and Tapia, L. (2010) *Imperio, multitud y sociedad abigarrada.* Buenos Aires: CLACSO/Waldhuter Editores.

Neumann F., Marcuse, H., and Kirchheimer, O. (2013) *Secret reports on Nazi Germany: the Frankfurt School contribution to the war effort.* R. Laudani (ed.) Princeton: Princeton University Press.

Samour, H. (2014) 'El concepto del 'mal común' y la crítica de la civilización del capital', in Tamayo, J.J. and Alvarenga, L. (eds.) *Ignacio Ellacuría: utopía y teoría crítica.* Valencia: Tirant Humanidades, pp. 104–22.

Santos, B. de S. (2014) *Epistemologies of the South: justice against epistemicide.* Boulder: Paradigm Publishers.

Saul, J.R. (2014) *The comeback*. Toronto: Viking.

Schavelzon, S. (2015) 'Podemos, Suramérica y la república plurinacional de España', *Rebelión*, 4 February. www.rebelion.org/noticia.php?id=195069 (Accessed: 17 June 2015).

Schmucler, H. (2014) *Rayuela: juicio a la literatura*. México: Fondo de Cultura Económica. (Originally published in *Pasado y Presente*, 9, 1965, pp. 15–58)

Tamayo, J.J. and Alvarenga, L. (eds.) (2014) *Ignacio Ellacuría: utopía y teoría crítica*. Valencia: Tirant Humanidades.

Vulliamy, E. (2015) 'The global extraction industry has become hallmarked by plundering, violence and political corruption', *The Observer*, 22 March, p. 31.

Chapter 7

Necessary deceptions

Kafka and the mystery of law

Peter Fitzpatrick

> 'Nothing that is not there and the nothing that is.'
>
> (Wallace Stevens 2006, p. 9)

Genres

To begin with an impossible beginning, and in a way that pervades this chapter, after finding that 'a focus on crime, but sometimes only its investigation' is all that distinguishes the genre, John Scaggs (2005, p. 1) decides that his engaging critical foray will 'employ the term "crime fiction" to classify an otherwise unclassifiable genre' (p. 1). And soon the crowded contraction of Scaggs' instances attests to the genre's 'flexibility and porosity' (p. 2). Not all prominent authors of fiction dealing with crime are accommodated (Kafka for one is not there), and with its diversity and immensity the 'otherwise unclassifiable genre' remains uncertain and unbound. Yet in Scaggs' account and generally, the genre is readily recognised. That is our initiating mystery.

It may well be the thousands of works carrying the label 'crime fiction' that endow it with a seeming solidity. That endowment may ensue also from the genre's 'golden age' (roughly between the two World Wars and centred in England) persisting as its paradigm. Contrary instances become exceptions or 'sub-genres'. So, 'the artificial gentility of the classical detective story' (Scaggs 2005, p. 57) would serve to set it, and especially its resolution, in contained locations apart from the *profanum vulgus*, focusing it through rituals of ratiocination and revelation towards a patterned *dénouement* which reaffirms order and right.[1] It was never quite that straightforward of course and the inheritors of the 'golden age' have managed at times to accommodate some ultimate irresolution as well as departures from the affirmation of right (e.g. Mann 2006; Leon 2001, pp. 279–80). But the exceptions to classical conformity can be starker than that. Detective fiction is typically now

1 'Ratiocination' here is purloined from Poe's reference to his 'tales of ratiocination' (see e.g. Rachman n.d.).

saturated with social realism and will often and amply accommodate the transgressive and the insistently unsettled.[2]

It is with detective fiction's becoming in this way intrinsically contrary that Kafka can be more confidently reintroduced. It is not uncommon for detective novels to be described as influenced by Kafka, and this goes beyond the trite invocation of the Kafkaesque (see Michaud 2013). More to the point, Laura Marcus (2003) finds that Paul Auster's *Trilogy* 'operates simultaneously . . . as both a detective and as an "anti-detective" novel drawing on the conventions of . . . Kafka' (p. 251) among others, and she instances Kafka's *The Trial* itself as an anti-detective novel (p. 261). The 'anti-' is not merely oppositional. It 'testifies . . . to the detective genre's openness to subversion and renewal' (p. 264).

This hardly looks like progress. We have the mystery of a generic classification of what cannot be classified, compounded now by a generative link between the genre and that which is quite contrary to it yet still somehow connects to it, the outcome becoming something in-between. This sub-mystery could be approached by way of Benjamin's relating another genre, that of poetry, to Kafka's notorious branding of his own works 'as failures' (Benjamin 1973, p. 129). What Benjamin specifically instances is Kafka's failed and 'grandiose attempt to convert poetry into doctrine' (p. 129). In a later piece, Benjamin (1973) emphasised Kafka's general realisation of the inevitability of failure: 'One is tempted to say: once he was certain of eventual failure, everything worked out for him' and that '[t]o do justice to the figure of Kafka . . . one must never lose sight of one thing: it is the purity and beauty of a failure' (p. 148; and see Murray 2004, p. 347). This is, in short, a productive failure, one which in a variety of ways can tell us something of what, for example, poetry 'is'.

Benjamin is less obliging when it comes to law. Gasché (2002) observes that Benjamin takes the 'laws' in Kafka to have 'mainly a semblance-like character', and that he sees Kafka as not having 'said anything determinate about the law or the laws' (p. 972). This is juxtaposed by Gasché to Gershom Scholem's remonstrating with Benjamin about one of his talks on Kafka: 'How, as a critic, you could manage to say anything about the world of this man without putting the doctrine, what Kafka called the law, into the center, is an enigma for me' (p. 972). And many after would affirm a comparable significance for law in Kafka's works (e.g. Minkkinen 1994, p. 350). Yet there is no abrupt resolution here. Gasché's (2002) own essay on 'Kafka's Law' affirms, aptly enough, that 'Kafka's world is a legal world' yet that 'Kafka's legal world is characterized by complete lawlessness . . . [I]n this world *Recht* and *Unrecht* blend without any way of distinguishing between them' (p. 973, p. 984).

2 Instances by now would be beyond calculation. For a recent extensive yet brief sampling see Lawson (2012), and somewhat more expansively Messent (2013, esp. pp. 50–9 and e.g. pp. 198–207).

As between law and lawlessness, Kafka's work is almost invariably typified by the latter. Such tokens of law as can be found are fragmentary, incoherent, unhinged. 'In Kafka,' adds Cixous (1991), 'the law is not figured by anyone' (p. 3). And for Banakar (2010) 'the legal images in Kafka's fiction' come with 'their bewildering, enigmatic, bizarre, profane and alienating effects' (p. 463). And that description would readily match Minkkinen's (1994) equating law and 'the Kafkaesque' (p. 353) – a word readily revealed by the Oxford English Dictionary (2nd ed. 1989) as denoting horror and despair in the face of the deepest existential uncertainty, a self-abnegation when confronted with an all-pervading, tentacular, inscrutable and inescapable power. It appears then that Kafka would not be contributing to that quest of an occidental jurisprudence forever seeking what an elusive law may be. But perhaps a part for Kafka can be intimated in his providing a formative force of negation in the making of the genre of crime fiction. And perhaps that part could be amplified in Kafka's seeing himself has having 'vigorously absorbed the negative element of the age in which I live' (as cited in Murray 2004, p. 272). Perhaps further, and finally, Kafka's composition of the genre 'law' may be revealed in terms not only of what law is, but of what it is not.

Another generic impasse to end this section. Within a work of crime fiction, at least 'classically', resolution comes only with conclusion. Within the genre of the academic essay, resolution comes with, or is explicitly anticipated in, the introduction. Matters for now, and here also, are left in-between. There are already plenty of clues.

The Trial

With *The Trial* the work of negative formation begins at the beginning.[3] There is no trial. Or the title could be translated as 'the process'. There is no process. And in a sense the novel itself is not 'there' in being reputedly unfinished. Yet incompletion is apt since, contrary to the constituent expectation of crime fiction, this novel insistently pursues irresolution. And the focal figure of this irresolution, and of the Law – where '[a]ll reality has become the Law' (Citati 1990, p. 132) – is 'the court'.

The court is everywhere and, as a result, is nowhere. Or reversing the emphasis, with Citati: 'The Court is secret and manifest: concealed and apparent, invisible and most visible – as is God' (Citati 1990, p. 132). 'Everything belongs to the court' – this said by way of explaining why certain licentious 'girls belong to the court' (p. 150). Character after character, location after location (attics, stairs, windows and doors, doors opening onto more or closing off more, being frequently singled out) are said to be of the court. Vivid and palpable as such people and

3 The version used here is the Schocken edition translated by Breon Mitchell (Kafka 1998). Page numbers without more in this part will refer to this edition.

places can be, it is not long before they fall out of contention or are implicitly set against their contrary. The windowless room acquires a window, or vice versa; or a 'reddish' beard becomes 'blonde' a few pages later (p. 13, p. 18). Even the usual indicia of a court – a courtroom, a hearing, officials – soon dissipate into something else. The official merges into an unofficial and quotidian inconsequence. Officialdom can only be approached unofficially – through 'influence' or 'connections' (e.g. p. 58, p. 90). Petitions to the court are unconsidered or they are incapable of being finished because one's 'entire life, down to the smallest actions and events, would have to be called to mind, described, and examined from all sides' (p. 127 and see p. 122). The courtroom dissolves into a scene of sexual improprieties or of mysterious and diverse groups. Any resort to certain levels of the court is eventually revealed as futile, only some highest court having any efficacy at all, but it never appears and the only relevant courts are 'inaccessible' (p. 121).

Yet the court has a 'strange attraction' (p. 29). The focal character, Josef K. assiduously seeks the court feeling that the law is something he has to effect – effect even to the point of knowing 'it was his duty' to carry out his own execution (p. 230).[4] He believes he lives 'in a state governed by law' where 'all statutes were in force' (p. 6). He seeks to obtain a hearing and is assured by his lawyer that his case 'had excited a great deal of attention at the court from the very start' (p. 124). But lawyers had already been shown to be irrelevant with 'everything' being 'laid upon the defendant himself' (p. 115, p. 121). And K. also finds himself trying to deal with 'an unknown system of jurisprudence' (p. 61). Not only is K. denied knowledge of his supposed offence, an offence of which he is usually assumed to be guilty, but as an 'accused' he can know nothing of the processes of the court or secure any significant hearing to present his defence, or to present anything at all (e.g. pp. 113–14, p. 121). His securing a hearing is something either effectively deferred or simply speculated about. 'Where was the judge he'd never seen? Where was the High Court he'd never reached?' (p. 132). And even if all that were as nought, there is in Benjamin's gloss the ultimate impasse: 'The court does not dare to admit that it cannot make up its mind' (Benjamin 2005, p. 68).

Benjamin also finds in *The Trial* an impasse that is potentially more productive. This entails another return to the in-between – now a condition in and between determinacy and evanescence, the graspable for now and the ever-elusive. For Benjamin, Kafka peoples this in-between with messengers and assistants, 'beings in an unfinished state,' beings for whom 'there is hope,' and beings in whose 'activities' law 'may be discerned, subtly and informally' (Benjamin 1973, p. 117). A contender for what Gasché (2002, p. 973, p. 974) calls this 'intermediate' or

4 Not only that, as he is dying, K. observes how his executioners 'drew near his face, leaning cheek-to-cheek to observe the verdict' somehow embedded in him (p. 231).

'intermediary' status could be the 'man from the country' coming in search of law in the parable beginning 'Before the Law' found towards the end of *The Trial* (pp. 215–17). Before adding to the numberless engagements with this homily, it may help to range somewhat more widely through Kafka's work in search of law.

The problem of our laws

The Trial has long provided the focal impetus for the content of the 'Kafkaesque' and for generalised accounts of Kafka's work, along with the pervasive part of an abject law within it. And there is much in this work sustaining that reduction, but there is also much else. First, some instances of the sustenance.

The Castle (Kafka 1983) offers something of a mirror image of *The Trial* even if the reflection is less sharply focused. Here, along with the main character K., and borrowing a summary from Brod (1995), we are involved with 'the inexplicable, unpredictable and unappeasable nature of the reigning powers' (p. 254). Despite K.'s insistent efforts, the decisions he needs from the castle are never forthcoming, and the holder of its ultimate authority is never seen. The quiescent populace do not even bother to seek 'official decisions' considering them to be 'as shy as young girls' (Kafka 1983, p. 317). The role of the in-between, drawing again on Benjamin's (1973) category, is filled by a messenger, Barnabas, who provides precarious connection between K. and the castle's officialdom (p. 117).

In the short stories and parables, unappeasable authority and its quiescent objects are evident, if not as extensively as standard descriptions of Kafka's work would allow. The instance most signalled has to be the terrifying exercise of paternal authority in *The Judgment* (Kafka 1988). And as Benjamin (1973) puts it: 'There is much to indicate that the world of the officials and the world of the fathers are the same to Kafka' (p. 113). With this short story, a son is becoming comfortably involved in life and in the family business in particular, taking over from his ailing father. Yet he kills himself in self-abnegation when the father, reasserting himself as a figure of complete authority, issues an insane judgement that the son must do so (Kafka 1988, pp. 87–8). To take just one more example, also a short story, there is 'The Refusal' (Kafka 1988) in which the custodian of the village's law compliantly succumbs whenever his petitions are refused by the representative of a remote authority.

Yet, always 'yet' with Kafka, matters become more mixitive when we add another helpful trio – this time all parables. *The Problem of Our Laws* (Kafka 1988) announces at the outset that '[o]ur laws are not generally known; they are kept secret by the small group of nobles who rule us' – nobles who 'stand above the laws,' laws 'entrusted exclusively into their hands' (p. 437). There is an imperative quality to the existence of this nobility: 'nobody would dare to repudiate the nobility . . . The sole visible and indubitable law that is imposed upon us is the nobility, and must we ourselves deprive ourselves of that one law?' (p. 438). Yet there is an ancient tradition, and an accessibility, to the law. It has been studied by the people so there is *a* knowledge of the law, a knowledge which discerns:

> certain main tendencies which permit of this or that historical formulation; but when in accordance with the scrupulously tested and logically ordered conclusions we seek to adjust ourselves somewhat for the present or the future, everything becomes uncertain, and our work seems only an intellectual game, for perhaps these laws we are trying to unravel do not exist at all.
>
> (pp. 437–8)

That supposition is held by 'a small party' who anticipate a brand of legal realism in also holding that '[t]he Law is whatever the nobles do' (p. 438). Nonetheless, 'the overwhelming majority of our people' would hold 'that the tradition is far from complete and must be more fully inquired into' (p. 438). And although it would be a conclusion to be long awaited, 'when everything will have become clear, the law will belong to the people and the nobility will vanish' (p. 438). But in the interim 'nobody would dare to repudiate the nobility': 'the sole visible and indubitable law that is imposed upon us is the nobility, and must we ourselves deprive ourselves of that one law?' (p. 438)

Before looking at the remaining two of our contrary trio, it could be emphasised that with Kafka the hold of remote power is usually neither clear nor complete. A stark illustration of the point is offered in *The Great Wall of China* (Kafka 1988) where we find that '[l]ong-dead emperors are set on the throne in our villages, and one that lives on in song recently had a proclamation of his read out by the priest before the altar' (p. 245). The very remoteness of authority puts the purchase of actual edicts in doubt, something vividly affirmed in the parable *An Imperial Message* (Kafka 1988) where a message issued by the emperor, and one on which he sets great store, fails to negotiate the compounded complexity of its passage leaving its intended recipient to 'dream it' to himself (p. 5).

Returning to our contrary trio, now the second parable where we are immersed in the contemplative calm of *The New Advocate* (Kafka 1988), Dr. Bucephalus. Once the mighty horse of Alexander the Great, this Bucephalus, remaining very much alive, no longer follows Alexander's precipitate path of violent assertion and acquisition – a path that inevitably reached its limit: 'Even in his [Alexander's] day the gates of India were beyond reach, yet the King's sword pointed the way to them. Today the gates have receded to remoter and loftier places; no one points the way' (p. 415):

> So perhaps it is really best to do as Bucephalus has done and absorb oneself in law books. In the quiet lamplight, his flanks unhampered by the thighs of a rider, free and far from the clamour of battle, he reads and turns the pages of our ancient tomes.
>
> (p. 415)

Benjamin (1973) again, after noting that Bucephalus actually 'does not seem to be practicing law,' continues: 'The law which is studied and not practiced any longer is the gate to justice' (p. 139).

The protagonist in the third parable, *Advocates* (Kafka 1988), is also unconstrained, ultimately able to range beyond limits, but initially he is deeply uncertain. In his search for advocates he is unsure whether a surreal court and its corridors, reminiscent of *The Trial*, house the law, whether an incessant and pervasive droning said to be characteristic of 'a law court' originated in 'the place where one happened to be standing', or whether that was an illusion 'for it came from a distance' (p. 449).[5] Yet he remains set on his search to find advocates for they are needed 'everywhere' because the 'verdict' is based on 'inquiries' that extend 'everywhere' (p. 450). Indeed, advocates are, 'if anything needed less in court than elsewhere' for a court, 'one assumes, passes judgment according to the law':

> If one were to assume that this was being done unjustly or frivolously, then life would not be possible; one must have confidence that the court allows the majesty of the law its full scope, for this is its sole duty.
>
> (p. 450)

Within the ambience of the seeming court with its unlikely and vaporous denizens, he fails to find advocates, realises that 'I cannot rid myself of the feeling that I'm not in the right place, I ought to be in a place where all kinds of people meet, from various parts of the country, from every class, every profession of all ages' (p. 450). Impulsively, he runs into a house and offers us a string of nostrums to the effect that in any existential search one cannot go back. These culminate in a beautifully buoyant passage which ends the parable:

> So if you find nothing in the corridors open the doors, if you find nothing behind these doors there are more floors, and if you find nothing up there, don't worry, just leap up another flight of stairs. As long as you don't stop climbing, the stairs won't end, under your climbing feet they will go on growing upwards.
>
> (p. 451)

In the Penal Colony

To claim that Kafka's short story, *In the Penal Colony* (Kafka 1988), extends that illimitable search could seem utterly perverse, but a proposition to that effect will come later. The usual response to this famed and lurid account of a penal colony

5 My use of the masculine pronoun is an assumption. The feminine would be more appropriate – something implicitly confirmed later.

and its mechanised mode of execution is that it renders the Kafkaesque gruesomely 'real' and 'portrays the horror of the world as it truly is' (see Minkkinen 1994, p. 352). But the specific inability of this regime to endure signals what is needed for there to be an enduring authority, and law (cf. Minkkinen 1994, p. 355, p. 361).

The setting is a penal colony in which there is a machine that executes those who break the law. It does this by inscribing the letter of the law on their bound bodies and doing so over a long period – twelve hours in all, the words eventually piercing all the way through the body. The story is about a particular execution or attempted execution. The law to be inscribed is 'HONOR THY SUPERIORS' (Kafka 1988, p. 144).[6] It is to be inscribed on the body of a condemned man whose duty it was throughout the night to salute the door of a captain at regular intervals. He sleeps through one saluting slot, is caught out by the captain, vigorously resists being arrested by him and, in all, is to be executed. The main character, however, is an officer who superintends the execution and who describes the machine to another character, a visiting explorer, in terms of its autonomy and functional perfection – 'it works all by itself' (p. 141): 'No discordant noise spoiled the working of the machine' (p. 154). 'It is effective in itself' (p. 154). '[M]ovements [of a key section] are precisely calculated' (p. 143). The machine was the invention of a former authoritarian Commandant of the colony. The officer proudly shows the Commandant's plan of the machine to the explorer who finds it entirely inexplicable.

The range of set determinations of which the machine is the symbol and instrument extends to the status of the condemned man. His 'guilt is never to be doubted' (p. 145). He is entirely submissive, even taking a compliant interest in the whole proceedings. And with executions generally, and as the officer claims, 'just about the sixth hour' of the machine's 'Harrow' inscribing the law, a luminous 'enlightenment' (more accurately translated as 'understanding') shines out of the face of the condemned when they 'begin . . . to understand the inscription' (p. 150) – 'the radiance of that justice, achieved at last and fading so quickly' (p. 154). This is for the officer '[a] moment that might tempt one to get under the Harrow oneself' (p. 150).

But with this particular planned execution, it soon becomes evident that all is not well with either the machine or the penal regime that it comprehensively characterises. For a start, the whole scene has a stark solitariness to it. There is only the officer, the explorer, the condemned man and a soldier who guards him, all set along with the machine in a desolate landscape. This contrasts to the glory days when '[a] whole day before the ceremony [of execution] the valley was packed with people' (p. 153) wanting to come to it. 'It was impossible to grant all the requests to be allowed to watch it from nearby' (p. 154).

6 In this section bracketed numbers without more are references to *In the Penal Colony* referenced here.

The lack of popular concern and commitment is not the only problem however. There is a new regime, a new Commandant, the colony is changing, and neither the officer nor the machine fit into the new scheme of things. So, whereas the machine inevitably required occasional replacement parts, now those parts are not so forthcoming and the machine creaks with mounting dysfunctions. Furthermore, both the condemned man and the soldier supposedly guarding him act in undisciplined, almost casual ways. Generally, the machine with its concordant regime are no longer the focal force of the colony but are increasingly marginalised and set apart with the officer now being its sole supporter. The new regime would seem to be humane, to accommodate some popular participation, and to have popular support (p. 158, p. 167). And it becomes evident, repeatedly so, and much to the chagrin of the officer, that the new Commandant is much influenced by 'the women' or 'the ladies' seemingly always around him (e.g. p. 153, p. 158).[7]

The *dénouement* is as gruesome as it is abrupt. The condemned man is strapped into the machine by the officer. Previously 'the condemned man was laid under the Harrow by the Commandant himself' (p. 153). But, with the explorer having refused the officer's request to seek the new Commandant's support for the machine, the officer decides that 'the time has come' (p. 160) and, perhaps seeking that enlightenment he found so tempting, frees the condemned man in a farcical scene and substitutes himself in the machine. With that sacrifice the machine may for one terminal time complete its intrinsic function of dealing death, of effecting finality. Which it proceeds to attempt, but in the process its functioning becomes a horrifying malfunctioning. As the machine fragments, it still kills but in an incoordinate way that fails to complete the old process. This also dissipates the ability of the machine itself to inscribe the law. So the legal text the officer wants to have inscribed in and through his body, 'BE JUST' (p. 161), itself dissipates as 'the machine was obviously going to pieces' (p. 165). It 'was not writing, it was only jabbing', and 'this was no exquisite torture' suffused with a radiant 'enlightenment' or understanding – 'this was plain murder': 'no sign was visible of the promised redemption' (p. 165, p. 166).

In the final scene, the explorer visits the hidden grave of the old Commandant which contains this inscription: 'There is a prophecy that after a certain number of years the Commandant will rise again and lead his adherents from this house to recover the colony. Have faith and wait!' (p. 167). This is something which 'the bystanders' seem to find 'ridiculous' (p. 167), perhaps a little uneasily. Then at the end of the story, when the explorer is leaving the colony, the once-condemned man and the soldier seem desperately to want to go with him. But he rejects them. He does not want to engage with them. Perhaps he is repulsed by the whole experience. But in any case he is only an observer, something he had been concerned to emphasise throughout.

7 There is also a mention of the old Commandant's having 'ladies' with him (Kafka 1998, p. 153), but no mention of their being influential. This is accommodated later.

Before the Law

And so we come, inevitably and finally, to Kafka's most famed engagement with the law, his parable *Before the Law* (Kafka 1998). For present purposes, this piece will serve to draw out the law, incipient in the series of works sketched so far. In *The Trial* the parable is told near the end when K. comes to place, or misplace, some trust in an ostensibly obliging priest who 'belong[s] to the court' (p. 215), and with whom K. engages in the hope of finding some way of influencing the court or avoiding its jurisdiction. The priest is quick to disabuse K., and having chastised him for seeking 'too much outside help, particularly from women,' the priest tells K. he is 'deceiving [himself] about the court' and continues with that now resonant opening: 'in the introductory texts to the Law it says of this deception: before the Law stands a doorkeeper' (p. 213, p. 215). The parable tells, or seems to tell, of someone persistently denied any access to the law, to a law that seems ever beyond him. The parable is tightly packed, but a summary could go like this: 'A man from the country comes to this doorkeeper and requests admittance to the Law' (p. 215). The doorkeeper, a figure of official authority and the first in a hierarchy of keepers stretching beyond the door, asserts control over entry to the law. Despite the man's repeated, 'insatiable' efforts to obtain entry, this doorkeeper only allows him a glimpse beyond the door and refuses immediate entrance through what is an ever-open doorway to the law (p. 217). Yet he does not rule out the possibility of later entry. After a lifetime of waiting by the door and of seeking to persuade the official to let him enter, the man from the country is near death:

> [H]is eyes grow dim and he no longer knows whether it's really getting darker around him or if his eyes are merely deceiving him. And yet in the darkness he now sees a radiance that streams forth inextinguishably from the door of the Law. . . . Before he dies, everything he has experienced over the years coalesces in his mind into a single question he has never asked the doorkeeper. . . . 'everyone strives to reach the Law', says the man 'how does it happen, then, that in all these years no one but me has requested admittance.' The doorkeeper sees that the man is nearing his end and in order to reach his failing hearing, he roars at him: 'No one else could gain admittance here, because this entrance was meant solely for you. I'm going to go and shut it now.'
>
> (pp. 216–17)

With that the parable ends and the multitude of engagements with it begins, starting with a debate between K. and the priest which will eventually be drawn on after looking at some other contentions, those of Cixous and of Derrida.[8] 'Before

8 Despite Benjamin's marginalising of law's significance in Kafka, he did have much to say about Kafka and law that could be aptly and more extensively pursued here. However, that 'much' is such a mix of the ridiculous and the profound that it would, in the present setting, take reams to untangle and adapt it. For a beautifully nuanced substitute there is Gasché (2002).

the law' provides both the opening phrase of the parable and its title when Kafka published it separately. And in *The Trial* the priest tells K. that the parable is to be found 'in the introductory texts to the Law' (p. 215), in what introduces the law – in what would, by way of the etymology of 'introduce', bring it in and within (Skeat 1963, p. 266). So, from the many meanings attached to 'before', we can begin with what comes before the law in the sense of what there has to be before there can be law.[9]

Cixous (1991) then:

> The definition of the law can unfold only in relation to the question of the origin of the law. In order to get out of Kafka's text, we must ask: Where does the law come from? and not think that it has always been there.
>
> (p. 19)

Which may not be immediately promising since Cixous would add that the originary dimension of law is what impels a feminine law – a law which 'has no material inside,' 'does not exist,' 'does not take place,' 'cannot be defined' (p. 18). Furthermore, and in another setting, Cixous would affirm: 'Not the origin: she doesn't go back there' (Cixous and Clement 1986, p. 93). Not the origin, the origin as the delimited, appropriated, place of secure return to which 'he will go: she will go further, always beyond', 'to the unknown' (p. 93).[10] Hence, his eternally straitened law as against her 'wild', her 'savage' heart (Cixous 1991, p. 1, p. 3). Yet, even when contrary to the pathology of positivism, for law there is still a 'closing' as well as an 'opening' beyond (Cixous 1991, p. 18).

This generative irresolution 'before the law' links the man from the country with the feminine of Cixous – links them through their resolute seeking of the law: 'There are always men from the country with a little bit of femininity who feel like going in to see nevertheless' (Cixous 1991, p. 27). Like those 'women' in *The Trial* whose 'help' K. was chastised for seeking, the man is also 'outside', at least insofar as he comes from the country and the country is 'beyond of the reach of the court somewhat' (Kafka 1998, p. 94, p. 213). Likewise, it would seem, the new Commandant who brings a more open regime to the penal colony is faulted by the officer for being influenced by 'the women' and 'the ladies' (e.g. Kafka 1988, p. 153, p. 158) – the officer who is now the sole representative of the draconic old regime. Yet the old Commandant had 'his ladies' (Kafka 1998, p. 153), but nothing is said or could be said, about their ability to influence that regime.

9 The range in German for *vor* would include the meanings covered here, and much more. Thanks to Hannah Franzki for guidance on this.

10 For a luminous engagement with the thought of Cixous on this point see Ramshaw (2003). Derrida (1992) would help by adding that '[i]n French, the feminine determines a semantic contagion that we cannot forget' (p. 206).

It is time to return pointedly to Benjamin's (1973) finding in Kafka's writings 'beings' in between, beings who are 'in an unfinished state' in whose 'activities' law 'may be discerned,' and for whom 'there is hope' (p. 117). These are beings of embedded possibility, neither settled in a determinate world nor outside and dissipated indeterminately. Seen in such an 'intermediary' way (Gasché 2002, p. 974), this in-between is nonetheless attuned and related to the determinate and the indeterminate, and it is in and as this relation that we may find the formative force of law.

But another impasse, another denial of entry to the law, would seem to ensue from the impossible simultaneity of the determinate and the indeterminate, of 'an opening and a closing' (Cixous 1991, p. 18). Thence mystery compounded for, even if that one were solved, we would still find, having entered, a law which 'has no material inside', 'does not exist', 'does not take place' (Cixous 1991, p. 18). Perhaps then a return to the force of negative formation 'in' Kafka's works may help. The plan now is to tackle, in order, as it were, the determinate and closed, then the indeterminate and open, and then both in combination.

The determinate, or the seeming determinate, abounds in Kafka. As for law, it can somehow be found or accessed through a multitude of palpable sites – doors, stairs, attics, bedrooms, even courtrooms – and more. The guilt of both K. in *The Trial* and of the condemned *In the Penal Colony* is not to be doubted. And in the colony, the erstwhile machine effects the law in a complete calculability and cutting assertion. Here the law becomes a further variety of legal positivism, one where it is the creature of an entirely surpassing authority, much like the paternal 'sentence' in *The Judgment* (Kafka 1988). From that surpassing position, appeals to law can be arbitrarily and constantly rejected, as in *The Refusal* (Kafka 1988). And so, in *Before the Law*, the priest says that '[o]ne could almost argue that the doorkeeper exceeded his duty by holding out to the man the prospect of a possible future entry. At that time his sole duty appears to have been to turn the man away', that time being when the man from the country first requested entry to the law (Kafka 1998, p. 218). Kafka's evocative precision: 'one could almost argue', but not quite.

The doorkeeper may have some intuition of *The Problem of our Laws* (Kafka 1988). At the outset we would seem to be in the positivist's paradise where the laws 'are kept secret by the small group of nobles who rule us' (p. 437). Not only do the nobles 'stand above the laws', but such laws are 'entrusted exclusively into their hands' (p. 437). And this nobility is indispensable: 'The sole visible and indubitable law that is imposed upon us is the nobility' (p. 438). Yet this pellucid scene not only poses a problem, but it is also a 'problem of *our* laws'. Such laws are demotically generated – generated to the extent of discernible 'main tendencies which permit of this or that historical formulation', but also formulations that are taken as far as 'scrupulously tested and logically ordered conclusions' (p. 437). The focal 'problem of our laws' ensues when 'we seek to adjust ourselves somewhat for the present or the future' because then 'everything becomes uncertain, and our work seems only an intellectual game, for perhaps these laws we are trying to unravel do not exist at all' (pp. 437–8). The emphasis here would have to be on 'perhaps' because this is the view of 'a small party' who hold that 'the Law is whatever nobles do' (p. 438). '[T]he overwhelming majority' insistently think otherwise, however (p. 438). Even though 'nobody would dare to repudiate the nobility', still that majority would cling to their legal tradition because it 'is far from complete and must be more fully inquired into' to the extent that eventually 'everything will have become clear [and] the law will belong to the people and the nobility will vanish' (p. 438). And another of Kafka's frequent themes is the evanescence of imperative authority. In *An Imperial Message* the message disappears in its transmission (Kafka 1988, pp. 4–5). The Emperors in the instances taken from *The Great Wall of China* are fictive (Kafka 1988, p. 245). The father in *The Judgment* collapses on his issuing it (Kafka 1988, p. 87). And the all-presiding court in *The Trial* dissipates in the very effort to locate it, and 'in any case', Benjamin (2005) again, '[t]he court does not dare to admit that it cannot make up its mind' (p. 68). We are left, then, in a hyper-determinacy, in Rushdie's (2007) 'surreal'. 'The surreal is the strangeness of the world made visible: it's a court case that appears to have no end' (p. 274).

Perverse as it may seem, the road to resolution is opened up by Kafka's most spectacular, and most thorough, dissipation of determinate law – the demise of its mechanical exaltation *In the Penal Colony*. Dissolution ensues when the focal instruction given to the machine is 'BE JUST' (Kafka 1988, p. 161). This instruction proves to be entirely destructive of the machine's complete calculability. A more specific outcome is provided by *The New Advocate*, Dr. Bucephalus. Having reached a limit of Alexander's acquisitive violence, and in the recognition that there was more 'beyond reach', Bucephalus throws off restraint and serenely seeks the law – and returning to Benjamin (1973) yet again, and this time in relation to Dr. Bucephalus: 'The law which is studied and not practiced any longer is the gate to justice' (p. 139).

The justice here could, peremptorily for now, be found in one of Derrida's (2002) engagements with *Before the Law*. Here the law identified with justice is a law 'always to come, always promised', the antithesis yet necessary companion of a determinate law: '[o]nly the "to-come" . . . will produce the intelligibility or the interpretability of this law' – that is the law determinate (p. 270). So, for the demotic majority in *The Problem of Our Laws*, these laws have ever to 'be more fully inquired into' even as the attempt to bring them to bear intimates that they 'do not exist at all' (Kafka 1988, p. 438). A more optimistic scenario is adopted by the seeker of the law in *Advocates*. Although initially uncertain whether a manifestation of the law was in 'the place where one happened to be standing' or whether it came from afar, he proceeds irrepressibly to seek it 'everywhere' (Kafka 1988, p. 450). He could be disappointed. The 'force' of this law beyond, the law that is to come, is one of negative formation: it is 'not law'; (Derrida 2002, p. 254). So when seeking through various doors he anticipates finding 'nothing' (Kafka 1998, p. 451), much like the man from the country who would find that the door meant for him would 'open on nothing' (Derrida 1992, p. 206), 'has no material inside' (Cixous 1991, p. 18). It would follow, as Derrida (1992) notes of *Before the Law*, that this law is 'essentially inaccessible' (p. 199). But some relief may be found in Derrida's (2002) revealing that the distinction between this law ever beyond and the law determinate 'is not a true distinction,' and that the two combine in an 'aporetic structure' (p. 270). And to activate the combining of the two would depend upon a 'performative act by which' the man from the country 'institutes' the law, a law that always 'depends only on who is before it' (p. 270).

We are coming closer to the exact terms of *Before the Law* but before reaching them there remains a further obstacle besides that presented by the doorkeeper. *The Trial* has already given us something like a combining of these two dimensions of law: 'Everything belongs to the court' (Kafka 1998, p. 150). Everywhere there are palpable locations where law is, supposedly, to be determinately found. Yet, for all Josef K.'s performative searching, the law proves to be entirely malleable or ever elusive. A more dramatic outcome climaxes *In the Penal Colony* where a mechanistic mode of determination is to perform the illimitable injunction 'BE JUST', only for the machine to self-destruct in the process (Kafka 1988, p. 161). Apparently then, these two dimensions of law must not only be joined but also and decidedly kept apart. In solving this particular mystery, a conspicuous clue can be found in a return to Derrida's (2002) seeing these dimensions of law as combined in an 'aporetic structure' (p. 270). 'Aporetic', so they are not joinable. 'Structure', so they must be joined. A condition of there being such an aporetic structure would require the opposition itself to be connective. A further condition would require the connection to be constituted in terms of the opposition.

The antithesis of each condition can be found in *The Trial*. With the novel as a whole and its fusing the two dimensions of law, the aporetic opposition is lost and along with it the emergence of any resolving law. The trial, the process, is interminable. Then, towards the end of the novel the parable *Before the Law* provides the corrective by instating the enduring opposition between the determinate, limited law and the illimitable. But the effect of this opposition is suspended. The man from the country seeks a determinate law but is left before the law in its illimitability, before its taking determinate place. Although entry to such a law is 'open as always' the illimitable cannot be entered and any resolution is at best deferred from one doorkeeper to another; yet the immediate doorkeeper holds out future entry as 'possible' (Kafka 1998, p. 215). This is something which the priest affirms is not a deception. But before coming to this possibility of entry, a little more needs to be unravelled.

To appreciate how entry to and as law can take place by connecting the dimensions in opposition, that connectability could be considered a little more closely. What, in brief, it consists of is the necessity of one dimension for the sustained existence of the other. Should 'everything' belong to the law, as it does in *The Trial* by way of the court as law's proxy (Kafka 1998, p. 150), the law would be incapable of any differentiated existence. Should it be differentiated and seek to be purely and enduringly so, it would decline and disappear with its inability to respond receptively to change – as with the isolated and increasingly dysfunctional machine *In the Penal Colony*. Turning to the obverse, the illimitable, the law beyond the door cannot have any operative effect unless made determinate. And for this conjunction and disjunction of law's dimensions to work each has to remain distinct and untrammelled by the other. The determinate cannot persist inviolate in part any more than it can in its putative whole. And the illimitable cannot be delimited.

The illimitable, as itself and in its intrinsic necessity for the enduringly determinate, resists any connective reduction. And these dimensions of law (also) have to remain distinct from, and opposed to, each other. Whilst that opposition has been shown (I hope) to be connective, the formative and sustaining terms of that connection remain mysterious. Much of Kafka's work delved into here can be read 'in the quiet lamplight' with Dr. Bucephalus as a search for that connection (Kafka 1988, p. 415). Acutely appreciative of limits as he is, Dr. Bucephalus is surely not so intent on seeking that which can simply and never be found. Likewise, the joyous search in *Advocates*, starting with the uncertainty of whether the law was near or came from afar, is not one dedicated to futility. And in *The Problem of our Laws* the demos, or its majority party, seeks the law not as a vacuity but as ultimately realisable. Both K.s, in *The Castle* and especially in *The Trial*, are dedicated to the search for a palpable, a realisable connection. And the man from the country seeks its possibility, a possibility held out to him by the doorkeeper, and that same possibility pervades *The Trial*. K. does not find connection in the factuality of law's officials and locations, in the force of the state's statutes, or in any positive conceptual constraint, and he realises at times that he is dealing with 'an unknown system of jurisprudence', but he remains committed to the possibility of resolution (Kafka 1998, p. 61). Derrida (2002) finds the law 'whose presence always escapes' the man from the country to be quite beyond, to be 'transcendent' (p. 270). With the worlding of law, and with Blanchot (1992), this has to be a 'pure transcendence', one not tied to any determinate entity beyond the immanent (p. 25). The 'performative' connection is to a law that is 'always to come, always promised', (Derrida 2002, p. 270).

The existential challenge this poses is intimated by the priest in his response to K.'s claiming that the doorkeeper deceived the man from the country: 'One passage says: "that he can't grant him admittance now"; and the other: "this entrance was meant only for you"' (Kafka 1988, p. 217). But here 'there is no contradiction. On the contrary, the first statement even implies the second' (Kafka 1988, p. 218). Whilst the priest is surely being disingenuous in disregarding the deception involved in the doorkeeper's explanatory restraint, there is no delimitable, ultimately measurable moment in which we can enter, assuredly know or attain the law – a law ever receding from gate to gate and a law which, in its infinite deferral, cannot be finally 'entered'. Yet this is a law which holds out the possibility of determinate resolution for the time being – for a transient time being, the law as promised and as possibility being for the man from the country 'nearest to him . . . depends only on him, on the performative act by which he institutes it' (Derrida 2002, p. 270). The gateway, 'the entrance is meant solely for' him (Kafka 1998, p. 217). The law cannot be simply 'there', whether as fact, command or concept. It is 'a matter' of belief and commitment, and of their operative extent. And of hope – the hope of Kafka's 'beings in an unfinished state', those beings in between in whose 'activities' and for Benjamin (1973), law 'may be discerned', if 'subtly and informally' (p. 117).

As for obviousness and form, we are still before the law, before there can be law. The man from the country is performatively insistent, 'insatiable' (Kafka 1998, p. 217), but still there is no resolution. Yet again Kafka takes us further through the provocation engendered by absence. This time it is the absence of sociality. The man from the country is isolated. Although, unlike the country dwellers in *The Castle*, he is insistent, like them he does not challenge and transgress the existing authorities. And similarly to the populace in *The Refusal* and the son in *The Judgment*, there is no generative ground left for any resistant law. In *The Trial* K. is a solitary whose attempts to link with others are continually truncated or frustrated. There is also a stark solitariness to the officer in *In the Penal Colony* and to the regime which he represents, a regime that cannot withstand the contrary sociality the very existence of which now undermines it. More affirmatively, the seeker after law and its advocates in *Advocates* comes to realise that 'I ought to be in a place where all kinds of people meet, from various parts of the country, from every class, every profession, of all ages' (Kafka 1988, p. 450).

Even if that excess of instances did not counter the asocial, lawless element of the Kafkaesque, there would still be the culminating instance of *The Problem of Our Laws*. Here the laws become ours, and decidedly so. Whilst our efforts to know and adapt ourselves to the laws produce uncertainty, and whilst it remains obvious that we still depend on the nobles to determinatively know the laws – true to an etymology of 'noble' which would draw upon both the 'well known' and 'to know' (Skeat 1963, p. 349), there is still the expectation that the demotic 'tradition' of insistent enquiry into the law 'is far from complete and must be more fully' continued (Kafka 1988, p. 438). In this endeavour we are sustained by the messianic expectation that 'when everything will have become clear, the law will belong to the people, and the nobility will vanish' (Kafka 1988, p. 438). Here Kafka captures something of an impelling sociality in and as law – with Derrida (1997) again, 'a law of originary sociability . . . perhaps the very essence of law', a law 'prior to all organized *socius*, . . . *before* all "law"'. Prior to and before all law, in Kafka's sense of being 'before the law' (p. 231, his emphasis).

The radical reflection of this sociality within 'the process' of the law can be derived from *The Trial*, *Der Prozess*, again by way of negative inference. With law, there is always an 'opening' as well as a 'closing', a possibility somehow embedded, a 'pure transcendence' (Cixous 1991, p. 18; Blanchot 1992, p. 25). For this opening to exist and be sustained it must be distinct and self-sufficing, not dependent on or lost in a supposed social reality or any part of it. With the opening being held apart from this reality and being unreliant on any pre-existent differentiation, there is an equality before the law – unlike the condition of the shrunken denizens in *The Trial*. Being insistently apart also imports impartiality into the process. This again is in stark contrast to the world of corruption and expedience, of pervasive partiality in *The Trial*. Yet, a final 'yet', there cannot be this enduring opening without the promise and possibility of a determinate closing, a closing that in *The Trial* eludes the process to the point of its becoming non-existent. The opening and the closing fuse in our being drawn into the emanant radiance of the law – 'a radiance that streams forth inextinguishably from the door of the Law' (Kafka 1988, p. 216).

References

Banakar, B. (2010) 'In search of heimat: a note on Franz Kafka's concept of law', *Law & Literature*, 22(2), pp. 463–90.

Benjamin, W. (1973) 'Franz Kafka: on the tenth anniversary of his death' (pp. 111–40) and 'Max Brod's book on Kafka' (pp. 141–8), translated by H. Zohn, in Arendt, H. (ed.) *Illuminations*. London: Fontana/Collins.

Benjamin, W. (2005) 'The idea of mystery', translated by R. Livingstone, in Jennings, M.W., Eiland, H. and Smith, G. (eds.) *Selected writings, volume 2: part 1, 1927–1930*. Cambridge: Harvard University Press, p. 68.

Blanchot, M. (1992) *The step not beyond*. Translated by L. Nelson. Albany: State University of New York Press.

Brod, M. (1995) *Franz Kafka: a biography*. Translated by G.H. Roberts and R. Winston. Boston: Da Capo Press.

Citati, P. (1990) *Kafka*. Translated by R. Rosenthal. London: Secker & Warburg.

Cixous, H. (1991) *Readings: the poetics of Blanchot, Joyce, Kafka, Kleist, Lispector, and Tsvetayeva*. Translated by B.A. Conley. Minneapolis: University of Minnesota Press.

Cixous, H. and Clement, C. (1986) *The newly born woman*. Translated by B. Wing. Manchester: Manchester University Press.

Derrida, J. (1992) 'Before the law', translated by A. Ronell and C. Roulston (pp. 183–220) and 'The law of genre', translated by A. Ronell (pp. 223–52), in Attridge, D. (ed.) *Acts of literature*. New York: Routledge.

Derrida, J. (1997) *Politics of friendship*. Translated by G. Collins. London: Verso.

Derrida, J. (2002) 'Force of law: the 'mystical foundation of authority'', translated by M. Quaintance, in Anidjar, G. (ed.) *Acts of religion*. New York: Routledge, pp. 228–98.

Gasché, R. (2002) 'Kafka's law: in the field of forces between Judaism and Hellenism', *MLN*, 117, pp. 971–1002.

Kafka, F. (1983) *The castle*. Translated by W. and E. Muir, in *The collected novels of Franz Kafka*. London: Penguin.

Kafka, F. (1988) 'An imperial message' (pp. 4–5), 'The judgement' (pp. 77–88), 'In the penal colony' (pp. 140–67), 'The great wall of China' (pp. 235–48), all translated by W. and E. Muir; 'The refusal' (pp. 263–7), translated by T. and J. Stern; 'The new advocate' (pp. 414–15), 'The problem of our laws' (pp. 437–8), both translated by. W. and E. Muir; 'Advocates' (pp. 449–51), translated by T. and J. Stern, in *The collected short stories of Franz Kafka*. London: Penguin.

Kafka, F. (1998) *The trial*. Translated by B. Mitchell. New York: Schocken Books.

Lawson, M. (2012) 'Crime's grand tour. European detective fiction', *The Guardian*, 26 October. www.theguardian.com/books/2012/oct/26/crimes-grand-tour-european-detective-fiction (Accessed: 17 November 2015).

Leon, D. (2001) *Friends in high places*. London: Arrow Books.

Mann, J. (2006) *The mystery writer*. London: Allison & Busby.
Marcus, L. (2003) 'Detective and literary fiction', in Priestman, M. (ed.) *The Cambridge companion to crime fiction*, Cambridge: Cambridge University Press, pp. 245–67.
Messent, P. (2013) *The crime fiction handbook*. Oxford: Wiley-Blackwell.
Michaud, J. (2013) 'Hardboiled existentialism', *The New Yorker*, 9 September. www.newyorker.com/books/page-turner/hardboiled-existentialism (Accessed: 17 November 2015).
Minkkinen, P. (1994) 'The radiance of justice: on the minor jurisprudence of Franz Kafka', *Social & Legal Studies*, 3, pp. 349–63.
Mitchell, B. (1998) 'Translator's preface', in Kafka, F. *The trial*. New York: Schocken Books.
Murray, N. (2004) *Kafka*. London: Little, Brown.
Oxford English Dictionary (1989). Oxford: Oxford University Press, 2nd ed.
Rachman, S. (n.d.) 'Edgar Alan Poe and the origins of mystery fiction', *Strand Magazine*. www.strandmag.com/poe.htm (Accessed: 17 November 2015).
Ramshaw, S. (2003) 'Bearing the 'wild heart': the Cixousian 'feminine' and the quest for law's origin', *The Australian Feminist Law Journal*, 19, pp. 11–27.
Rushdie, S. (2007) 'Heraclitus', *Granta: The Magazine of New Writing*, 100, pp. 263–74.
Scaggs, J. (2005) *Crime fiction*. Abingdon: Routledge.
Skeat, W. (1963) *Concise etymological dictionary of the English language*. New York: Capricorn Books.
Stevens, W. (2006) 'The snow man', in *Collected Poems*. London: Faber and Faber.

Chapter 8

Suspending democracy

Vigilante justice and the rule of law in Christopher Nolan's *Dark Knight* trilogy

Chris Boge

1 Introduction

About 20 minutes into *The Dark Knight* (2008), the most interesting part of Christopher Nolan's film trilogy about comic book vigilante Batman, the audience witnesses a conversation between Bruce Wayne, a certain Natasha, who is the prima ballerina from the Moscow ballet, and Gotham City's district attorneys, Harvey Dent and Rachel Dawes.

Natasha: How could you want to raise children in a city like this?
Wayne: I was raised here. I turned out OK.
Dent: Is Wayne Manor in the city limits?
Wayne: The Palisades? Sure. You know, as our new DA you might wanna figure out where your jurisdiction ends.
Natasha: I'm talking about the kind of city that idolizes a masked vigilante.
Dent: Gotham City is proud of an ordinary citizen standing up for what's right.
Natasha: Gotham needs heroes like you: elected officials. Not a man who thinks he's above the law.
Wayne: Exactly. Who appointed the Batman?
Dent: We did. All of us who stood by and let scum take control of our city.
Natasha: But this is a democracy, Harvey.
Dent: When their enemies were at the gates, the Romans would suspend democracy and appoint one man to protect the city. It wasn't considered an order, it was considered a public service.
Dawes: Harvey, the last man that they appointed to defend the republic was named Caesar, and he never gave up his power.
Dent: OK, fine. You either die a hero, or you live long enough to see yourself become the villain. Look, whoever the Batman is, he doesn't wanna do this for the rest of his life, how could he? Batman is looking for someone to take up his mantle.

Natasha: Someone like you, Mr Dent?
Dent: Maybe. If I'm up to it.[1]

The mention of the Palisades at the city limits emphasizes Gotham's need for a bulwark against aggressive intruders. The figure of the blonde ballerina from Russia, on the other hand, a country that according to *The New York Times* has recently ordered the United States 'to end its financial support for a wide range of pro-democracy . . . programs . . . in an aggressive step . . . to halt what it views as American meddling in its internal affairs' (Herzenshorn and Barry 2012), reminds Western(ized) audiences of antiquated bloc conflicts and the possibility of the existence of other, morally inferior non-democratic systems of government. The analogy between Rome and America reiterates the truism that the rise of the neo-colonial American empire will be followed by its fall, but it also establishes a false origin story to some degree, referring as it does to rather different legal and social forms.[2] The Old World precedent lends respectability to the present decision of empowering the vigilante. Educated viewers may also notice that the scene appears to have been directly inspired by passages from Jean-Jacques Rousseau's *Le contrat social* (1762), thus promoting the idea of a social contract protecting

1 Like all subsequent quotations of movie dialogue, this is my transcript.

2 Although repeatedly Romanized, common law (also referred to as Anglo-American law) is not coextensive with Roman law, which gave rise to civil law, and differences between common law and civil law traditions, such as the absence or presence of legal codification, the role of precedents and judges or the function of equity courts (maintained in some US states even today) in the common law system should be acknowledged. However, this is hardly something you would expect to find in a superhero movie, even of the more sophisticated sort, targeting markets expecting a lot of action on screen rather than 'tedious' academic discourse. In some cases, the American legal system has indeed used Roman civil law examples as precedents for decisions e.g. in the 1805 case of *Pierson v. Post*, mainly through the influence of Blackstone's *Commentaries on the laws of England* (1765–9) which discusses Roman law examples, and Cooper's 1812 English translation of Emperor Justinian's *Institutes*, dating back to the sixth century CE and known in sixteenth century Europe as *Corpus iuris civilis:* see Kiralfy and Glendon 2012; Simpson 2008; The Robbins Religious and Civil Law Collection 2010. As regards differences between the democratic institutions in the Roman Republic and the United States, it is worth noting that Roman assemblies excluded the majority of citizens 'who did not live in or near the city itself' and were thus 'unable to participate and . . . effectively excluded from the *demos* . . . Two millennia later, the solution – electing representatives to a Roman legislature – would seem obvious' (Dahl 2012). Moreover, the Romans used:

> not only an extremely powerful Senate but also four assemblies [in which] votes were counted by units (centuries or tribes) rather than by individuals; thus, insofar as a majority prevailed in voting, it would have been a majority of units, not of citizens. Although they collectively represented all Roman citizens, the assemblies were not sovereign. Throughout the entire period of the republic, the Senate – an institution inherited from the earlier era of the Roman monarchy – continued to exercise great power. [During the monarchy, Senators were] exclusively drawn from the privileged patrician class, though later, during the republic, members of certain plebeian families [common people] were also admitted (Dahl 2012).

citizens from (the fall back into) a state of nature that is red in tooth and claw, while establishing a tenuous connection between the French and the American revolutions as democratization movements. In Book IV of *The social contract*, titled Dictatorship, Rousseau (2004) muses on the 'inflexibility of the laws, which prevents them from bending to circumstances', and which may 'in certain cases make them injurious, and bring about in a time of crisis the ruin of the state' (p. 147). He goes on to say that, if the 'danger is such that the apparatus of law is itself an obstacle to safety, then a supreme head must be nominated with power to silence all the laws and temporarily suspend the sovereign authority' (p. 148). The nomination of such a supreme head, Rousseau explains in a footnote, 'took place by night and in secret, as if . . . [the consuls] were ashamed to put a man above the law' (p. 149). This is congruent with Natasha's contention that Gotham needs 'elected officials', ordinary citizens working 9 to 5, not 'a man who thinks he's above the law' (*The Dark Knight* 2008), crawling the rooftops at night. 'Dark knight' is, of course, a homophonic play on words: it is a dark night of unreason in which Batman is (constructed as being) forced to hunt criminals, and the proverb 'the night is always darkest before the dawn' springs to mind, as does Francisco Goya's painting *The sleep of reason produces monsters* (1796–7), in which bats figure prominently. Gotham, the argument goes, is not yet ready for a White Knight, such as Harvey Dent, which is why it gets what it deserves, a Dark Knight who instils fear in his opponents and may not appear to be 'the person who is most worthy' (Rousseau 2004, p. 148) to defend the realm.

2 'Vigilance is the price of safety': an American nightmare

By definition, a vigilante is a 'self-appointed guardian of law and order',[3] but Harvey Dent's analogy implies that the people of Gotham appointed their 'silent guardian' and 'watchful protector' (as Detective Commissioner Gordon calls Batman) democratically, if apparently not consciously casting votes. As O'Connor (2010) highlights, social acceptance or inclusion is what separates the vigilante from the (ordinary) criminal. Society may disapprove of the means to which the vigilante resorts, but the result of his actions proves that he is friend not foe, a benefactor humbly and silently working for the maintenance of the social order, fostering the common good.[4] He is the *über*-citizen and ultra-patriot.

3 As defined in the New Penguin English Dictionary (Allen 2000).

4 In *Strain of violence: historical studies of American violence and vigilantism* (1975), R.M. Brown:

> attempted to define vigilantism, saying it represented *'morally sanctimonious' behavior aimed at rectifying or remedying a 'structural flaw' in society*, with the flaw usually being some place where the law was ineffective or not enforced. This is a complex socio-legal definition. It treats vigilantism as a societal reaction and not as a social movement. It also implies that the phenomenon of vigilantism will be

As a representative of the American legal system, Dent uses precedents in order to lay claim to a constitutional ancestry that seems rather too remote to be taken seriously, and may be indicative of the current insecurity of the US as regards its

---

> short-lived since once a flaw is remedied, there is no reason to continue, and in any event, 'sanctimonious' morality is unlikely to be sustainable. For criminological purposes, this definition treats the vigilante the same as the criminal. Both are victims of the same social forces, the same 'structural flaw,' and vigilantes are the victim of a flawed society in the same way a criminal can be considered a victim of society. The difference, of course, is that the criminal is an enemy of society while the vigilante acts as a friend of society. The notion that VIGILANTES ARE VICTIMS of society seems to be a dominant thrust in criminological thought on the subject . . . Psychologists, as well as some criminologists . . . are . . . likely to consider the vigilante's noble motive and premeditation toward curbing evil as important, making it the ultimate act of good citizenship (i.e. '*autonomous citizenship*').[In *Vigilantism: political history of private power in America*] Culberson (1990) also points out the importance of distinguishing between domestic terrorism – which seeks to harm the social order; and vigilantism – which seeks to help the social order (i.e. '*popular sovereignty*'). The notion of VIGILANTE AS GOOD CITIZEN appears to have some currency in the literature. Vigilante violence is the opposite of revolutionary violence as vigilantism always seeks to restore order or preserve the status quo (O'Connor 2010, italics and caps in original).

Without making it explicit, A. Graham-Bertolini (2011) at first seems to equate vigilante justice with vengeance, before interpreting vigilantism as a socio-legal reaction to political oppression and a means of self-protection originating in frontier societies: 'Western epic and drama', she writes:

> reverberate with scenes of bloody vengeance and righteous atonement. From Greek tragedy on, the theme of vigilante justice has been reproduced and developed, from Homer's *Iliad*, to Shakespeare's *Hamlet*, demonstrating the attraction of moral controversy as a literary focus. Retaliating against oppressive forces has always been understood and condoned by men, at least to some degree. Vigilante literature tells the stories of individuals who rectify injustice by taking matters into their own hands. Examples of this plot can be found in American literature dating from colonial times, when settlers made an effort to preserve their moral code without the aid of an established justice system. The popularity of this theme finds further currency in tales of the frontier and Wild West. More recently, Hollywood has capitalized on its popularity by drawing from the myth of American pioneer culture and the theme of the lone avenger (p. 1).

On the historical context of American vigilantism, see also L. Johnston (1992), who explains how vigilance committees came to be seen as an extralegal rather than illegal means directed at eradicating outlawry:

> The first American vigilante movement appeared in 1767, and from then, until about 1900, vigilantism was a constant factor in American life. Typically, vigilantist ideology subscribed to the view that, on occasions, it was necessary to 'break the law in order to uphold it', the vigilante being committed to circumventing the law of the land, but never [to] harming or destroying it . . . 'Vigilance committees' possessed defined goals, rules, and regulations. Their duration varied, but few persisted beyond a year, and most had exhausted their energies within a period of weeks or months. At least 326 movements have been documented for the period from 1767 to 1910. Most contained a few hundred people (a large proportion of the community in many frontier towns), though groups varied in size from the dozen or so members found in Pierre, South Dakota in 1880, to the 6,000-plus belonging to the San Francisco vigilance committee

foreign and domestic policies. The country's most persistent foundation myth is of course, the American Dream, usually cited as an umbrella term for 'the ideals of democracy, freedom, equality, material prosperity, and social welfare on which

---

> of 1856 . . . Membership reflected the social structure of American communities at the time. Leaders tended to be drawn from an elite of businessmen, professionals, and affluent farmers, the middle layer of farmers, craftsmen, tradesmen, teachers, and lower professionals providing the rank-and-file . . . Alienated and marginalized elements of the lowest sections of society – 'outlaws' and 'lower people' rather than the 'honest poor' – were the main targets of vigilantism. Outlaws rejected the respectable values of life and property adhered to by the elite, and in a frontier society where social bonds were fragile and weak, such rejection threatened the brittle social fabric. Fearing the takeover of newly settled areas by such alienated elements, vigilante or 'Regulator' movements responded with vigour against groups of horse thieves, robbers, counterfeiters, arsonists, murderers, slave stealers, and land pirates in areas such as East Texas in the 1830s, Northern and Southern Illinois in the 1840s, and Northern Indiana in the 1850s . . . Whipping and expulsion were common punishments in the early years, but as time passed hanging became the customary sentence . . .In total, it is estimated that organized vigilante groups executed more than 700 people between 1767 and 1910, though if the activities of unorganized lynch mobs, Ku-Klux-Klansmen and others are included, the total for the period probably exceeds 6,000. . . . [V]igilantism was directed at both moral and criminal transgressions, as well as to activities arising in both public and private domains (pp. 12–14).

L. Arellano's (2012) *Vigilantes and lynch mobs* is interesting in that it helps explain how the construction, maintenance and refashioning of images of fictitious vigilantes like Batman serves as a 'narrative justification' (p. 23) of the fact that, although it has become 'considerably less common for present-day Americans to make recourse to vigilantism as a means of taking control over ruptures in the social order than it was in the nineteenth century', the phenomenon may still be interpreted by some local communities in terms of an 'earlier narrative in which vigilantism and even lynching are characterized as heroic' (pp. 131–2). Moreover, there may be continuity in the costumes/masks of American superheroes, reaching back to historical dress codes of vigilantes, making them 'universally heroic, interchangeable with valorous characters from other periods and regions' (p. 46). Vigilante violence is justified by a rhetoric of necessity: it is depicted as a form of execution rather than murder (p. 46). As a rule of thumb, superheroes don't kill their foes, but even in streamlined Hollywood adaptations there has been a recent shift towards the theme of execution. In Snyder's *Man of Steel* (2013) – story and production by Nolan – after what feels like an eternity of traumatizing sequences showing crumbling high-rise buildings threatening to bury civilians, Superman brings his adversary 'to justice' by breaking his neck. In the showdown leading up to the 'execution' scene, set in a building supported by Roman columns, the evil Kryptonian, who is thus established as a perpetrator of 'crimes against humanity' and evil anthropomorphic alien, insists he will not stop attempting to exterminate the human race. Cutting the pillars of the hall with a laser beam shot from his eyes and threatening to kill a group of parents and children, the biological unit of the nuclear family thus becomes synonymous with the 'pillars of society'. Superman, whose countless incarnations have ranged from subversive 'socialist-anarchist' figure in the 1930s to 'government toady' in the 1980s (see Saunders (2011) and F. Miller's (2002) revisionist graphic novel *The Dark Knight Returns*) is here reconstructed along the lines of vigilante rhetoric. Nolan and Snyder's *Man of Steel* (2013) has been socialized in Kansas and therefore claims to be 'as American as it gets', but he's also biologically superior and a misunderstood 'outcast' answerable to no one: Superman embodies American exceptionalism's claim to moral superiority, which serves to 'justify' America's world policing activities (see next footnote as well as Boge 2015).

the USA was founded' (Allen 2000, p. 40).[5] However, what happens to the notion of progress and your personal aspirations if the American Dream comes true? Where's the *telos* when you've achieved what is deemed the ideal state? Taken at face value, ideals like liberty and democracy must allow, contain even, the

5 Closely related to the myth of the American Dream is that of American exceptionalism, referring to:

> the special character of the United States as a uniquely free nation based on democratic ideals and personal liberty. Sometimes this special character is inferred from the nature of American political institutions founded in the 1776–89 period – the declaration of independence (1776), revolution (1776–83), constitution (1787) etc. Thus the 'revolution' and its aftermath freeing the US from British control are important in ideas of American exceptionalism. But often the political differences are said to be underpinned by material differences brought about by the wealth/resources of the United States, sometimes seen as a direct product of the freedom of the American people, but by others as the product of the inheritance of the North American continent's abundant resources. This is the frontier version of the theory, and this and the ideas of social mobility and immigrant assimilation are closely tied to this set of ideas of American material prosperity (Tyrell n.d.).

It is in recent discussions on American exceptionalism that we find bland iterations of 'key American values and virtues' but also increasing levels of self-consciousness and self-doubt. In what reads like propaganda material issued in the first half of the twentieth century, while in fact published in 2013, G. Shapiro, without the slightest trace of irony, propagates an exclusionist form of biological racism that is supposed to justify American cultural imperialism. Unless you're born into it, you can't join the club of superior beings, who, by right of birth, colonize the globe physically and conceptually:

> America is an exceptional nation, in part because we lead the world in innovation . . . [Innovation] is in our culture and our DNA. Every breakthrough Internet company is American . . . Not only that, but our technology companies . . . lead the world. Let's not forget that we also have success in the motion picture, biotech, music, theater and publishing industries . . . While we have reason to be cautious, our supremacy today cannot be seriously questioned . . . Americans are independent thinkers. They create. They challenge the status quo. They make a difference. They solve problems . . . Indeed, our nation may be the most successful experiment in behavioral genetics in human history. We are an amazing case of people having the mental agility and willingness to overcome fear of the unknown and the unpredictable in order to raise their station in life. We are an exceptional nation of innovative entrepreneurs. We must recognize this, celebrate it and make sure that our comparative advantage, especially in innovation, is one we continue to enhance rather than destroy (Shapiro 2013).

In *Time no longer: Americans after the American century* (New Haven: Yale University Press) Smith maintains that:

> America was exceptional during the decades when westward land seemed limitless – from independence until 1890, if we take the census bureau's word for the latter date. For roughly a century, then, Americans were indeed able to reside outside of history – or pretend they did (Smith 2013, which is excerpted from *Time no longer*).

Yet he also reflects on:

> a truth that had been a long time coming: The world does not require America to release it into freedom. Often the world does not even mean the same things when it speaks of 'freedom,'

possibility of their own disintegration. In a(n ideal) democracy, the state's executive forces cannot prevent protest marches because they must uphold the ideal that freedom of thought and expression may become revolutionary, possibly resulting in the system's dissolution. In Alan Moore's complex 1980s graphic novel *Watchmen*, adapted for the screen in 2009, superhero vigilantism is starting to turn into the systematic oppression of civilians. Having just tear-gassed protestors in the streets of New York demanding 'reg'lar cops' instead of 'vigilantes', one masked crime-fighter wonders: 'The country's disintegrating. What's happened to the American Dream?' To which the other, called the Comedian, replies: 'It came

---

> 'liberty,' and 'democracy.' . . . Do Americans have a democratic mission? Finally someone has asked. And the only serious answer is, 'They never did'(Smith 2013).

The enduring myth of American 'specialness' 'does not rest on one particular creation story or narrative derived from a specific series of events. It is more akin to a cluster of stories that provides buttresses for pseudo-analytical judgments about American national identity' (Tyrell n.d.), and the cluster of American superhero stories, with its curious amalgam of ideological and metaphysical aspects, which cannot be discussed in detail in this chapter, helps foster, (re)fashion and maintain the myth at home and abroad. H. Zinn (n.d.) explains the myth of American exceptionalism in terms of a self-congratulatory feeling of superiority, whose origins he sees in the context of religious fanaticism and territorial expansionism in the early white settler colony:

> We are fond in the United States of congratulating ourselves for how wonderful we are, how we are the best, we are the greatest, we are the strongest, we are the most prosperous, we are the freest, we are the most democratic, and yes, we are number one . . . This notion of superiority and exceptionalism starts early . . . in the Massachusetts Bay colony [as early] as 1630. The colony had just begun, and Governor Winthrop utters those words . . . [of] the Massachusetts Bay colony as a city on a hill . . . The idea of a city on a hill is a nice one, because it suggests a model, it suggests setting an example, it suggests what in fact George Bush has spoken of, when he said, 'We are a beacon of liberty and democracy.' And if that's . . . [what] we are, we're a city on a hill that people can look to, and that people can learn from and that people can admire and that people can emulate, then that is a wonderful thing to be. But it doesn't stop there, with being a city on a hill . . . [J]ust a few years after Governor Winthrop utters these words about being a city on a hill, just a few years later, the people in the city on a hill move out to massacre the Peacock Indians who seem to think they belong on this land . . . [T]here's a description of that [by] William Bradford . . . one of the early settlers in Massachusetts at that time . . . [who] wrote a history of the Plymouth Plantation, and he talks about Captain Mason attacking a Peacock village [who] said, 'We must burn them.' And then Bradford reports, 'Those who've escaped the fire were slain with the by sword, some hewed to pieces, some run through with rapiers. As they were very quickly dispatched, and very few escaped, it is conceived that they thus destroyed four hundred at this time. It was a fearful sight to see them frying in the fire, and the streams of blood quenching the same. But the victory seemed a sweet sacrifice, and I gave prayers thereof to God, who had wrought so wonderfully for them, and given them so speedy a victory over so proud and insulting an enemy.' And very early on there is an association between what the government does and what God approves of. And . . . that process of not being just a city on a hill but of moving out, of expanding, continued. That's a persistent fact of American history, going all the way back to these first settlers, and coming down to the present day, the persistence of expansion into somebody else's territory, and occupying that territory, and dealing harshly with the people who resist that occupation (my transcript).

true. You're looking at it. Now c'mon . . . let's really put these jokers through some changes' (Moore and Gibbons 2008, pp. 16–18).

In the Comedian's line of reasoning, Western democracies need watchmen – vigilantes – to protect the citizens, not so much from external threats to the community, but 'from themselves', thereby preventing the system's collapse in a manner that is no different from Soviet and Chinese tanks mowing down civilians. The vigilantes act as an extension of the state's reach, widening the circle of constraints on the rights and liberties of the *demos*. As reactionary forces safeguarding the powers that be, they are reminiscent of Rousseau's thoughts on dictatorship turning into tyranny, of ultra-nationalism as the single-most defining feature of fascism (Passmore 2002, p. 31). In *Watchmen* (Moore and Gibbons 2008), a woman spray paints a phrase on a brick wall before she is shot by the Comedian and carried off by other protestors. The half-finished question reads WHO WATCHES THE WATCHMEN? and is a translation of a line from Juvenal's *Satires*, also translated as 'But who wards the warders?' (Juvenal 1918, VI, p. 347). 'Vigilance is the price of safety', Gotham's mayor states in *The Dark Knight* (2008), but it is easy to see that the price he asks for is too high.

Except for its middle episode, the *Dark Knight* trilogy proves less daring and radical than *Watchmen* as regards the vigilante's doubtful complementary function to state-controlled law and order, resulting in an 'excess of governmentality' (Arellano 2012, p. 21). Yet, Nolan too sketches the American Dream as having temporarily collapsed into its correlative nightmare. Characters like the Scarecrow and the Joker expose the hidden relations of conventions, roles and institutions, thus drawing the viewer's attention to democracy's intrinsic potentiality for internal dissolution. These characters release the suppressed darker implications of the civilizing process by telling the side of the story commonly not told, by laying bare the madness at the foundation: the Scarecrow is a psychiatrist inducing psychoses in his patients, the Joker a 'terrorist' who sets fire to fire trucks and turns laughter into slaughter. When robbing the Gotham National Bank, he uses school buses. Later, he blows up a hospital dressed as a nurse and puts inmates of the Arkham asylum in police uniforms, thus connecting these institutions in a Foucauldian reading with the omnipresent (possibility of im)prison(ment) as a signifier of (bodily and mental) discipline, punishment, order, regulation, control, and surveillance (Foucault 1995).

Our obsession with grounding our judgments in (legal) precedents to lend them (the illusion of) respectability might be called the Derridean archive fever, which exposes the human 'nostalgic desire to return to the origin, to a most archaic place of absolute commencement' (Constable 2012, p. 21). As such, it is a self-deceptive undertaking and an impossibility, an illusion congealing into foundation myths like the American Dream, mirrored in the audience's desire to know how to deal with a Dionysian force like the Joker, who subverts but, as we shall see, also reaffirms an Apollonian rage for structure. Knowing a person's history offers (the illusion of) seamless social control(ability), but the fulfilment of the audience's desire to return to archaic places of absolute commencement is cleverly denied in this part of the trilogy. In spite of the title and content of the first instalment, *Batman Begins* (2005), *The Dark Knight* (2008) offers no *Joker Begins*, and the villain's constantly changing origin story – he asks his victims: 'Do you know how I got these scars?' to which he gives different answers – renders questionable the validity of other characters' victimization stories before the concluding part of the trilogy, *The Dark Knight Rises* (2012), establishes Bane as a victim of circumstance, the pitiable monster with clear-cut origins.

Critics tend to believe the claims made by him, and regurgitated by other characters, that the Joker 'just does' things, that he is a 'mad dog chasing a car' who 'can't be bullied or reasoned' with because he 'just [wants to] watch the world burn' (*The Dark Knight* 2008). However, the Joker is in fact an accomplished liar and unreliable narrator of his own life story, not at all unreasonable or indifferent to the game of telling lies (see Frankfurt 2005). He is not just a reaction or an effect to a cause who cannot be held accountable, but someone feeding on the fear and gullibility of others. His true motives are revealed in the last of his thought-experiments-put-to-practice which makes apparent the strains between liberalism and communitarianism. Meticulously planning what he claims is introducing anarchy into society, he is an extremist thinker and doer who puts a lot of effort into proving his points, and it is precisely his successful veiling of this fact that creates uncertainty in audiences craving the fictitious comfort of the circumscribable, locatable origin story.

One of the test tube situations he creates involves evacuees caught on two boats rigged with explosives, which the passengers weren't aware of when boarding. One boat contains convicts and their warders, the other is crowded with Gotham's good or ordinary inhabitants. Each party is given the detonators for the bombs on the other ship, and the Joker announces that both ships will be blown up on the stroke of midnight unless one blows up the other beforehand. The good citizens decide to cast votes as to what to do: this is the democratic majority principle, resulting in representational government, and it seems the natural way of resolving a moral dilemma involving more than one decision maker. However, are you obliged to make any decision at all?

3 Justice and the rule of law

One common definition of justice results in the term's conflation with fairness, famously by Rawls (1999), who thinks that 'the rule of law is . . . closely related to liberty', and that legal systems are intimately connected with 'the precepts definitive of justice as regularity'. A legal system, Rawls asserts, 'is a coercive order of public rules addressed to rational persons for the purpose of regulating their conduct and providing the framework for social cooperation'. According to him, 'just rules' and 'legitimate expectations' go hand in hand, constituting 'the grounds upon which persons rely on one another' (p. 207). However, what if legitimate expectations are ungroundable when the law, that 'basic structure' framing 'the pursuit of all other activities' (p. 207), proves as vacuous as the American Dream?

What if Honderich's (2006) question about the legitimacy of the rule of law, any rule of law, proves more than mere rhetoric?[6]

> What of the more general idea of going by what is called *the rule of law*? That is the idea, presumably, of always going by some or other body of . . . law, as distinct from what may be supposed to be the body of . . . law at a particular time . . . We cannot suppose that there is *no* conceivable body of law, however monstrous, such that we should abide by it rather than break it. It cannot possibly be true, despite a certain amount of ancient wisdom to the contrary, that any rule is better than no rule. It cannot possibly be true that every conceivable law should be kept in order to serve or support the whole institution or fabric of the law.
>
> (pp. 11–12, italics in original)

6 In *Modernism and the grounds of law*, Peter Fitzpatrick (2001), taking as his starting point Freud's attempt to provide a consistent genealogy of society in *Totem and Taboo*, traces the posited origin of (the rule of) law as one that in legal modernity – that is in 'positivist and other assertions of law's stability, fixity, implacability, finality' – is ideally non-contingent or 'self-grounding . . ., self-generating and self-regulating' (pp. 5–6, 70–1). However, what Fitzpatrick finds is in fact a complex dialectic between determinacy and responsibility (which he also spells responsability), or universalism and particularism/openness and finitude:

> For law to rule, it has to be able to do anything, if not everything. It cannot, then, simply secure stability and predictability but also has to do the opposite: it has to ensure that law is ever responsive to change, otherwise law will eventually cease to rule the situation which has changed around it. So, how could the rule of law be complete if it must ever respond to the infinite variety of fact and circumstance impinging on it? How could it be closed when it must hold itself constantly responsive to all that is beyond what it may at the moment be? And how could law, in extending to what is continually other to itself, avoid pervasive contradiction? . . . [E]very tale of law's bringing order to disordered times and places, along with the triumph of such things as modernity or capitalist social relations, can be matched by others where it created uncertainty and inflicted massive disorder in the same cause (pp. 7–71).

By the same token, whereas Nolan sets out to convince the viewer that the League of Shadows' occupation and (partial) destruction of Gotham in *The Dark Knight Rises* (2012) is not only unjust and illegal – the war they wage would not be construed as legal or just[ifiable] in international law – the disorder it causes in the eyes of the audience would be seen as the (re)establishing/restoration of (a global) order from the point of view of the League members. Whereas 'we' would regard their rule of law as either oppressive or altogether non-existent, from their vantage point it would be responsive/a necessary reaction to Western decadence and *de facto* lawlessness. Thus, here too we're faced with questions of perspectivalism and the justification of the rightness and wrongness of a course of action, questions that narrow frameworks such as legal positivism – whose methodology is based on the preference of one set of values over another, which it must account for if the selection is to be acknowledged as reasonable, and since the justification of values traditionally (though not exclusively) falls in the field of ethics, it is a circular move – cannot accommodate. 'Was the Holocaust legal in Germany, by the way?' Honderich (2006, p. 9) asks rhetorically.

The Joker's experiment, by which he means to prove that it takes no more than a little push to restore mankind to the state of nature, is based on the premise that someone in charge of a situation thinks he is justified in setting up what to him is a reasonable scenario for proving the validity of his thesis, hiding from us the fact that he is conducting a laboratory experiment contingent on selected factors and values. The evacuation scenario is only brought about by the Joker's threats in the first place; the people would never have been crowded on the boats faced with such a strange proposal if he hadn't initially forced them to flee, nor would the boats have been rigged with explosive oil drums. Let us assume for a moment that the whole set-up is meant to serve the Joker – and, by extrapolation, Nolan – as a metonymy for the American way of life, or perhaps even for Western civilization as such. The threat of blowing up the vessels at midnight implies that those forms of social coexistence are doomed, and that only some will survive by exterminating the others in time. However, this claim is prophetic, and its truth content unverifiable. If we read the separate boats as signifying different nation states, locked in mortal combat or fierce economic competition, the implication is that individuals are forced together, that the nation is not an imagined community that citizens voluntarily subscribe to but a deadly coercive, real-life entity. Moving one step up the scale, the scenario sketches mankind as doomed unless some peoples exterminate others (as e.g. natural resources become scarce and living space is limited). But who should justly kill who?

If it is true that ethical reasoning is fundamental to law, as there may exist a 'gulf . . . between what is right and what it is legal' and that moral or ethical reasoning is fundamental to 'the question of humanity, decency or justice' in that it gives rise to what becomes law (Honderich 2006, pp. 2–9), the notion of justice would appear to be not so much situated in the realm of legal but ethical thinking. That is to say, if we assume that justice is fairness and that right decisions are also fair decisions, the terms *right* and *just* must be correlated. Yet, how do we determine what is right and wrong? Do we have an innate moral compass or 'ethical framework, much as we have an innate predisposition for language', a 'moral faculty' that is part of our mental and biological make-up as humans, leading us 'to judge situations based on notions of fairness' (Monroe 2012, pp. 296–300)? It sounds almost too simple – and, anyway, who's the homogeneous *we* these sentences claim to refer to?

In *Batman Begins* (2005), (criminal) justice is variously defined as: (1) a form of vengeance that has a cathartic psychological function in that it keeps the individual who feels wronged from being torn apart by the anger pent up inside (see criminal mastermind Ra's al Ghul); (2) a form of revenge that is coextensive with justice in times when the purportedly impartial system 'is broken' (see Bruce Wayne); (3) as something other than revenge, which is only an attempt to make 'yourself feel better'. Justice requires an 'impartial system' and looking 'beyond your own pain'; it brings about 'harmony' (see district attorney Rachel Dawes, and later, Wayne who admits: 'I was a coward with a gun. Justice is about more than revenge'). However, harmony, though not specified, does not seem to come into existence through *quid pro quo*, an exact equivalence of crime and punishment. 'Justice is balance,' the leader of the League of Shadows, Ra's al Ghul (Arabic for 'the demon's head', see Langley 2012), claims before setting Wayne Manor on fire: 'You burnt my house and left me for dead. Consider us even.' Wayne's reply to this at the end of *Batman Begins* (2005), in a variant of the thought experiment known as The Runaway Trolley Car, is that, although he won't kill Ra's al Ghul, he is under no obligation to save his life either.[7]

All of these claims on justice are calculations along similar lines. All of them are based on premises of desert or merit, the idea of a social contract and the notion of causality. You deserve reward or punishment according to how you behave. Put differently: your past action *x* determines your present treatment *y* by others, much as your present action determines the future in the same way. Yet, the categorical assumption that the vigilante's reasoning is flawed because he is not disinterested and his treatment of others – unlike the seemingly neutral decisions made by representatives of an 'impartial system' – is therefore unjust is problematic: even a judge and jury's omniscience and omnipotence would not logically preclude bias or guarantee their absence of self-interest. So the question *By whom?* remains: whose justice and whose law are we talking about, what are their standards of right and wrong, and can they give good reasons to support them?[8]

7 'Justice is a concept. Like all concepts, it is a tool invented and refined by human beings – by many human beings, for most of whom any contribution toward shaping or transmitting the concept of justice is an unintended by-product of thoughts and actions that aim at other purposes . . . If we want ideas about justice to be recognized and accepted as ideas about justice, rather than as arbitrary fabrications, we must respect the intuitions that are fundamental to the sense of justice. A sensibility for reciprocity in relations among human beings is integral to that sense. It is commonplace for people who have received significant benefits from others to feel that they ought to requite those benefits in some fashion, if they are able to do so. Perhaps even more strikingly, people will often go to great lengths to retaliate against others who have inflicted harm, if they are able to do so. It is not unusual for people to retaliate against perpetrators of harm even if they are not the victims and the act of retaliation is costly to themselves . . . [B]oth monocultural and cross-cultural studies of behaviour related to fairness have found that people generally are motivated by considerations of reciprocity and are willing to make personal sacrifices in order to satisfy the demands of reciprocity' (Johnston 2011, pp. 224–6).

While the idea of reciprocity is alluded to in utterances such as 'Justice is balance' or Dawes's idea of harmony, one of the major problems in Nolan's trilogy – from an academic point of view – is that, like so many other superhero narratives, it makes no clear distinctions between terms like revenge, vengeance, retaliation, or retribution.

8 This can be illustrated by an example from British imperial history: the proclamation board of Lieutenant Governor Gordon Arthur of Van Diemen's Land (Tasmania), issued around 1830. At first glance it would appear a fair and reasonable arrangement to settle the frontier violence and establish the legal foundations for the peaceful intercultural coexistence, cohabitation even, of Aborigines and white Australian settlers. Irrespective of their 'racial' characteristics or cultural affiliations, transgressors will be equally – *justly* – punished: the same type of action/crime (murder) elicits the same type of punishment (hanging). But is symmetry – or this type of symmetry – the same as justice? Obviously not. As Stuart Macintyre (1999) points out, the:

In the boats-rigged-with-explosives experiment, the theme of desert repeats itself: 'Those men had their chance', one of the 'good' citizens in favour of detonating the bomb on the convict ship argues. But who can say that's true? And what of the warders, the non-transgressive, law-abiding watchmen? Do they deserve to die in the collateral damage? The Joker does not reveal the construction lines of his experiment but, even if he did, he could not be trusted to speak the truth on account of his unreliability. Yet, the passengers on the boats simply believe that what he says is true without asking if pushing the button on the detonator might cause the bombs on their own boat to go off; if the possibility exists that the Joker won't blow up any boat if the crew and passengers simply bide their time; or how likely it is that he is going to blow up the boat that they are on anyway shortly after they've detonated the bombs on the other boat exactly to prevent this scenario from becoming real.

That the selection, distribution and form of presentation of information influences our perception of the world and our decision-making processes is as much a

---

> ostensible even-handedness of British justice . . . rested on a fundamental inequality. In both panels it was the white man who prescribed the rules and meted out the punishment. The Aboriginal rejoinder to such one-sided justice was delivered in the year that Arthur conducted his Black Line: 'Go away, you white buggers! What business have you here?' (pp. 64–6).

It is the white man's idea of law and order, hardly ever questioned at the time *as* just that, a Western principle. The fundamental unfairness – or *injustice?* – is to impose upon the indigenous inhabitants a system they have nothing to do with, that is not in accordance with their worldviews and ways of life, one they never asked for and simply do not want. To conceive of the principle of justice as a calculation of merit and desert may be viable, but it may equally be just someone's way of doing things and, thus, cannot, perhaps, claim universality, unless supported by valid reasoning, good arguments and the consent of those to be ruled and judged according to principles mutually agreed on. It is perhaps also worth noting that symmetry (read equilibrium or balance), though perhaps biologically rooted in human evolution (experiments show that most people instinctively prefer faces whose left and right halves are rather symmetrical) is as much an aesthetic as an ethical ideal and as such not necessarily justifiable in terms of logic. Yet, we need not resort to cynicism or an uncritical 'anything goes' as regards our standards of justice, or become 'post-Enlightenment persons' as Alasdair Macintyre (1988) puts it in *Whose justice? which rationality?* To him, a post-Enlightenment person is someone for whom 'no set of beliefs proposed for acceptance is . . . justifiable' and who treats the:

> everyday world . . . as one of pragmatic necessities. Every scheme of overall belief which extends beyond the realm of pragmatic necessity is equally unjustified. There is no such scheme of belief within which such an individual is able to find him or herself at home, and the imaginative assumption of beliefs not actually held is not and cannot be for the purpose of investigating the rationality of that scheme, for it has already been concluded that all such schemes fail. Such an individual therefore views the social and cultural order, the order of traditions, as a series of falsifying masquerades (p. 395).

Perhaps the Joker can be seen as someone playing out extreme versions of such falsifying masquerades, as he has become cynical about pondering the nihilistic implications of this worldview. One alternative to postmodern indifference lies in an engagement in the dialectic of thick and thin moral descriptions, of particularities and universalisms (see e.g. Walzer 1994).

commonplace as is the observation that the manipulation of data for propaganda purposes is a standard procedure in both democracies and non-democratic forms of government. What is disturbing in this scene in the movie is that no one even attempts to verify the given information or, for instance, tries to make contact with the other boat to reach a consensus. The panic the Joker creates through the time constraint coupled with the threat to life – the horror intrinsic to the word deadline – appears to induce gullibility and suspend critical thinking, creating monsters through drugging reason and putting it to sleep. This is another aspect of the injustice of the situation, as is its artificiality uncritically accepted by the viewers. It turns out the Joker intended to blow up the ships in any event, so the individual and collective autonomy he pretends to offer the involuntary participants in his experiment is an illusion he creates. It amounts to a wicked play on robbing people of their freedom of volition, proving that his rule is totalitarian. However, how non-authoritarian is democracy, commonly known as the rule of the people?

Despite its 'doubly flawed' or even 'perverse' logic, as Russell Hardin (1995) puts it, democracy is 'virtually universally revered as the best or the right form of government'. The system's flaws have been pointed out by public choice theorists, who argue that 'orderly individual preferences do not generally aggregate into orderly collective preferences', and that 'individual motivations for action are incompatible with collective preferences even when the latter are well-defined' (Hardin 1995). Other criticisms undermining justifications for democracy include the fact that 'a winning party in a democratic election can be elected with fewer votes in total than the losing party' or that the uneven distribution of wealth and power makes it a 'hierarchic' or 'primitive' system fostering inequality (Honderich 2006, pp. 42–8). More often than not, however, the story of Western democracy is told uncritically as one of inevitable progress, as Sharp's (2010) title *From dictatorship to democracy* suggests. It is not only an ideal but also an ideological story. In Nolan, the rule of law and the forms of government depicted are defined negatively as the better choice in a contrastive pair. Rather than being shown as enabling the good life – whatever that may be – and promoting equality, the law in these films protects, prevents and curbs evil; the state system, supported by the vigilante, keeps at bay worse choices and forms of government. This is similar to Churchill's quip, referring to Aristotle's *Politics*, that 'it has been said that democracy is the worst form of government except all the others that have been tried'.

4 To be there with you, o my true guardian!

To make the audience believe that the *de facto* rule of the powerful few (the billionaire-turned-vigilante as protector) over the many is necessary, the threat to life (of the 'good' characters, and, by extension, to the audience themselves) must be perceived as real; the absence of the vigilante must be perceived as producing worse results than does his presence. While the latter is doubtful in *Watchmen* (Moore and Gibbons 2008), Nolan invests much time in his *Dark Knight* trilogy to construct the vigilante as beneficent. Indistinct fears of anarchy, terror, and even the threat of military occupation are a constant presence throughout the films: in *The Dark Knight Rises* (2012), Detective Commissioner Gordon is sentenced to death in a mock-military tribunal that is sharply contrasted with the notion of due process in a regular civil court, before he is saved by the Batman.[9]

9 Interestingly, the *New Oxford Companion to Law* has no entry for 'due process' but refers the reader to 'fair trial, right to' instead. In its first 10 lines, the entry opens up a semantic field of the following bold print terms for cross-referencing: human rights, democracy, rule of law, human, common law, natural justice (Jackson 2008, p. 442). Strauss (n.d.) lists 10 'kinds of procedures that might be claimed in a "due process" argument, roughly in order of their perceived importance' which, he goes on to say, do not however constitute 'a list of procedures that will in fact be required'. This ideal list consists of (1) an unbiased tribunal, (2) notice of the proposed action and the grounds asserted for it, (3) opportunity to present reasons why the proposed action should not be taken, (4) the right to present evidence, including the right to call witnesses, (5) the right to know opposing evidence, (6) the right to cross-examine adverse witnesses, (7) a decision based exclusively on the evidence presented, (8) opportunity to be represented by counsel, (9) requirement that the tribunal prepare a record of the evidence presented, (10) requirement that the tribunal prepare written findings of fact and reasons for its decision. At a recent Foundation for Law, Justice and Society conference held at Wolfson College, University of Oxford, Judge R. Sharpe of the Court of Appeal for Ontario argued that 'democracy is a richer concept than majority rule, and that courts have the mandate to protect minorities . . . [as] judges enrich [and] strengthen democracy by sitting in judgement on the decisions of the elected representatives – the politicians' (Wolfson College, University of Oxford 2012). This discussion might be of greater importance in the common law system, which, while perhaps offering greater flexibility, may also exhibit potential dangers in giving judges legislative power to some extent: 'The precedents to be applied in the decision of each new case are determined by the presiding judge. As a result, judges have an enormous role in shaping American and British law' (The Robbins Religious and Civil Law Collection 2010). Due process procedures, such as those listed by Strauss (n.d.), are meant to define, control and limit judicial powers, but the scene from *The Dark Knight Rises* (2008) stands the following dichotomic line of reasoning on its head by showing that, far from constituting of necessity, 'an essential element of society's machinery for keeping peace' and keeping at bay the spectres of anarchy, courts, probably more so in the common law system than in civil law, bear in themselves the potential for turning into fickle, wilful affairs. Thus, there may be potentially less difference between the vigilante's meting out of punishment and a court doing so than Karlen, Gibson and Smentkowsi's (2012) reactionary and progressivist text (state-of-nature primitivism versus orderly civilized proceduralism as a motor for worldwide democratization) suggests:

> If there were no institution that was accepted by the citizens of a society as an impartial and authoritative judge of whether a person had committed a crime and, if so, what type of punishment should be meted out, vigilantes offended by the person's conduct might well take the law into their own hands and proceed to punish the alleged miscreant according to their uncontrolled discretion. If no agency were empowered to decide private disputes impartially and authoritatively, people would have to settle their disputes by themselves, with power rather than legitimate authority likely being the basis of such decisions. Such a system might easily degenerate into anarchy. Not even a primitive society could survive under such conditions. Thus, in this most basic sense, courts constitute an essential element of society's machinery for keeping peace . . . While countries that have democratized more recently still lag behind Western democracies in terms of both the usage and the independence of the judiciary, courts globally have become important agents of legal, political, and social change. Because courts are often viewed as the 'guardians of

'The fear of imminent destruction by an enemy of boundless evil' is a common device exploited for propaganda purposes: 'Such perceptions are deeply rooted in American popular culture, coupled with faith in the nobility of purpose', Noam Chomsky (2006) asserts, and the 'demons' about to destroy Americans have ranged from American 'Indians, blacks, [and] Chinese workers' to 'Arab terrorists lurking everywhere' (p. 213).

Like most post-9/11 superhero films, Nolan's *Dark Knight* trilogy re-examines the undercurrents of American patriotism and nationalism, depicting an America casting itself in the role of the victim of destabilizing and aggressive forces in a dog-eat-dog world; an America that is easy prey for invasive elements which, like alien parasites, worm their way into and undermine the country's democratic foundations. According to this reading, Nolan's America is not only unsure of the validity of its origin myth, its legal and institutional grounds and the values and morals underpinning them, but also of its economic and political place in an international network that is conceived as a hierarchical pecking order. This xenophobic and paranoid America, whose self-image as a safe haven for immigrants serves as a substantial pillar for perpetuating the matrix of the American Dream (see Gerber 2011), is shown as under attack and defenceless by legal means, thus unconsciously summoning extralegal help in the form of the patriotic vigilante serving as protector of the realm and restoring the country to peace, order and liberty.[10] At the same time, the feelings of paranoia created instil in audiences the

> democracy', powerful and independent judiciaries throughout the world are increasingly seen as necessary components of a successful democratic system.

The text also leaves strikingly undefined the differences between authority and power. Although authority is sometimes treated as 'a subset of power' and while the concepts may overlap in theory and practice, authority arguably is 'a *de jure* or normative concept' whereas power is 'a *de facto* or causal concept' (Downie 1995) – hence the vigilante in Nolan's films as *de facto* but not *de jure* ruler of the people/'guardian of democracy'.

10 Perhaps one can read Nolan's trilogy in this regard as the visual embodiment of libertarian philosopher Robert Nozick's idea of a 'night watchman state' in *Anarchy, state, and utopia*:

> Justice, Nozick argues, requires a 'night watchman' state, which provides basic security for all but, beyond that, refrains from intervening in people's choices. Just distributions, in his analysis, are whichever distributions are arrived at when people acquire things in a fair way and then engage in free market exchanges with one another (Hayward and Swanstrom 2011, p. 8).

It is easy to see that the (rather naive or optimistic) premise of (the just institution of) a free market is contingent on fundamental historical inequalities, as Hayward and Swanstrom (2011) continue to explain with regard to American colonial history:

> Think back to what is often (still) called 'the discovery of America'. Original acquisition took the form of outright expropriation. At the start of black-white relations in the United States, first distributions were rooted in enslavement, coerced labor, and exploitation. Even if we confine our historical analysis to black-white relations in the twentieth century metropolis, we cannot

desire for means of social control that would guarantee security by enabling the supposed readability of the other.

Though shrewd at times, Nolan's critique eventually proves reactionary, providing the prospect of the restoration of the status quo, safeguarded by the hero who as a principle – as a trope – is potentially eternal. Shying away from a more radical, un-Hollywoodesque solution, Nolan's storytelling devices are at times reminiscent of political propaganda techniques that were borrowed 'from business doctrines and practices that were mostly pioneered in the Anglo-American societies', resorting to 'simple "symbols and slogans" with "tremendously reiterated impressions"' appealing to 'fear and other elementary emotions in the manner of commercial advertising' (Chomsky 2006, p. 210).

The resolution to the crisis at the end of *The Dark Knight Rises* (2012) inscribes the former vigilante as a hero, presumed to have sacrificed his life for the greater good, into the national(ist) narrative. At the same time, America emplaces itself in a progressivist narrative of Western democratic constitutionalism by depicting Wayne as finding private fulfilment in Italy, that land feeding the dreams of British and continental European romantics like Shelley or Johann Wolfgang von Goethe (2004), whose lyrical I claims in his poem Mignon: 'It's there I'd be gone, / To be there with you, O my true guardian!'

References

Allen, R. (ed.) (2000) 'American dream', 'vigilante', *The new Penguin English dictionary*. London: Penguin Books.

Arellano, L. (2012) *Vigilantes and lynch mobs: narratives of community and nation*. Philadelphia: Temple University Press.

Batman Begins (2005) Directed by Christopher Nolan [Film]. USA: Warner Bros. Pictures.

Boge, C. (2015) 'Crimes against (super)humanity: graphic forms of justice and governance', in Giddens, T. (ed.) *Graphic justice: intersections of comics and law*. Abingdon: Routledge, pp. 219–35.

Brown, R. M. (1975) *Strain of Violence: Historical studies of American violence and vigilantism*. New York: Oxford University Press.

Chang, H.J. (2011) *23 things they don't tell you about capitalism*. London: Penguin.

Chomsky, N. (2006) *Failed states: the abuse of power and the assault on democracy*. New York: Metropolitan Books.

Constable, M. (2012) 'Incitement to justice: Fitzpatrick's citations as counter-imperialism', in Buchanan, R., Motha, S. and Pahuja, S. (eds.) *Reading modern law: critical methodologies and sovereign formations*. Abingdon: Routledge, pp. 15–23.

help but conclude that contemporary distributive patterns are not the product of free and fair exchange (p. 8).

It is easy to see in historical perspective why, if 'there is no such thing as a free market' (Chang 2011, p. 1), distributive justice – hinted at in the Joker's thought experiments – faces manifold challenges, as the unequal distribution of resources is based on heavily entrenched power imbalances.

Dahl, R.A. (2012) 'democracy', *Encyclopædia Britannica: ultimate reference suite*. Chicago: Encyclopædia Britannica.

Downie, R.S. (1995) 'authority', in Honderich, T. (ed.) *The Oxford companion to philosophy*. Oxford: Oxford University Press.

Fitzpatrick, P. (2001) *Modernism and the grounds of law*. Cambridge: Cambridge University Press.

Foucault, M. (1995) *Discipline and punish: the birth of the prison*. Translated by A. Sheridan. New York: Vintage. (Original work published in 1975)

Frankfurt, H. (2005) *On bullshit*. Princeton: Princeton University Press.

Gerber, D. (2011) *American immigration: a very short introduction*. Oxford: Oxford University Press.

Goethe, J.W. von (2004) 'Mignon', *Goethe: selected poems*. Translated by A.S. Kline, in Kline, A.S. (2015) *Poetry in Translation*. www.poetryintranslation.com (Accessed: 25 October 2012). (Original work published in 1795–6)

Graham-Bertolini, A. (2011) *Vigilante women in American fiction*. New York: Palgrave Macmillan.

Hardin, R. (1995) 'Democracy', in Honderich T. (ed.) *The Oxford companion to philosophy*. Oxford: Oxford University Press.

Hayward, C.R. and Swanstrom, T. (2011) 'Introduction: thick injustice', in Hayward, C.R. and Swanstrom, T. (eds.) *Justice and the American metropolis*. Minneapolis: University of Minnesota Press, pp. 1–29.

Herzenshorn, D.M. and Barry, E. (2012) 'Russia demands U.S. end support of democracy groups', *The New York Times*, 18 September. www.nytimes.com/2012/09/19/world/europe/russia-demands-us-end-pro-democracy-work.html?_r=0 (Accessed: 23 September 2012).

Honderich, T. (2006) *Humanity, terrorism, terrorist war*. London: Continuum.

Jackson, J. (2008) 'fair trial, right to', in Cane, P. and Conaghan, J. (eds.) *The new Oxford companion to law*. Oxford: Oxford University Press.

Johnston, D. (2011) *A brief history of justice*. Chichester: Wiley-Blackwell.

Johnston, L. (1992) *The rebirth of private policing*. London: Routledge.

Juvenal (1918) *Satires*. Translated by G.G. Ramsay, in Pearse, R. (2015) *The Tertullian Project*. www.tertullian.org/fathers/index.htm#Juvenal_Satires (Accessed: 11 November 2012). (Original work written in ca. 112–30 CE)

Karlen, D., Gibson, J.L. and Smentkowski, B.P. (2012) 'court', *Encyclopædia Britannica: ultimate reference suite*. Chicago: Encyclopædia Britannica.

Kiralfy, A.R. and Glendon, M.A. (2012) 'common law', *Encyclopædia Britannica: ultimate reference suite*. Chicago: Encyclopædia Britannica.

Langley, T. (2012) 'Batman's case files: immortality versus extinction', *Psychology Today*, 9 August. www.psychologytoday.com (Accessed: 16 October 2012).

Macintyre, A. (1988) *Whose justice? Which rationality?*. London: Duckworth.

Macintyre, S. (1999) *A concise history of Australia*. Cambridge: Cambridge University.

Man of Steel (2013) Directed by Zack Snyder [Film]. USA: Warner Bros. Pictures.

Miller, F. (2002) *Batman: The Dark Knight Returns*. New York: DC.

Monroe, K.R. (2012) *Ethics in an age of terror and genocide: identity and moral choice*. Princeton: Princeton University Press.

Moore, A. and Gibbons, D. (2008) *Watchmen: international edition*. New York: DC.

O'Connor, T. (2010) 'Vigilantism, vigilante justice, and self-help', *drtomoconnor*, 26 August. http://drtomoconnor.com (Accessed: 24 September 2012).

Passmore, K. (2002) *Fascism: a very short introduction*. Oxford: Oxford University Press.

Rawls, J. (1999) *A theory of justice*. Revised edn. Oxford: Oxford University Press.

Rousseau, J-J. (2004) *The social contract*. Translated by M. Cranston. London: Penguin. (Original work published in 1762)

Saunders, B. (2011) *Do the gods wear capes? Spirituality, fantasy, and superheroes*. London: Continuum.

Shapiro, G. (2013) 'American exceptionalism: it's in our genes', *U.S. News and World Report*, 26 April. www.usnews.com/opinion/articles/2013/04/26/american-exceptionalism-its-in-our-genes (Accessed: 28 May 2013).

Sharp, G. (2010) *From dictatorship to democracy: a conceptual framework for liberation*. 4th U.S. edn. Boston: The Albert Einstein Institution. www.aeinstein.org (Accessed: 16 September 2012).

Simpson, A.W.B. (2008) 'common law' in Cane, P. and Conaghan, J. (eds.) *The new Oxford companion to law*. Oxford: Oxford University Press.

Smith, P. (2013) 'American exceptionalism is a dangerous myth', *Salon*, 26 May 2013. www.salon.com (Accessed: 12 July 2013).

Strauss, P. (n.d.) 'due process', in *Wex: Legal dictionary and legal encyclopedia*. Legal Information Institute, Cornell University Law School. www.law.cornell.edu (Accessed: 27 November 2012).

The Dark Knight (2008) Directed by Christopher Nolan [Film]. USA: Warner Bros. Pictures.

The Dark Knight Rises (2012) Directed by Christopher Nolan [Film]. USA: Warner Bros. Pictures.

The Robbins Religious and Civil Law Collection, School of Law (Boalt Hall), University of California at Berkeley (2010) 'The common law and civil law traditions', www.law.berkeley.edu (Accessed: 19 October 2012).

Tyrell, I. (n.d.) 'What is American exceptionalism?', *Ian Tyrell*. http://iantyrrell.wordpress.com (Accessed: 3 April 2013).

Walzer, M. (1994) *Thick and thin: moral argument at home and abroad*. Notre Dame: University of Notre Dame Press.

Wolfson College, University of Oxford (2012), 'Leading judges and academic experts ask: are courts representatives?' [Panel discussion] 22 October. www.wolfson.ox.ac.uk (Accessed: 26 November 2012).

Zinn, H (n.d.) *The myth of American exceptionalism* [Opening lecture], *MIT World lecture series: myths about America*. http://video.mit.edu (Accessed: 4 April 2013).

Chapter 9

Lawless

Fiona Macmillan and Chris Boge

1 Introduction

The film *Lawless* (2012), directed by John Hillcoat, was released in 2012. It is based on a prohibition era novel by Matt Bondurant, originally (before its republication in the wake of the film's release) called *The Wettest County in the World* (Bondurant 2008). As things typically go in the commodified world of cultural production, immediately prior to the release of the film, Bondurant's novel was republished under the title *Lawless* (Bondurant 2012), with a cover photo of the central characters from the film and a foreword by John Hillcoat.

The book has two parallel stories. The one depicted in the film is that of the Bondurant brothers – grandfather and great uncles of the author – and the culture in which Franklin County, Virginia, became the largest producer of illegal whiskey in the US, and thus 'the wettest county in the world'. Hillcoat (2012), as he notes in his foreword to the renamed novel, locates this story in those of:

> the Western legends such as the Daltons and the Jameses . . . [it] portrays the next generation of country outlaws – the men and women who gave birth to the big-time urban mobsters like Capone by supplying the Prohibition cities with their illegal liquor . . . [It is] the story of the little guys out back, the foot soldiers and the worker bees who propped up the urban criminal empire, like a behind the scenes view of the lower ranks that supported a ruthless machine relentlessly pursuing the American dream in what became crime's first major gold rush.
>
> (p. *x*)

And these worker bees were, it appears, swarming. According to the *Official Records of the National Commission on Law Observance and Enforcement 1935* (quoted in Bondurant 2012, p. 1):

> In one county (Franklin) it is claimed 99 people out of 100 are making, or have some connection with, illicit liquor.
>
> (National Commission 1935, vol. 4, p. 1075)

While being wary of loading too much significance onto a title, the genesis of which may reflect preoccupations other than those addressed here, this chapter focuses on the concept of lawlessness. Specifically, it considers this concept through an examination of the extent to which the story told in Bondurant's book and Hillcoat's film can be considered 'lawless'. Addressing this question in relation to both works introduces a certain level of complication because, while the book uses a parallel story to reflect on the question of the role of legal institutions, the film as already noted does not depict this parallel story and, accordingly, is less concerned with this matter. The book's parallel story, which is also based on fact, is the story of the writer Sherwood Anderson[1] who, contemporaneously, is trying to complete a series of newspaper articles on 'the wettest county'. Using the vehicle of Sherwood Anderson's story, Bondurant's book gives an account of some significant criminal trials in the period, particularly the so-called Great Franklin County Moonshine Conspiracy Trial of 1935. The absence of representations of these trials in Hillcoat's film perhaps tends to give more literal force to the idea of it being lawless. Nevertheless, it might be argued that the film's central thesis of lawlessness is less concerned with specific legal instances, such as trials, and more focused upon the combination of endemic corruption in law enforcement and a popular state of disregard for the law as promulgated by the government and enforced (or not) by its agents.

In considering the obvious questions raised by this particular thesis of lawlessness, it is clear that this chapter generates more questions than good answers about the nature of law and lawlessness. The subsidiary questions, of whether to be lawless means to be without law or whether it means a state of non-compliance with the law, tend to dissolve into a much bigger consideration about the nature of law itself as an object of presence or absence. In order to find some point of entry to this very large question, this chapter pursues a form of inductive reasoning, using both versions of *Lawless*, to consider in what, if any, circumstances law may be said to be absent. Proceeding from this consideration, the chapter draws some conclusions about the way in which fiction may cast light on the significance of law's presence or absence in the context of social relations. The fact that, as this chapter demonstrates, good arguments may be made in favour of either the presence or absence of law in *Lawless* tends to suggest that in this endeavour we are treading on very uncertain ground. Whether the walk is worth it is another question and one to which we will return in the chapter's conclusion.

1 Sherwood Anderson, 1876–1941, is perhaps is less well known than other writers on whom he is said to have been a major influence, such as Hemingway, Faulkner and Steinbeck. According to Wikipedia, he does have a degree of fame as a result of having died of peritonitis after accidentally swallowing a toothpick, which was attached to martini olive, while on a cruise ship in South America ('Sherwood Anderson' 2015).

2 Against the proposition that law is absent in *Lawless*

The story of a legal paradigm shift?

On one reading, *Lawless* depends absolutely on the presence of law because it is the legal context, in the form of the US Prohibition Act of 1920 and its associated legislation, which creates the story's environment. In other words, without the law there is no story here at all. Unlike its counter proposition, this argument does not address itself to the possibility of a law that is itself lawless or illegitimate. Instead it depends upon the suggestion that laws enacted on the authority of the state are legitimate because they express the state's assertion of the monopoly of violence.[2] This is not the same thing, of course, as arguing that all laws are right, just or good. In fact, the lack of rightness, justice and/or goodness of this law, the Prohibition Act of 1920, is a central theme of the story.

Developing further this line of thought, the story of *Lawless* – a story of extreme violence on the part of both law enforcement officers and the moonshiners – could be read as an instantiation of a paradigm shift in the law-producing community, which eventually leads to the repeal of the prohibition laws and the end of the prohibition period. On this reading, not only is the story not lawless, but in fact it is precisely about law, the process by which it changes and the significance of its change. In his foreword to the republished book, Hillcoat (2012) writes that in the film 'we wanted to hone in and explore the ideas of the myths of immortality and the cycles of time, the transition from one age to another and the rupture, violence, and brutality that often accompanies such transitions' (*ix–x*).

The reference to a paradigm shift and its accompanying rupture invokes, of course, Kuhn's famous theory of paradigm shifts in scientific thought.[3] We are (painfully) aware of the possibility that, not only does this continue to be a contested theory,[4] but also its application to a change in the law is either an extension or an over-extension of Kuhn's proposition. The specific problem is that Kuhn's theory seeks to explain changes in the dominant theoretical tradition of an intellectual community, rather than being focussed on the phenomena that community is seeking to explain. As a result, in academic legal discourse, extensive use has been made of this theory to explain changes in prevailing theoretical traditions governing the organisation of law as a discipline.[5] The use of the theory to explain changes in the law itself has been much thinner,[6] but it is arguable that it is nevertheless quite capable of being used in this way.

2 See further Benjamin 2004; Tuitt 2006; Douzinas 2013, pp. 87–8.

3 See, for example, Kuhn 1996 and Kuhn 1977.

4 See Macintyre 2006.

5 See further Collier 1993, 841n.

6 For an example of such work, however, see Moffitt 2009.

It is clear, of course, that there is a distinction between changes in the law itself and the way in which its relevant intellectual communities theorise both those changes and the process by which they are made. However, it is also important to understand the reflexive links between changes in the law and the theorisation of those changes. This has certain parallels with Macintyre's (2006) observation, in the course of a critical appraisal of Kuhn's theory that:

> What the scientific genius . . . achieves in his transition is . . . not only a new way of understanding nature, but also and inseparably a new way of understanding the old science's way of understanding nature. It is because only from the standpoint of the new science can the inadequacy of the old science be characterised that new science is taken to be more adequate than the old. It is from the standpoint of the new science that the continuities of narrative history are re-established.
>
> (p. 18)

But law is not nature, or at least it is not nature in the way that Macintyre is writing about it. It is as much the product of a community as is a theory explaining why it should be understood as a product of a community. In this sense, prevailing legal norms might be thought of as paradigms that may shift in certain circumstances in response to a new discovery or a new understanding of certain phenomena. It is such a shift that establishes what Macintyre calls 'new science' or, in this case, new law. One aspect of a study, like the present one, considering a major shift in the law in the light of non-legal texts (such as the two *Lawless* texts) is the possibility of using those texts as a particular instantiation of the continuity of a narrative history. In some quite literal way, Macintyre's (2006) insistence on the importance, in understanding paradigmatic shifts, of 'constructing an intelligible dramatic narrative which can claim historical truth' (p. 22) can in this way be realised.

Viewed through these spectacles, Hillcoat's (2012) reference to 'the transition from one age to another and the rupture, violence, and brutality that often accompanies such transitions' (quoted above) sounds a lot like what one might write if one was describing the turbulence that precedes the shift in a prevailing paradigm. The paradigm in this case would be the concept of prohibition and its legislative realisation. To fit the story of *Lawless* into this type of reasoning would be to argue that the prohibition legislation represented, amongst the communities that produce law, the acceptance of the proposition that alcohol consumption should be regulated and that a ban on the production and sale of certain types of alcoholic beverages was the best way to achieve this result. Continuing with this argument, the eventual repeal of the prohibition laws, marking the transition from one age to another, was represented by a change in the dominant paradigm amongst the relevant law-producing communities.

According to Kuhn, a paradigm shift is provoked by a type of turbulence in the relevant community, which cannot be absorbed by the prevailing paradigm and, thus, puts the validity of the paradigm into question. In the scientific context, such turbulence might arise as a result of the observation of phenomena in the physical or natural world that are inconsistent with the dominant paradigm. In the extended reading of paradigm theory asserted here the signs of paradigm-shifting turbulence might be argued to lie not only in the specific social consequences of the legislation, but also in a more general disturbance of the social contract as it is mediated through, or produced by, law. Correspondingly, one would expect to see a reduction of turbulence and the normalisation of social relations in the period after the paradigm shift.

In is not difficult to find in both versions of *Lawless,* evidence of exactly this type of phenomena both before and after the paradigm shift. As should be clear at this point, the pre paradigm shift period is characterised by turbulence generated by widespread non-compliance with the law, accompanied by acts of startling violence committed both by the moonshiners and by the law enforcement agents, and a substantial level of corruption on the part of the latter. After the repeal of the prohibition laws, even though the bottom falls out of the moonshine market, the turbulence produced by, and associated with, this non-compliance with the law disappears. However, even apart from the specific depiction of violence and non-compliance with the law, there is also another way in which the movement in the prevailing legal paradigm is reflected in the story of the Bondurant brothers. Perhaps more interesting, because it is less obvious, this is the depiction of social and familial relations in the pre and post paradigm shift periods.

In the period in which prohibition is the prevailing legal paradigm, social relations, including intimate and familial relations, are stunted, contingent or impossible. Both texts of *Lawless*, in slightly differing ways, depict this state of affairs through the private lives of the three Bondurant brothers. Howard Bondurant, the oldest of three brothers, has particular responsibility for the process of producing the moonshine whiskey. Since this responsibility seems to also encompass acting as a taster, he is in a constant state of inebriation. In the book, this state of inebriation has a highly deleterious impact, not only on his relations with his wife but also on the health of their offspring. The film, however, tends to focus more on the intimate relationships of the other two Bondurant brothers. The middle brother, Forrest, the boss and brains of the enterprise, has some sort of relationship with the elusive Maggie. The exact nature of the relationship is a mystery, probably even to Forrest and Maggie. The control that Forrest has to exercise in order to maintain the monopoly of fear on which his power is based – and more on this below – renders him almost completely repressed in all respects when it comes to Maggie. The other important sexual dynamic in the film is the relationship between the youngest brother, Jack Bondurant, and Bertha, the daughter of one of the elders of a fundamentalist religious sect. The impossibility of their relationship in the period leading up to the paradigm shift is mirrored by the social division in Franklin County between the moonshiners, who live on the wrong side of the law, and the members of the religious sect who live within the law. (This reading, of course, reinforces the essential presence of the law in this story.)

The post paradigm shift depictions of the lives of the Bondurant brothers and their intimates are really by way of a coda to the main point of the film. All of these unhappy variations on human relations – familial, intimate and social – that characterised the pre paradigm shift period are depicted as normalised and relatively harmonious. The final scenes of the film show a family gathering at the home of Jack and Bertha, by now married with the obligatory collection of children. Also present are Howard, his wife and their now healthy offspring. Admittedly, the relationship of Forrest and Maggie retains some ambiguity, but they are clearly part of the family and the children joke with 'Uncle Forrest' about the fact that he refuses to dance. In the end, Uncle Forrest, the charismatic and apparently indestructible boss of the family's prohibition (pre paradigm shift) empire, dancing drunk and alone on the edge of a frozen lake, falls in and dies as a consequence. Even this melancholy event can be read as part of the necessary adjustment to the post paradigm shift situation: Forrest is a relic of the previous paradigm, he has no place now, he represents dissonance, he is part of an old order that must be swept away to make space for the new.

Corruption and the violence of the law

Reading the two texts of *Lawless* as instantiations of a paradigm shift in the law, suggests not only that law is present in this story, but also provides some type of framework for understanding the relationship between law, violence and corruption. There is also another way in which the level of violence and corruption depicted in the story of *Lawless* suggests a foundational engagement with law, which tends to negate the suggestion that law is absent.

A key feature of both the book and the film is the corruption and violence of the law enforcement officers. Unsurprisingly, these two phenomena are closely related. For a time, there is a sort of unstable truce between the moonshiners and the law enforcement officers, according to which the latter derive material benefits from the moonshine business in return for turning a blind eye to the extensive non-compliance with the law. Things start to turn nasty when Forrest refuses to accede to the inflated demands on the part of the sheriff and the Attorney General for a cut of takings in the moonshine trade. They get really nasty with the arrival of Special Federal Agent Charlie Rakes. In the film, the role of the Federal Agent is given much greater prominence than in the book. He represents – at least in the context of this story – a paradox, an exception to the apparent rules of engagement: he is the law enforcement officer who relies on a justification of the importance of the law to commit acts of violence apparently outside the law, but not related to personal financial gain and therefore not dictated by a recognisable logic of greed. One might disingenuously argue that he is motivated to excess by the desire to enforce the law, but the level of his excess suggests that this would be a tenuous conclusion. What, it seems, moves Federal Agent Charlie Rakes is the love of violence, the fear that violence creates, and the power that fear carries. This connection between enforcement of the law, violence and fear, makes Charlie Rakes a character of particular interest.

In the case against the proposition that the wettest county is lawless, one might say that what makes the attorney general, sheriff, deputies and special federal agent a force to be reckoned with is that they carry the authority of the state. One might, therefore, assert that they represent the founding violence of the law, famously comprised in which is law's insistence on a monopoly of violence (Benjamin 2004; Derrida 2002). However, in the case of *Lawless*, the illegality of the acts of the law enforcement officers creates an impossible relationship with law's assertion of the monopoly of violence. Paradoxically, the law's own enforcers appear here to be challenging the juridical order and thus potentially undermining it. With the possible exception of the conduct of Special Agent Charlie Rakes, the illegality in question goes beyond excessive violence in the enforcement of law and comprehends a level of personal corruption that presents a fundamental challenge to prevailing legal norms. The sense of outrage that this type of corruption produces is critical to the story in *Lawless*. It is, perhaps, one of the reasons why the sympathies of viewer and reader lie with the moonshiners, who are just as surely as the law enforcement officers committing illegal acts tainted by excessive violence. *Lawless*, therefore, asks us some particular questions about the nature of the relationship between the founding violence of the law, law enforcement and individual violence.

As Tuitt (2006) observes, '[t]he idea that individual violence and the preservation and authority of law are fundamentally incommensurable is one that lies at the heart of western philosophies of violence' (p. 5). Thus, as Benjamin (2004) famously argued, to be justified violence must be law-creating or law-preserving (p. 243). However, while Tuitt does not contest this proposition, she argues that it involves an insufficient problematisation of the nature of law. A consequence of this, to which Tuitt turns her attention, is that the idea that individual violence always sits outside the law is, itself, problematic. Reflecting on Benjamin's distinction between sanctioned and unsanctioned violence, Tuitt considers the circumstances in which violence should be properly considered law-creating or law-preserving.

Tuitt's (2006) argument is that unsanctioned individual violence is by its nature law-preserving, but that this law-preserving function of violence 'becomes *most* urgent not when the citizen threatens to challenge the law but when the law that is always violent and equally *more* than violent, threatens to become no more than the external violent forces it seeks to repress, thereby inviting new law' (p. 8). When the law complies with this description then:

> It is revolutionary violence (historically sanctioned violence) that brings such a state to an end, replacing it with new law, thus serving the first function of violence. It is the non-revolutionary, individual, always unsanctioned violence that 'corrects and represses' the excessive violence of the law, thereby protecting it from revolutionary violence and change, serving the second function of law.
>
> (p. 9)

To be non-revolutionary and law-preserving, such violence must be committed by 'those not aspiring to or capable of acquiring a monopoly of violence' (Tuitt 2006, p. 9). Not only is this non-revolutionary, individual, unsanctioned violence by those not aspiring to or capable of acquiring a monopoly of violence important in serving the second, law-preserving, function of violence, it also makes law more responsive to its ('often tenuous, uncertain and highly contingent' (Tuitt 2006, p. 9)) relationship with justice because the law is brought to 'experience its own violence' (Tuitt 2006, p. 10). Since this type of violence is, by definition, not carried out by people capable of, or aspiring to acquire, a monopoly of violence, acts of violence that constitute an unequivocal assault on justice are acts that can only be committed in the name of the law.' In such a situation 'the relation between law and justice . . . can only be restored by bringing the law to experience its own violence – but to experience its own violence without fear of its authority being undermined by another act of law-making violence' (Tuitt 2006, pp. 9–10).

For Tuitt, however, this function of unsanctioned individual violence as making law responsive to justice depends on the violence of law being what Fanon describes as 'violence in its natural state' (Fanon 1961, p. 61). This type of violence only occurs in circumstances where law 'denies or excludes the multiplicity of choices of avenues of resistance that contemporary political ideology would suggest are always open' (Tuitt 2006, p. 11). Unsanctioned individual violence by those not aspiring to, and incapable of acquiring, a monopoly of violence:

> prevents the law from losing its responsiveness to justice by giving it back a minute proportion of its own violence, such that law can recognise and reflect upon the suffusing potential for violence and marshal internal resistance against this potential.
>
> (Tuitt 2006, pp. 12–13)

In these circumstances, the law-preserving function of violence is fulfilled because 'law's instinct for self-preservation would, in most instances, balk at removing itself entirely from the claims of justice, thereby opening itself to new law' (Tuitt 2006, p. 13).

How then are we to understand the orgy of violence that takes place in *Lawless* on the part of both the so-called law enforcement officers and the moonshiners? Is this violence law-creating or law-preserving? Does it serve the cause of making law responsive to justice? Does it have anything to do with law at all? Taking the last of these questions first, it has already been argued above that without law, in the form of the prohibition legislation, there would be no story here. It seems plausible to suggest a similar conclusion in relation to the violence that is crucial to this story. In other words, without the prohibition legislation this violent confrontation would not have taken place. But this is the easiest of the questions posed at the beginning of this paragraph. Attempting to answer the others requires a more nuanced application of Tuitt's theoretical framework to the story portrayed in *Lawless*. In particular, locating the violence of the law enforcement officers in this framework is challenging. It is tempting here to argue that the law enforcement officers represent the violence of the law, which is pitted against the non-revolutionary, unsanctioned violence of the moonshiners. But both characterisations seem problematic.

While there may be circumstances in which one might argue that law enforcement officers represent or embody the violence of the law, the phenomenon of police violence has tended to create a crack in this argument that cannot easily be papered over. Just as famous as Benjamin's distinction between founding and preserving violence is Derrida's (2002) critique of the distinction based partly on the problem of police violence, which he argues mixes founding and preserving violence 'as if one violence haunted the other' (p. 276). For Derrida, it seems, Benjamin's concession that founding violence may be 'represented' in preserving violence is not enough to explain the challenge that police violence presents to his argument (p. 290). In fact, this concession on Benjamin's part might well be no more than the proposition with which this paragraph commenced: that is, that law enforcement officers represent or embody the violence of the law. Derrida's argument is a different one:

> In democracy . . . violence is no longer accorded nor granted to the spirit of the police. Because of the presumed separation of powers, it is exercised illegitimately, especially when instead of enforcing the law, it makes the law . . . the police violence of democracies denies its own principle, making laws surreptitiously, clandestinely.
>
> (p. 281)

Lawless provides an interesting framework in which to consider the question of the violence of law enforcement officers. This is because, with the exception of Special Agent Charlie Rakes, their violence is not simply an excess of zeal in the enforcement of the law but part of a wider pattern of corruption enabled by the authority in which the law has clothed them. Despite this representation of legal authority, their violence might be seen as a means of enforcing, not the law, but rather their ability to profit personally from the widespread breaches of the law. It is not clear, on the other hand, that this observation applies to Special Agent Charlie Rakes. His violence in apparent pursuit of the enforcement of the law clearly exceeds any mandate that the law has given him and yet, at the same time, is an exercise of the authority conferred upon him by law. His case, therefore, appears to fall more squarely within Derrida's critique of the distinction between founding and preserving violence. But is it really the case that the behaviour of Charlie Rakes makes law, even 'surreptitiously, clandestinely', as Derrida would have it?

At this point, rather than abandoning completely the distinction between founding and preserving violence, it is worth returning to Tuitt's more nuanced treatment of this distinction. Within this framework, one might argue, with respect to the conduct of all the law enforcement officers, their behaviour is neither sanctioned at the time it occurs nor, as in the case of revolutions, historically sanctioned. On the other hand, while the violence of the law enforcement officers is unsanctioned, it is not clear that it is being committed by those who are not seeking, or are incapable of attaining, a monopoly of violence. In fact, we might argue that the law enforcement officers, unlawfully misusing the authority in which the law has clothed them are both seeking, and capable of attaining, a monopoly of violence. Testing the violence of the law enforcement officers in *Lawless* against Tuitt's framework in this way leads to the conclusion that – being neither law-creating, nor law-preserving – the violence of the law enforcement officers has no legitimate function. This is the first demonstration of the robustness of this framework because it refuses the proposition that corruption and abuse of their power by those in positions of legally conferred power is a type of violence which can be understood or justified on the basis of its law-preserving function. The refusal of this proposition is, we argue, philosophically sound.

What about the very considerable violence perpetrated by the moonshiners? Can it be understood as either law-preserving or law-creating? Its characterisation as law-preserving presents some challenges. According to Tuitt's framework, such violence must be perpetrated by those not seeking, or capable of attaining, a monopoly of violence. Whether or not the moonshiners were capable of attaining a monopoly of violence is open to question, but it does not seem impossible to suggest that they were seeking such control. As will be further discussed below, in a particularly suggestive scene of the film, Forrest Bondurant says 'we control the fear. And without the fear we are all as good as dead'. Can we read this as an assertion of control over the constitutional order, at least so far as it applies in Franklin County, Virginia, during the prohibition era? Certainly, it seems tendentious, in light of subsequent history, to argue that the violence of the moonshiners was law-preserving, at least so far as the preservation of the prohibition laws were concerned.

However, if we think of law here as being the US constitutional order in general, which enjoys a monopoly violence, then our conclusions might be different. First, we might say that the unsanctioned violence of the moonshiners was committed by those incapable of, and not wishing to obtain, a monopoly of violence. Further, it would be argued that the violence of the moonshiners had the effect of drawing the law's attention to its own violence and causing it to, in Tuitt's (2006) words, 'recognise and reflect upon the suffusing potential for violence and marshal internal resistance against this potential' (p. 13) through, in this case, the repeal of the offending portion of the law, that is (obviously), the prohibition legislation. The only doubt that remains in such an application of Tuitt's framework is whether the prohibition laws were 'violence in its natural state' (Fanon 1961, p. 61; Tuitt 2006, p. 11). Here we would tentatively argue that the monopoly of power held by the US constitutional order, which not only promulgated the prohibition legislation but which also tolerated widespread corruption in its enforcement, constituted the type of violence that effectively denied or excluded other avenues of resistance. Such an argument suggests that the violence of the moonshiners was justified and, ultimately, law-preserving in the sense that it forced the constitutional regime to marshal its resistance against the threat posed by this widespread corruption and to defuse it through the repeal of the prohibition legislation.

While this specific argument on the nature and function of violence in *Lawless* reinforces the proposition that, far from being without law, *Lawless* is actually all about law, or more precisely the relationship between law and violence, it also opens another path of enquiry: if the toxic mixture of the prohibition legislation and its corrupt enforcement really can be taken to be 'violence in its natural state' then can we say that the holder of the monopoly of violence, the law itself, is lawless. And what would it mean to say so?

3 For the proposition that law is absent in *Lawless*

At first blush the proposition that law is absent in *Lawless* seems almost impossible to sustain. This is particularly so if one considers Hillcoat's film version in the light of his, immediately prior, 2009 film (*The Road* 2009) of Cormac McCarthy's (2006) post-apocalyptic novel, *The Road* (2006). Both texts, of *The Road*, the book and the film, tell us the desperate story of a father and his small son travelling south through a landscape that has been almost reduced to lifelessness – the life that remains being mainly only 'human', and almost only in the barest sense of that word. Thinking about Hillcoat's two films, *The Road* and *Lawless*, together suggests the possibility that Hillcoat, a filmmaker characterised by subtlety and nuance, might have been having a moment of irony. If *Lawless* is lawless, that is without law, how can we describe the dystopia of *The Road*? A place where the immediate imperative is physical survival and where any notion of common humanity has almost been forsaken; a place where at least three great fears reign – cold, starvation and the atavistic terror of cannibalism; a place where there is no state, corrupt or otherwise, and no legislation, legitimate or not. Compared to *The Road*, one might say *Lawless* has a super-abundance of law (Macmillan 2015).

Nevertheless, we would like to further strain the reader's patience by proposing two arguments that might be used to test the hypothesis of lawlessness. The first, and more obvious, of these arguments is that if one understands lawlessness as being based on widespread failure to comply with the law, then the behaviour of all the law enforcement officers, which goes well beyond their legally authorised power and into the realm of extensive criminal activity, could well be seen as prime evidence of lawlessness. And a similar observation might be applied to the conduct of the moonshiners. We have some doubts, however, about whether illegality or unlawfulness is an equivalent concept to lawlessness – although we accept, unconditionally, that in the world of commodified cultural products *Lawless* sounds more engaging than *Unlawful* or, even more unexciting, *Illegal*.

The second argument in favour of the proposition that the story of *Lawless* is correctly described by its title depends upon the idea that law itself can be lawless or illegitimate (Boge 2009, pp. 335 and 409n, citing Eagleton 2005, p. 65; and Douzinas 2013, pp. 87–8). Characterising the prohibition legislation in this way depends upon the argument that state coercion in this case, both through the enactment of the legislation and its enforcement, failed to achieve consent and failed to determine what should be considered right or just in society. Consequently, there is a breakdown of order in which the moral line between those said to be enforcing the law and those breaking it disappears. In such circumstances, the argument would go, a society can be said to be effectively without law.

A striking aspect of *Lawless*, both the book and the film, is that those entrusted with law enforcement have no greater, and possibly less, claim to legitimacy than the alleged criminals – and therefore apparently lack any authority with which the law might have otherwise clothed them. Of course, as has already been discussed above, the explanation of this intuitive sense of what is legitimate and illegitimate in the story of *Lawless* may be that, while the violence of the law enforcement officers cannot be understood or justified on the basis that it is law-creating or law-preserving, the violence of the moonshiners has some claim to being law-preserving. This, perhaps, tells us something about the genre of the 'Western', which is where Hillcoat (2012) has located his interpretation. In the Western we are used to the idea that the good guys and the bad guys change places – and that our sympathies might sometimes lie with the 'outlaws' due to the corruption of the law enforcement authorities. Traditional Westerns, of the sort that have been such major business for the Hollywood studios since the 1930s, are, of course, telling the story of the frontier, in which the role of law is always in play as one of the markers of the advance of (American) settlement and 'civilisation'.[7] In this sense, at least, some Westerns have something in common with the dystopia of *The Road* – although one of the features of the Western is that typically law arrives and imposes itself as the new organising principle. Even though Hillcoat locates his version of *Lawless* in the genre of the Western, the story (perhaps) lacks this aspect of the frontier, both physical and metaphysical. Nevertheless, this idea that a state of lawlessness might exist where law is not the organising principle of society can also be found in both texts of *Lawless*.

The relationship between Forrest and Jack Bondurant expresses a number of the central themes of *Lawless*. In particular, Forrest represents the past – or, at least, the paradigm that is passing – while Jack, the baby of the family, represents the future. Their relationship, therefore, is the site of the conflict and turbulence produced as the past dissolves and the future arrives. And it is Forrest, speaking to Jack after the latter has been savagely beaten up by Special Agent Charlie Rakes, who articulates what may be one of the strongest claims to lawlessness. As has already been noted above, he says, speaking of the bloody conflict between the moonshiners and the law enforcement officers: 'we control the fear. And without

7 It is interesting to note that the word 'lawless' made a number of appearances in the titles of, particularly early, Western films e.g. *The Lawless Frontier* (1934), *Lawless Range* (1935), *The Lawless Nineties* (1936). And, as Mithani (2007, especially pp. 115 ff.) shows there was a more general preoccupation with the concept of 'lawlessness' in Hollywood films of the 1930s.

the fear we are all as good as dead.'[8] In *Lawless*, an argument might be made that law, as the organising principle of conduct, has given way to fear. Not the fear of the law as state-authorised violence, but the fear of random acts of unauthorised violence. Understood like this, the similarity between *The Road* and *Lawless* becomes evident since both are concerned with a state of affairs in which fear of random acts of unauthorised violence is the organising principle. The essential difference, perhaps, between *Lawless* and *The Road* is that in *The Road* there is no yardstick, however bent and skewed, of authorisation. No basis, it seems, at all for distinguishing between authorised and unauthorised violence, between random and non-random violence. While in both texts it might be argued that law is absent as an organising principle, it might also be argued that in *Lawless* it is present through its explicit failure to authorise violence. In *The Road*, on the other hand, it seems law exists only as a shadow, as the desire for a higher authority – or any authority – which is apparently absent.[9]

But fear in Franklin County, as represented in both the book and the film of *Lawless*, is also the ally of another organising principle, which has a different but equally ambiguous relationship with law. This is the principle of justice. Whether the presence of law is a prerequisite for the existence of justice is a big question and one that we will not consider in any detail here.[10] Rather, what is evident here is that the idea of justice, without law, exposes itself in the text of *Lawless* as a form of tit-for-tat violence, as a free-standing unconstrained force. This theme of justice as retributive violence/retributive violence as justice is a recurring theme in Hillcoat's work. This was particularly the case in his film, *The Proposition* (2005).[11] However, there are subtle differences in this respect between the two films. In *The Proposition*, in the context of a spiral of violence and 'retributive justice', justice is linked to the force (and violence) of the law in the form of its authorised representatives and their attempts to uphold the rule of law. This link is missing in *Lawless*. Further, the concept of tit-for-tat violence as a form of justice, already problematic, is further complicated.

The relation between fear, violence and justice in *Lawless* is epitomised in an episode of critical importance in both the book and the film. In the book, the consequences of this episode mark the beginning of Sherwood Anderson's search for 'truth' and/or a good newspaper story. The episode is central, it seems, to the

8 Cf. Orwell (2008) *Nineteen eighty four:* 'Power over matter – external reality as you would call it – is not important . . . We control matter because we control the mind. Reality is inside the skull' (p. 277).

9 On this aspect of *The Road*, see further Macmillan 2015. On the desire for law, see Aristodemou 2014, especially chap. 2.

10 In the dystopia of *The Road* justice, like law, is a dead letter. But in e.g. Rousseau's famous pre-law utopia the organising principles of virtue, *amour propre* and the general will are argued to produce justice, humanity and community. This is a vision that has been hotly contested by, amongst others, Hobbes and Burlamaqui: see further Macmillan 2015.

11 The screenplay of which, like that of *Lawless*, was also written with Nick Cave.

case in favour of lawlessness because it represents the use of fear to displace law and maybe vindicate some free-standing idea of justice. In the episode in question Forrest and his elder brother, Howard, wreak awful 'justice' on two men – working at the behest of Special Agent Charlie Rakes – who have slit Forrest's throat and left him for dead. The episode is important in both the texts because the fact that Forrest survives this, allegedly by walking 20 miles in the snow holding his throat together, adds to his myth and the fear that he commands. The 'punishment' that is meted out for this crime once the culprits have been located is the removal, without the benefit of anaesthetic, of their testicles (which, in the film, are subsequently delivered to Special Agent Charlie Rakes in a brown paper bag). Only after this punishment has been meted out does Forrest come to know that these same men sexually assaulted Maggie on the evening they slit his throat. Thus any notion that this is a particularly appropriate punishment to the crime in a world of 'eye for an eye' justice is subjectively impossible yet subsequently seems to operate on Forrest as an objective justification for this violent act. In the end, then, the question of the justice of 'eye for an eye', or maybe the law of 'eye for an eye', is left hanging. What remains is the fear.

4 (In)Conclusion

In the end, despite our best attempts to convince ourselves that law is absent from *Lawless*, this seems to be the weaker of the two hypotheses. Perhaps the reason for this is that even the arguments in favour of this proposition seem to bring us back to some engagement with the legal context of the story. Further, an analysis of these arguments tends also to reinforce the importance of the connection between law and justice. As has already been suggested, this connection is – in practice – tenuous and problematic, but abandoning the attempt to make law responsive to the call of justice is to condemn ourselves to something just as bad as, if not worse than, Hobbes' (1651) famous state of nature in which life is 'solitary, poor, nasty, brutish and short'.

The question of the connection, or disconnection, between law and justice is at the heart of the argument that law itself can be lawless because of its failure to determine what is right or just in society. While not (here, at least) disputing the arbitrary nature of all rules and norms, we take it as unarguable that law can have, and has often had, the character of failing to determine what is right or just. As it is common – but still important – to note in this context, colonialism was legal, slavery was legal, apartheid was legal and so on. In the post-colonial period, legal regimes have also been turned to a wide range of unjustified practices of appropriation, legitimated through appeals to political concepts such as development or through the discourses of other disciplines such as economics or anthropology.[12]

12 See e.g. Mattei and Nader 2008.

But the problem is not that such law is not law – in the sense that it is lacking the character of law. (To think otherwise would be, apart from anything else, to ignore the effect of politicisation.[13]) In fact, it has exactly the character of law because it expresses the state's claim to the monopoly of violence, but it is law that has been detached from justice. In the specific context of *Lawless* the combination of a law that does not command social support and a system of (alleged) enforcement that was illegal and corrupt produces the detachment of law and justice that tells us something about, not the absence of law, but of its infidelity to its too infrequent bedfellow, justice.

It is the turbulence produced by this detachment between law and justice that permits fear of unauthorised violence to emerge as what we have described as an organising principle in the story of *Lawless*. While it seems reasonable to argue that fear was, therefore, for a period more important than law in determining the relevant social relations, it is harder to assert that it displaced it completely. When Forrest Bondurant claims that 'we control the fear' he may be right, but he also knows that it matters so much exactly because he is tilting at law's claim to have the monopoly of violence. The acts of violence committed by Forrest and his fellow moonshiners in support of the claim to control the fear are, in the end, the means by which law is brought to know its own violence and inoculated. Further, it also seems to be the case that the dissolution of fear as an organising principle is part of the paradigm shift that occurs with the repeal of the prohibition legislation. Under the new paradigm, law and justice have somehow been re-attached.

Examining the question of law's presence, or absence, in the context of the two texts of *Lawless*, has allowed us to reflect on the relationship between violence, law and justice. One of the implicit, but we hope obvious, consequences of this reflection is to demonstrate that law exists within a wider political and social context, which can itself never be contained or fully reflected by law.[14] In this context law is not an unchangeable artefact, not a truth in itself, not the definer of social relations, not a guarantee of justice or security, and not – most importantly – a substitute for politics.

13 'Politicization . . . is interminable even if it cannot and should never be total. To keep this from being a truism, or a triviality, one must recognise it in the following consequence: each advance in politicization obliges one to reconsider, and so to reinterpret the very foundations of law such as they had previously been calculated or delimited. This was true for example in the French Declaration of the Rights of Man, in the abolition of slavery, in all the emancipatory battles that remain and will have to remain in progress, everywhere in the world for men and for women. Nothing seems to me less outdated than the classic emancipator ideal' (Derrida 2002), pp. 257–8.

14 See (much) further, Christodoulidis 1998.

References

Aristodemou, M. (2014) *Law, psychoanalysis, society: taking the unconscious seriously*. Oxford: Routledge.

Benjamin, W. (2004) 'Critique of violence', translated by E. Jephcott, in Bullock M. and Jennings, N. (eds.) *Walter Benjamin: selected writings, volume 1: 1913–1926*. Cambridge: Harvard University Press, 2004, pp. 236–52. (Original published in 1921)

Boge, C. (2009) *Outlaws, fakes & monsters*. Heidelberg: Universitäsverlag Winter.

Bondurant, M. (2008) *The wettest county in the world*. New York: Scribner.

Bondurant, M. (2012) *Lawless*. Edinburgh: Canongate.

Christodoulidis, E.A. (1998) *Law and reflexive politics*. Dordrecht: Kluwer.

Collier, C.W. (1993) 'Interdisciplinary legal scholarship in search of a paradigm', Duke Law Journal, 42(4), pp. 840–53.

Derrida, J. (2002) 'Force of law: the "mystical foundation of authority"', translated by M. Quaintance, in Anidjar, G. (ed.) *Acts of religion*. New York: Routledge, pp. 228–98.

Douzinas, C. (2013) *Philosophy & resistance in the crisis*. Cambridge: Polity Press.

Eagleton, T. (2005) *Holy terror*. Oxford: Oxford University Press.

Fanon, F. (1961) *The wretched of the earth*. Translated by C. Farringdon. Reprint. New York: Grove Press, 1963.

Hillcoat, J. (2012) 'Introduction' in Bondurant, M. *Lawless*. Edinburgh: Canongate.

Hobbes, T. (1651) *Leviathan*. Reprint, Peterborough: Broadview Press, 2002.

Kuhn, T.S. (1977) 'Second thoughts on paradigms' in Suppe, F. (ed.) *The structure of scientific theories*. 2nd edn. Chicago: Illini Books, pp. 459–82.

Kuhn, T.S. (1996) *The structure of scientific revolutions*. 3rd edn. Chicago; London: University of Chicago Press.

Lawless (2012) Directed by John Hillcoat [Film]. USA: The Weinstein Company/FilmNation Entertainment.

Lawless Range (1935) Directed by Robert N. Bradbury [Film]. USA: Republic Pictures.

Macintyre, A. (2006) 'Epistemological crises, dramatic narrative and the history of science' in Macintyre, A. The tasks of philosophy: selected essays, vol. 1. Cambridge: Cambridge University Press, pp. 3–23.

Macmillan, F. (2015) 'Is there voice without law? On The Road', Pòlemos, 9(2), pp. 331–40.

Mattei, U. and Nader, L. (2008) Plunder: when the rule of law is illegal. Malden, Blackwell.

McCarthy, C. (2006) *The road*. London: Picador.

Mithani, S. (2007) *The Hollywood left: cinematic art and activism in the 1930s*. PhD thesis. University of South California.

Moffitt, R. (2009) 'Resistance is futile', Journal of World Intellectual Property, 12(1), pp. 75–87.

Orwell, G. (2008) *Nineteen eighty four*. London: Penguin.

'Sherwood Anderson' (2015) https://en.wikipedia.org/wiki/Sherwood_Anderson (Accessed: 7 December 2012).

The Lawless Frontier (1934) Directed by Robert N. Bradbury [Film]. USA: Monogram Pictures.

The Lawless Nineties (1936) Directed by Joseph Kane [Film]. United States: Republic Pictures.

The Proposition (2005) Directed by John Hillcoat [Film]. Australia: Sony Pictures.

The Road (2009) Directed by John Hillcoat [Film]. USA: The Weinstein Company/Dimension Films.

Tuitt, P. (2006) 'Individual violence & the law', *Studies in Law, Politics & Society*, 39, pp. 3–14.

In memoriam

Our colleague Professor Patrick McAuslan passed away on 11 January 2014. At the time of his death, amongst many other projects, he was working on his contribution to this book but had not yet completed it. We have lightly edited the version of the chapter that appears below, seeking to ensure that it still speaks clearly in Patrick's own distinctive voice.

Attitudes to law and legal systems in crime fiction in Africa

An overview with special reference to Kenyan crime fiction

Patrick McAuslan[1]

1 Introduction

Over the years I have read several crime novels set in different countries in Anglophone Africa; in particular Botswana, Kenya, Nigeria and South Africa. In beginning the process of trying to discover whether there was any critical writing on the subject, I have discovered that there is an African Crime Fiction Project located in Indiana University, Bloomington, a major work published in Germany in 2012 on African Crime Fiction (Oed and Matzke 2012)[2] based on a conference on the subject a few years back, a conference at Yale University in 2012 (as to which no papers are yet available), several recent articles on the subject in academic journals and in June 2010, an article in the *Guardian* by Michael Stanley (2010) (an amalgam of two self-styled native Africans (with European names)) on 'his' top 10 African Crime Novels, only two of which I had read.

There is then a significant academic industry writing about African crime fiction that I never knew existed. If the publication of the latest book on the subject – *Life is a Thriller: Investigating African Crime Fiction* (Oed and Matzke 2012) – is anything to go by, most of this writing seems to be by literature scholars or Africanists rather than by lawyers.[3] A major theme is the relationship between fictional writing about crime and the criminal justice system and the reality of crime in the country of the author, with particular regard to the colonial and the postcolonial criminal justice systems. This chapter will attempt an overview of this body of work both by reviewing some recent writing on the subject and by considering the approach to the subject of some specific authors of crime fiction set in Anglophone Africa to try and discover whether the approach to law and legal systems in these novels

1 I would like to thank Ambreena Manji and my wife, Dorrette McAuslan, for reading through a first draft of this paper and thereby greatly improving it.

2 None of the chapters in the book are by lawyers.

3 Ambreena Manji was probably the first lawyer in the UK to write about the subject in her: 'Like a Mask Dancing': Law and Colonialism in Chinua Achebe's *Arrow of God* (Manji 2000). Kieran Dolin (2007) is not a lawyer but has an excellent chapter: 'Rumpole in Africa: law and literature in post-colonial society' to which I will refer later.

differed depending on whether the authors are expatriate or African or diasporic-African; colonial or postcolonial. My chapter will be an introduction to a particular part of a much wider field of study. I had originally thought to concentrate on Botswana, Kenya, Nigeria and South Africa, with respect to which there are both African and expatriate authors, to explore the authors' familiarity with and approach to the law and legal systems in their work and the interplay of Europeans and Africans but the wealth (meaning quantity rather than quality) of crime and detective fiction set in Kenya was such that I have concentrated principally on that country, with the South African, Botswanan and West African crime fiction being something of a coda to Kenya. I have also had the advantage of living in Nairobi for three years and visiting the country frequently which gives me some familiarity both with Nairobi, where most of the novels are set, and with the realities of crime in the country. Apart from anything else, to do anything like justice to the other countries would have meant a major programme of reading of detective novels based on those countries – not in itself disagreeable, even if some of the novels are rather slight, but difficult to combine with writing a chapter on all four countries.

The authors I will be reviewing in Kenya are: Elspeth Huxley, the doyenne of writers about colonial Kenya from the settlers' perspective; Nick Brownlee, Richard Crompton, Ralph Palmer, all postcolonial Englishmen who write Kenya-based crime fiction; US-based Mukoma Wa Ngugi (son of Ngugi wa Thiong'o), referred to by critics as a diasporic-African writer; Hilary Ng'weno; and Meja Mwangi. Other writers to which I will be referring are: Robert Wilson, an Englishman who wrote some excellent crime novels based in West Africa, and Deon Meyer, an Afrikaans writer whose books are then translated into English; Angela Makholwa and Diale Tlholwe, two black South African crime writers; Malla Nunn, a South African/Swaziland writer now based in Australia; and, Unity Dow from Botswana.

The definition of African Crime Fiction set out at the beginning of the African Crime Fiction Project (Keil 2012) is a useful introduction both generally and to this chapter so I have no qualms in purloining it:

> For the sake of this project, it must be noted that African Crime Fiction refers to *crime, detective, and mystery novels that are set in Africa or feature African characters*. However, other related sub-genres include legal thrillers and courtroom dramas, and many novels focus not only on the crimes and their detection, but also on criminals and their motives. True crime works and strict political thrillers have been excluded, though true incidents and politics are definitely part of many works of African Crime Fiction. In the context of this project, as with other geographically oriented topics, the use of the term 'African' is complex due to the numerous ways that identity can be understood, shaped, and constructed. Consequently, *labeling works as 'African' is difficult and highly politicized*, especially due to tensions wrought by colonialism, immigration, and skin color. For the sake of this project and being as inclusive as possible, all works of crime fiction that are set in Africa or feature African characters,

> regardless of authorship, are considered to be 'African Crime Fiction.' Also included are works by African authors that may not be heavily set in Africa or focused on African characters, though many are. Works by Western authors that fit those parameters are considered to be part of the genre.[4]

The notion of 'African characters' is somewhat unclear both as to its intrinsic nature and its quantitative element. Does it mean the 'Africanness' of a setting or a crime or does it refer to the possibility that someone from Africa may feature in the novel, and if so as a main character or with just a 'walk on' part? This chapter will not explore these matters further as it will be concentrating on novels based in Kenya, South Africa, Botswana and West Africa written either by citizens of those countries, diasporic-Africans or English authors living in either of those countries.

2 Colonial and postcolonial criminal justice: a brief note

Let me start off with two classic descriptions by Akiga (1939) and Alexander (1936) drawn from the heyday of colonialism as a way of setting the scene for those who might not be familiar with the reality of criminal justice in colonial and independent Africa:

> At that time the whole land of Tiv was shaken. When the Tiv saw that the Shitire elders were severely dealt with by the District Officer they were glad, for they were given a great chance to avenge themselves on their enemies, by falsely accusing them before him. One would come and say, 'So-and-so killed my brother to set right by an *imborivungu.*' When the District Officer heard this he would send to the chief to have the man brought before him. The policemen went to fetch him and before they even started from his home they would give him a thorough beating. When they brought him in, the white man asked him where was the *imborivungu* for which he had killed the man. When he began to deny it, the District Officer violently upbraided him and accused him of hiding the truth, until he finally admitted his guilt and asked to be allowed to fetch it. Policemen were sent with him. In some cases, when a man arrived at his home he would ask to be allowed to go into his house, and when he found nothing he could give up, took an arrow and stabbed himself, saying that death was better than so much undeserved misery . . . At that time

4 I suppose that there is also the issue of who is a Western author and who is an African author. Is Mukoma wa Ngugi an African author, or, as he was born in and lives in the USA, (though brought up in Kenya) a Western author? Is his *Nairobi Heat* (Ngugi 2011) African crime fiction, since much of it is set in Madison, Wisconsin and involves a US detective? Is Malla Nunn an African or an Australian author? On this issue see the thought-provoking article: Mengiste (2013).

> all officials working under the European claimed to have a good knowledge of the Tiv, and the white man acted on their advice without question. In this way they had great opportunities to hoodwink him, and many obtained promotion in consequence. (Akiga 1939, quoted in Dathorne and Feuser 1969, pp. 111–15). It was from this gaol [*Morogoro*] that a native convict called Ali bin Kassiki had escaped not long before. He was a man of powerful physique and unbridled passion – a most dangerous man to be at large. In him was to be found, I fancy, one of the rebels against society whom the savage system of *kiboko*, the indiscriminate application of the lash, in his earlier days had driven to desperation and reckless devilry. Later I was told his back was found to be scarred and seared with the marks of his earlier punishments. He broke into the gaol store, stole a rifle and 250 rounds of ammunition and ran amok . . . He committed three murders and was eventually captured by the stratagem of a *jumbe* (native chief) who employed a woman as a decoy. I tried him for murder and sentenced him to death, and I have never seen a more determined and savage-looking man in the dock.
>
> (Alexander 1936, pp. 43–4)

These were descriptions of colonial justice as it was perceived and practiced in the mid-1930s but Hailey (1957),[5] writing on the eve of the era of independence 20 years later offered a broadly similar, if more objective, analysis of the differences between African and European systems of justice:

> The student of jurisprudence who may seek to add to the history of the evolution of law in the Roman and the British Indian Empires a chapter tracing its development in Africa will enjoy the advantage that he will have before his eyes a living process. In his approach to this study, however, he will meet one initial difficulty. He will find little evidence that there was in indigenous Africa the conception of law as an organ of authority to be deliberately employed for the purpose of preserving social order or safeguarding private rights.
>
> As will have been gathered, it is in the Law of Public Order (to use a convenient French expression) rather than in the field of civil law that there is the greatest divergence between the European and African concepts of justice. The difficulty of securing from the African a ready acceptance of the European system of criminal law is increased by the apparent incompatibility of European ideas of penology with African traditional usage. The African practice was to compensate the injured party in such a way as to leave him no

5 Interestingly, whereas Hailey had a chapter of 55 pages on 'Law and Justice' (pp. 587–642) neither of two later books (Hunter 1962; Herskovits 1962) published just after the era of independence (in Africa) commenced (generally considered to have begun in 1960 although Sudan (1956) and Ghana (1957) became independent before that date) surveying Africa had any discussion of the subject.

> worse off than he was before; it did not embrace, except in special circumstances, the idea that an offence was committed against the State . . . The Bantu had no prisons . . . they had no system of fines . . . They had no public executioner; the relatives of the injured party were usually permitted to execute a murderer in whatever way they thought best.
>
> (Hailey 1957, pp. 624–5).

This then was the system of criminal justice taken over by independent countries at the outset of the era of independence. A major conference held in Dar es Salaam in 1963 (ACLCCL 1963)[6] considered that:

> Every country accepted the principle that the penal law should be written and that the present position in some countries, whereby unwritten criminal offences existed side by side with a written Penal Code, must be altered . . . Thus in Kenya customary criminal offences have been recorded in writing and were likely to continue in effect, but in statutory form.
>
> (p. 24).

> Existing provisions in regard to jurisdiction of the local courts vary widely both as to persons and subject matter. In the past, the common pattern for local court jurisdiction was the limitation of such jurisdiction to causes and matters in which all parties were 'natives' . . . always excluding Europeans . . . The Conference noted the trend away from race as a test for jurisdiction over persons in local courts and commended this as an ultimate objective.
>
> (p. 39)

Over the years that followed this conference many of the recommendations were acted upon so that now a uniform system of criminal justice applying to all persons equally is provided for by the law.

In the case of Kenya however, it is not too much to say that any 'system' of policing and criminal justice based on law has more or less broken down and this state of affairs is a relevant factor to bear in mind when considering crime novels set in that country and written in the last few years. A report to the UN Human Rights Council by its Special Rapporteur on police killings in Kenya in 2009 (UN Human Rights Council 2009) had this to say on the situation:

> The Special Rapporteur concluded that police in Kenya frequently execute individuals and that a climate of impunity prevails. Most troubling is the

6 I was one of the rapporteurs at the conference; an excellent introduction to the politics of law reform in Africa.

> existence of police death squads operating on the orders of senior police officials and charged with eliminating suspected leaders and members of criminal organizations. Such groups do harass and kill Kenyans, and strong policing is required to counter the threat. But carte blanche killing by the police does nothing to eradicate such criminality. Rather it perpetuates the sense that the police are good at killing and bad at law enforcement. For policing to truly create security, it must be conducted with respect for the human rights of all, including suspects and victims. A lack of police accountability for killings results from the absence of effective internal or external investigation or oversight mechanisms.
>
> Those responsible for the post-election violence, including those police responsible for extrajudicial executions, and officials who organized or instigated violence, remain immune from prosecution almost 18 months later. Witnesses to many of these killings are terrified to speak out. A witness protection program that has already absorbed significant resources, has yet to protect a single witness. Many of the human rights defenders who testified before the Special Rapporteur during his mission were threatened and harassed by members of the security forces, and other Government officials. Two activists who had been particularly active in reporting on police death squads were assassinated just two weeks after the mission ended.
>
> (pp. 2–3)

So much for the facts and their description and analysis. What of fiction? It's a lot harder for an amateur in literary criticism to know where to start. There are three possible starting points. The author, the novel, and the location, to say nothing of the implications and hidden meanings of the novel. I'll take what is hopefully an easy way out in discussing crime novels set in Kenya[7] by adopting a typical legal approach to literary criticism: first set out the facts of the case (novel); then comment on the novel (case); then try and draw some conclusions on the cases (novels) discussed.

3 Crime fiction in Kenya

Elspeth Huxley's (1988) *Murder at Government House* involves the murder of the governor of Chania (clearly Kenya) at a dinner party given by the governor in honour of the governor of Totseland (almost certainly Uganda) with whom negotiations were ongoing about a federation in which the sticking point was the valuation of

7 I should emphasise 'set in Kenya'. Kurtz (1998) dismisses Huxley as a Kenyan writer 'because even though the writers themselves [Huxley and Dinesen and others] were arguably *from* Kenya, their writing targeted an expatriate non-African audience and addressed specifically expatriate concerns. Theirs is the literature of Kenya's settler community'.

the two railways.[8] Amongst the guests was an anthropologist, Olivia Brandeis, who 'divided her time between field work among Central and East African native tribes and lecturing on functional anthropology at the London School of Economics' (almost certainly based on Lucy Mair, who was a social anthropologist at LSE undertaking research at that time in Uganda and Nyasaland).[9] There was no love lost between her and the governor's ADC (*Adjutant-chef*) – between the outsider 'meddling' in native affairs and the ex-public school boy on his way up. The details of the crime are not particularly relevant. What is of interest are the various characterisations and relationships between different levels of colonial officialdom.

First, there is the relationship between the Police Commissioner, a Major Armitage, an ex-army officer and Superintendent Vachell, the Canadian head of the investigation branch of the police. The Commissioner automatically assumed that a 'native' had murdered the governor ('You're not suggesting that one of our senior civil servants strangled the King's representative are you? . . . No, no. This is the work of some maniac – one of these degenerate crime-sodden swine from Chinyani [Nairobi]' (Huxley 1988, pp. 29–30)) and set the uniformed branch to seek out the most notorious of such persons. Vachell is not convinced on the basis of the evidence but this was initially brushed aside by Armitage.

Second, there is the relationship between the Colonial Secretary, Pallett, the senior colonial official in a British dependency after the governor, and Vachell:

> Mr. Pallett was annoyed . . . In him suddenly reposed the dignity and authority of the Crown. And his first experience was to be kept waiting for over an hour, without news or consultation by a policeman. He and he alone was now the supreme authority in Chania. It was his right and duty to direct the progress of the investigation. He explained this coldly and precisely to Vachell who stood in the doorway of the tearoom offering apologies.
>
> (p. 31)

It is relevant here to note that while practically all colonial officials were ex-public school and Oxbridge, colonial police certainly in the 1930s were not and a Canadian policeman would have been regarded as no better than a colonial himself. The governor of Totseland is, as a result, taken aback by the blunt questioning of Vachell. Nevertheless, throughout the novel, there is no suggestion of any attempt by the colonial officials, or indeed Armitage, to influence the course of Vachell's

8 There were constant differences between Kenya and Uganda in the 1920s and 1930s over the management and finances of the railway that ran from Mombasa to Port Bell in Uganda stemming largely from the fact that Kenya was a settler society and wanted the railway to serve settler interests whereas Uganda was not and objected to paying various levies from which it gained no benefit (Hill 1961).

9 Mair (1934) *An African People in the Twentieth Century* was her first book.

investigation, other than pressure arising from the need to solve the murder as quickly as possible.

The plot becomes a little far-fetched as the book progresses with the governor of Totseland also dying, having flown a plane into a mountain. Vachell makes several false steps in trying to find the murderer, although he never wavers in believing that it was one of the colonial officials. Eventually, as a result of the good relationship that emerges between the anthropologist and Vachell – both outsiders to the colonial establishment – she tells Vachell of a riddle, told to her by an old witch doctor in the village in which she was working, that indicates who the murderer was. Vachell takes some time to puzzle the riddle out but when he does so, he realises that the Secretary for Native Affairs, Victor Moon, is the murderer (he had been responsible for the death of the murdered governor's brother many years before when they were both working in the same colony and the governor was about to discover this). This is an interesting twist to the plot: it is an unlettered 'native' that finally leads to the uncovering of the culprit. Although Huxley was, at least until the 1960s, an advocate of colonialism, this ending suggests that even then she had some doubts about settler society – settlers are portrayed as lacking in intelligence and common sense – and colonial officialdom – few of the colonial officials are portrayed very sympathetically.

The second novel is Hilary Ng'weno's (1975) *The Men from Pretoria*. Ng'weno is a Harvard educated nuclear scientist born in Nairobi. After graduating from Harvard with a degree in nuclear physics, Ng'weno worked as a reporter for the *Daily Nation* for nine months before his appointment as the newspaper's first Kenyan editor-in-chief. He resigned in 1965 and established a successful career as a journalist.

This book is more of a political thriller, the main character of which is Nelson Naeta, a journalist who enjoys good relations with a CID Inspector as a result of which they uncover a South African plot to kidnap or murder a dissident South African scientist who had fled South Africa to Kenya on his way to Europe where he intended to disclose South African attempts to develop nuclear weapons. The main character and most of the action are clearly based much more on Ng'weno's life and activities as a journalist than on aspects of policing. However, there are interactions between 'Scoop' Naeta, a crime reporter, and the Special Branch which warns him off but is also prepared to give him some information and, finally, to ask Naeta and his editor for some assistance (mainly to back off from the story so as not to compromise the activities of the Special Branch). The homicide division of the CID also become involved, with Kilonzo, its head, being on quite good terms with Naeta but also warning Naeta not to muddy the waters by trying to do the CID's work:

> Both he [Naeta] and Inspector Kilonzo were concerned with the same thing; discovering the truth about crimes and criminals. But Kilonzo was more interested in the larger issue of maintaining law and order. Scoop was interested only in keeping the public's interest in the news satisfied. Kilonzo could not afford to settle for half-truths and tentative conclusions.
>
> (Ng'weno 1975, p. 104)

Scoop is finally arrested for getting in the way of Kilonzo's investigations but released when the Special Branch recognise and thank him for his assistance in locating the dissident South African scientist. The fact that this scientist has been located protects him, in the end, from being kidnapped or killed by South African agents based in Nairobi and headed up by Harold McLeod,[10] a white Kenyan who is killed in a shoot-out at a small station on the Nairobi-Mombasa railway line.

Coming back to this book after reading all the other crime novels discussed below, I found this to be a more authentic Kenyan crime novel than those because there were more matters which seemed to me to be based on reality. At the time it was written it was quite possible that the persons such as Naeta and Kilonzo would have known each other at school and would have continued meeting quite frequently. In the mid-1970s, the Kenyan police may not have been as efficient and pleasant as they are made out to be, but they had not yet sunk to their current depths. Insofar as there is any kind of political message in the book it is far more about apartheid South Africa than about Kenyan police practices, which are portrayed as quite efficient and responsible. Ng'weno as editor of the *Daily Nation* had a reputation of being something of a self-censor on political and social matters so he would not have wanted to cross the line in a novel.

Not so Meja Mwangi (1973) whose *Kill Me Quick*[11] will be briefly discussed through a reading of Kehinde's article (2004). The book examines Nairobi through the lives of Meja and Maina, two street boys. They become part of a gang and Maina is alleged to have murdered someone and spends some time in prison. Meja avoids becoming involved in crime although also ends up in prison. But the book is a vehicle for a strong criticism of the neo-colonial society that Kenya had become, even by 1973, a decade after independence:

> The neo-colonial African society depicted in *Kill Me Quick* is in a stage of stultifying poverty. The wealth is in the hands of a privileged minority . . . which surrounds itself with all the consumer durables that are associated with an acquisitive middle class . . . Life for the masses of the dog-eat-dog world of the Nairobi back streets (symbolized by Meja and Maina) is a living hell characterized by extreme poverty, fear, land shortage, crimes, famine, drought, hunger, unemployment and a very limited horizon . . . The novel

10 Possibly based on Bruce Mckenzie who was a British intelligence operative and Minister for Agriculture in Kenya under Jomo Kenyatta, to whom he was an adviser. He was assassinated by a time-bomb, placed in a gift of a lion head carving on his plane in 1978 over Ngong Hills outside Nairobi. General opinion at the time was that the bomb had been placed in the plane by Amin's goons while McKenzie was on a visit to Kampala. As with all other political assassinations in Kenya, no one was ever brought to book for the killing.

11 Kehinde (2004); Kurtz (1998, chap.7, especially pp. 123–24). This was Mwangi's first novel and ironically won the 1974 Jomo Kenyatta Award for Literature. One assumes that Kenyatta did not read the book.

> sums up Mwangi's concern for the prevalent social anomalies in neo-colonial Kenya . . . The novel is a public parade of crime and social alienation. This is no longer an external oppression, but an internal recolonization, in which certain individuals oppress their compatriots . . . The slide into crime in Mwangi's novel can thus be regarded as merely one dimension of a wider and deeper struggle between the exploiters and the exploited . . . the real issue is to see beyond their acts (which are only symptoms) and identify the circumstances that could have turned once normal and innocent young men into such recidivists . . . Mwangi does not lay all the blames for the avalanche of pains in Africa at the doorstep of the colonial masters, rather he believes that the neo-colonial indigenous rulers are even worse than the white colonialists. The lives of Meja and Maina in the text suggest that independence in African nations has not been very beneficial to the masses.
>
> (Kehinde (2004), pp. 231–2, 234–5, 238)

Mwangi's novel is more about the social conditions of the Kenyan urban poor than about crime as such but that is not to say that it cannot properly be classified as a crime novel. Of all the Kenyan crime novels that I have read and commented on in this chapter, this is the only one that addresses social issues head on. What general conclusions may be drawn from this apparent reluctance to address such issues will be considered later.

The fourth Kenyan novel to be considered is *Nairobi Heat* by Mukoma Wa Ngugi (2011). This is set partly in Madison, Wisconsin and partly in Nairobi and involves two detectives, David Odhiambo of Kenya CID and Ishmael, an African-American detective from Maple Bluff, an 'extremely white' town – we do not learn of his other name until he discloses it rather unwillingly to Lord Thompson in Kenya: Fofona. A young blonde woman, Macy Jane Admanzah, is found murdered on the doorstep of Joshua Hakizimana's house, a hero of the genocide in Rwanda who has accepted a position at the university. There appears nothing to connect Hakizimana to the murder although Ishmael regards him as the prime suspect. He receives an anonymous phone call telling him that if he wants to get to the truth, he must go to its source. 'The truth is in the past. Come to Nairobi.' He is given a fortnight by his chief to come up with 'the truth' in Nairobi.

Again, as with Huxley, the plot is very involved and becomes less and less credible as it goes on, but essentially it turns on the exploitation of the guilt of the genocide in Rwanda. Ishmael is kidnapped in Nairobi and meets with the man, Abu Jamal, who made the telephone call that got him to Nairobi on the instructions of a Samuel Alexander who worked for the Never Again Foundation. However, when Odhiambo and Ishmael visit Alexander he is dead in his bath having committed suicide leaving a note saying 'Sorry Joshua'. The call, it transpires, had been made to get Ishmael to Nairobi so he could be killed as he was becoming a thorn in the side of certain corrupt persons in Kenya:

> 'All right, say you are a savvy businessman who realises that there is money to be made out of this guilt . . . a lot of money. Say you have a white face, but you

> find a black man, a hero who helps you tap into the community of refugees from this country [Rwanda] that owns the guilt of the world, and you start a Refugee Centre. Say you then start a foundation called Never Again to tap into this guilt all over the world' . . . This man was some sort of middleman in a corrupt corporation fronted by the Refugee Centre and the Never Again Foundation, with Samuel as the acceptable white face and noble Joshua the stirrer of guilt. Together they preyed on the world's conscience ever since the genocide. 'Did Joshua do the things they say he did?' I asked . . . [Jamal]: 'I believe so. When he was offered money and fame for his good deeds, he felt entitled to them. It was Samuel who found Joshua'.
>
> (Ngugi 2011, p. 108)

It transpires that Joshua has not killed Macy Jane but had ordered the killing of her parents who had been missionaries in Rwanda and were also running an 'underground railroad' to get Tutsis out of Rwanda and who were therefore competitors of Joshua who wanted the Admanzahs out of the way both for that reason and because, according to Joshua, they were racists who treated escapees as little children. Joshua was in fact luring Tutsis out of hiding, saving some of them, but allowing many more to be killed by the genocidaires. In Kenya he is treated as a hero and recruited by Alexander as the poster boy for the corrupt foundation. Macy Jane went to Kenya to discover the truth about her parents' killing, learned of Joshua's true role and was going to expose him. Alexander told her where Joshua was, paid for her air ticket back to the US (an odd 'mistake' in the narrative since she would have bought a return ticket when leaving the US) and then arranged for her to be killed with the finger pointing at Joshua as he was costing the corrupt foundation too much money and Alexander wanted him out of the way too.

When Ishmael finally gets back to the US and tells his chief everything, they realise that they cannot arrest Joshua so, instead, they tell the tale of his involvement to the press. Even then, the story does not end. The Foundation collapses. The world's fury turns on Joshua. The International Criminal Court launches its own investigation into his role in the genocide:

> However as the weeks rolled into months the stories about the board and the trials got smaller and smaller until nothing more was heard of them. And as for Joshua, well it wasn't long before Johnnie Cochran type lawyers came crawling out of the woodwork – he was an American citizen after all and there was due process . . . no one could say for sure that he had ordered the murder of the Admanzah family. Even my [Ishmael's] testimony was questioned in light of the evidence that I had 'engaged in extra-judicial killings' in Kenya. And his confession, told to a detective 'who had just been tortured and killed four men' was 'agitated' and 'without a warrant' was inadmissible.
>
> The world never fully lets go of its heroes and slowly Joshua was rehabilitated, slowly students and professors came to his defence – claiming there was no evidence of his involvement in the genocide. Finally, sensing the turning

> of the tide, the Madison black community weighed in, speaking of Joshua's contribution to their development programmes . . . I had a front row seat to a genocidaire getting away with it.
>
> But so it was. The Chief was promoted to Police Commissioner and I to Chief Detective. Everyone except the dead came off better.
>
> (Ngugi 2011, pp. 176–7)

But Ishmael is not finished. He goes to the Ku Klux Klan, arranges for them to kill Joshua, which they did, and then he kills the Ku Klux Klan killers. His Chief knows what he has done but does nothing.

What can one make of this novel? Margie Orford, a leading South African detective writer, is quoted on the back cover of *Nairobi Heat* as saying that it is 'a gripping evocation of the collision of two intertwined worlds – the USA and Kenya – which are unraveled by violence, greed and prejudice.' Well, I'm not so sure of that.

Here is one quotation that I think tells one quite a bit about the author and his feelings about Kenya and the USA:

> "[Odhiambo asks] How do you [Ishmael] feel being here? I mean here in Kenya . . . as a black man from America?
>
> Now that was a tough question.
>
> 'Look, man, I like to keep it simple' I began. 'I like you but I like your wife better. I like the food and the beer, but I detest Mathare [a large informal settlement/slum in Nairobi] and whatever it is that keeps people there. I hate your city, with its skyscrapers that are trying to reach the white man's kingdom, and I sure as hell hate your justice system. How do I feel? I want to find my killer and bring him to justice . . . that's all.' "
>
> (Ngugi 2011, p. 81)

Here is Ngugi's ambivalence about Kenya, its slums, its corrupt legal and police system, its pretentiousness. But at the same time, he likes the informal socialising that is perhaps not so readily available in the United States. But he is also deeply critical of the US justice system as the earlier quotation about the Johnnie Cochrans crawling out of the woodwork shows. He is critical of the willingness of the system to forget the injustices uncovered by Ishmael, and the use of the same level of unlawful violence in the United States as in Kenya to achieve 'justice'. He seems to be saying that neither *system* can be relied upon and it is only the lone ranger acting on his own definition of right and wrong that can achieve justice:

> [Odhiambo]: 'Private detectives . . . let us set up shop. We shall be the first international private eyes, you and I . . .'
>
> I remained silent.
>
> 'Imagine all the assholes we can bring down . . .' he said, trying to convince me. 'For a hefty fee, of course.'

> I started weighing up the offer as soon as he hung up . . . I had to move. It made sense. I could belong anywhere. I would choose Africa . . . There were things to do there . . . I called the Chief, told him I was done and hung up before he tried talking me into staying. I wanted to live at one hundred degrees centigrade – all or nothing all of the time – and maybe do some good while at it.
>
> (Ngugi 2011, pp. 203–4)

South Africa's *Mail and Guardian* sums up the book: '*Nairobi Heat's* biggest triumph is the way it forces us to re-examine accepted narratives and received truths.' But do we really believe that a privatised justice system is the way to go? This seems to be neither a postcolonial Kenyan novel as discussed by Kurtz nor an example of American black crime fiction as analysed by Pepper (2003). It is, in my view and I am sorry if this seems a bit harsh, a book written by someone who is not sure where he belongs.[12]

How if at all have things changed in Ngugi's (2013a) second novel and the fifth novel to be discussed, *Black Star Nairobi*? It is a common place that after a successful first novel – and there are many reviews that would testify to *Nairobi Heat* being regarded as a successful first novel – it is often very difficult to follow up with an equally successful second novel. I regret to say that I don't think Ngugi has pulled it off. As my comments indicate, I do not share the enthusiasms of many reviewers of Ngugi's first novel so I would have to say that his second novel is – and this requires you to continue reading this chapter – more Brownlee than Crompton with perhaps even a touch of Palmer in it.

It does not help that the reader really needs to have read *Nairobi Heat* to get to grips with this novel. Detective Odhiambo is referred to from the beginning, and almost throughout the book, as O – as he was referred to in *Nairobi Heat* – and he and the American detective, Ishmael Fofano, have teamed up as a private detective agency in Nairobi as forecast in the earlier novel but with O still semi-attached to the Kenyan police, which throws the odd bone to the couple. The plot is too far-fetched to be worth describing in any detail so only its bare bones will be given. The Norfolk Hotel – probably still the best known, and best, hotel in Nairobi – is blown up.[13] Many people, including Americans, are killed. It quickly becomes apparent that an American group was responsible although an official from the US embassy, Paul, involved in the investigation, insists that Al Qaeda/Al Shabaab

12 A somewhat critical review is by Ross (2011).

13 As it was in 1981. This takes place in line 1 of the first page of the book when O and Ishmael are looking at the half-chewed body of a dead black American in the Ngong Hills. Thereafter, apart from eating and drinking in various well known places in Nairobi with excursions to Kisumu and Limuru, the Kenyan reality is in short supply.

are the culprits. To cut a very long and involved story short, the American group in question is led by a key person – known as Sahara – in a body called the International Democracy and Economic Security Council (IDESC), which turns out to be dedicated to killing off the corrupt leadership of countries – Kenya being the first as a result of the 2007 election – so that a new non-corrupt leadership under the tutelage of IDESC can take over and give the country good governance. The IDESC team discover that O and Ishmael are on to them; there is a shoot-out in O's house in which O's wife is killed as are three of the four bomb planters, but Sahara gets away on a scooter driven by a naked white man in the midst of Nairobi's traffic. The bulk of the book is about O and Ishmael chasing Sahara from Kenya to Mexico (where O, Ishmael and Ishmael's girlfriend enter the USA on false Kenyan passports supplied by Jason, the Section Chief of the CIA in Kenya) to the US to Kenya, with copious shoot-outs and killings on the way – all committed in total disregard of any law in any country in which O and Ishmael happen to be. Eventually they catch up with Sahara in the Kenyatta Conference Centre where the leaders of the main Kenyan political parties are meeting, in the wake of the copious quantity of post-election killings, to seal their power-sharing pact. Sahara is about to blow up the leaders so that a new IDESC-tutored government can take over and lead Kenya to the promised land. O mortally wounds Sahara. And later, after discovering from the dying Sahara that Paul, the US embassy official, is one of the IDESC supporters, he kills him too.

What can one say of this novel? In *Nairobi Heat*, there is some contact with the realities of policing in Madison, Wisconsin where Ishmael was a detective and in Nairobi where O is a detective. In this novel there is none. There is just non-stop killing with Ishmael very occasionally feeling slightly guilty, but O apparently not. As has been noted above, there is a considerable amount of extrajudicial killing by the police in Kenya, but the killings that take place in this novel do not seem to me bear any relationship in their nature, their quantity, their location nor the reaction to them that occurs in real-life Kenya. It seems to me that the novel represents a complete disillusionment with Kenya – apart from places where O and Ishmael eat and drink in Nairobi, there is nothing positive said about Nairobi or Kenya.[14]

The sixth novel to be examined is, in my view, a much more colonial, even if more complicated, affair: it is the third crime novel set in Mombasa by Nick Brownlee (2010), *Machete*. As with the other books, there are multiple plots with two detectives of sorts trying to sort them out: Jake Moore, an ex-English policeman invalided out of Scotland Yard after being shot and now running a failing

14 There are some elements in the novel which suggest that the author may have read one or two of Chester Himes' novels about the black detectives, Coffin Ed Johnson and Grave Digger Jones and how they operated in the Harlem of the 1940s and 1950s, particularly *A Rage in Harlem* (Himes 1957) where there is a considerable amount of violence and shootings. On the other hand, in *Cotton Comes to Harlem* (Himes 1965), there is much more discussion of police procedures with the two detectives more or less following the rules.

fishing boat operation in Mombasa, and Daniel Jouma, a somewhat maverick detective in the Mombasa police force. An apparent madman known as the Headhunter is killing persons by decapitating them and leaving notes with the heads in and around Mombasa. He is in fact a seven foot Maasai, called Isiah Oulu who had been a patient in a secure mental hospital near Malinidi. He calls himself Athi, son of Ngai, the Divider of the Universe and Lord of Nature. It was wrongly assumed that he had died. His *modus operandi* is to use a few dreadlocked minions to go and capture people for beheading. He, in turn, is controlled by the deputy head of the mental hospital, Dr Lutta, who uses him to kill the members of The Syndicate, a group of four poker players who had won Dr Lutta's father's business in a poker game. Three persons have been killed and decapitated. Jouma discovers that two of the persons were part of The Syndicate. Another member of The Syndicate, the European manager of a hotel, is saved from being captured by the Headhunter's minions by a mate of Jake's from Scotland, who had been hired to provide security for the hotel, but who is himself killed in the ensuing gun fight. The third person to be killed and decapitated is the son-in-law of a naval officer, who is in fact killed by the lover of the wife of the naval officer who had him decapitated to make it appear as if he had been killed by the Headhunter. The naval officer's wife had not thought him worthy to be the husband of her daughter.

Confused? I'll carry on and muddy the waters a little more. There are various subplots, some of which do not seem to add very much to the main plot. There is tension between the Mayor of Mombasa and the Coast Province CID headed up by Elizabeth Simba as the former wishes to be able to claim credit for the eventual capture of the Headhunter. There is tension between Simba and Jouma; tension between the father-in-law of one of the murder victims, a senior naval officer, and Jouma; tension between the Mayor and the local reporter from the *Daily Nation* newspaper, Katherine Rapuro. Eventually, all is sorted out. The Headhunter is killed. Dr Lutta, one of The Syndicate, who tried to kill the hotel manager, is arrested. The hotel manager wins a poker game, rigged by Jake, so that he can give the money to the widow of Jake's friend as he had promised.

Machete is not a good crime novel; it has too many plots and subplots. There is insufficient characterisation of the main characters. It is very colonial in its use of a seven foot Maasai as a kind of African God-cum-prophet. It would have been more realistically Kenyan if such a person were to have been a Pope or an Archbishop of a Christian sect of which there are many in Kenya. One interesting throwback to Huxley's novel is the clear contempt that the senior naval officer has for Jouma, a mere policeman, and I suppose one could also see a throwback to the mayor's concern to score over the police. I lived in Nairobi for three years and do not in any way pretend to have mixed with the kind of people Brownlee is writing about – my peer group were colleagues from UN-Habitat and former students who were senior lawyers – but the book did not give me the impression that Brownlee knew Kenya as a person who had lived there and there is indeed nothing in his CV to suggest that he has lived there. Kenya is just a location for a novel with quite a lot of bloodthirsty killings.

The seventh Kenyan novel is *The Honey Guide* by Richard Crompton (2013b) who does live in Nairobi and sets the novel in the run up to and the immediate aftermath of the disputed Kenyan elections of 2007, which led to a great deal of mayhem and killings in Nairobi and many deaths from intertribal fighting over land in the Rift Valley (De Smedt 2009). It has had excellent reviews in the British and South African press as an efficient police procedural. It is more believable than Brownlee's book but, from my point of view, that may be because it is set in and about Nairobi, which I know much better than I know Mombasa. His main protagonist is a Maasai detective, Mollel, a good deal more convincing, though not entirely credible, than Brownlee's Maasai. Crompton however states:

> [F]or the policeman in Mollel, I relied upon the assistance of an off-duty Nairobi detective who gave me many insights into a side of the city that a Westerner would never normally see. We holed up in a cafe on K-Street just as Mollel does to watch the street girls at work . . . He gave me a lot of the details about the inner workings of the police department . . . And it was with him that I took night-time visits to some of the more dangerous districts – visits which I had to stop when my friend got word that I'd been seen too often and my presence would no longer be tolerated . . . Mollel's Maasai backstory comes from another real person, a man my own age whom I befriended while living a few hours away from Nairobi, in Arusha, Northern Tanzania. We both became fathers at about the same time and while I was living in an unfamiliar country and adapting to parenthood, he was coming to terms with the transition from Warrior to Elder.
>
> (Crompton 2013b, pp. 330–1)

Mollel is something of a local hero for the work he did pulling people from the wreckage caused by the bombing of the American embassy in 2007 while looking for his wife who was killed in the bombing. He and his partner, Kiunga, are set to investigate the murder of a Maasai prostitute, Lucy, found in a storm drain in Nairobi's Uhuru Park by their boss, Otieno, the head of Central CID.[15] Otieno finds Mollel somewhat insubordinate but cannot sack him because of his past. Their investigations involve: Honey, another Maasai prostitute (her name is anglicised from Maasai) who was a friend of Lucy (both of them operated in Koinange Street (K-Street) in central Nairobi); David Kingori, the most powerful and influential businessman in Nairobi (a Kikuyu); the Reverend George and Dr Wanjiku Nalo, of the George Nalo Ministries, a large and well-heeled evangelical movement much patronised by the Nairobi middle classes; James Letherbridge, a

15 For those who would not otherwise know, Kiunga is a Kikuyu, and Otieno is a Luo.

gopher and procurer for Kingori (they were at school together in England); the GSU, the fearsome General Service Unit, nominally a part of the Kenyan police but in practice at the beck and call of the ruling party, which uses extreme force to break up demonstrations against the government and ruling party; and, Orpheus House, a derelict building in a highly desirable part of central Nairobi, owned by Kingori but wanted by the Nalos for their Ministry.

Mollel makes several false moves. He first of all suspects Kingori of Lucy's murder, arrests him and takes him to the Central Police Station in Nairobi on a slightly trumped up charge. When Otieno finds Kingori in the police station he greets him effusively as an old friend and warns off Mollel from harassing him. (The latter would be believable but the arrest is not). Then Mollel breaks into Orpheus House, finds evidence of illegal abortions (quite possible in Kenya) being organised and carried out by Dr Wanjiku Nalo and the illegal delivery of babies, which are then taken from their mothers and sold to those who are prepared to pay up to Kshs 100,000 (about £800) for a baby (again not too far-fetched in Kenya). He then wants to arrest Wanjiku for taking a baby from Lucy and killing Lucy to cover up what she did. That too proves a false trail. Then he decides that Letherbridge, who is a punter who frequents K-Street, is the culprit and goes to arrest him. Letherbridge more or less breaks down and confesses that he was involved in disposing of Lucy's body but not in murdering her.

Then Mollel suddenly and finally hits upon the truth: Honey who has been 'helping' him all along is the murderer of Lucy; the baby was Honey's, the father being George Nalo. The baby had a defect at birth that made it highly unlikely that it could have lived and indeed it died more or less at birth. Honey refused to believe that and thought that Lucy had conspired with Wanjiku to sell her baby away and split the proceeds. Honey pretends to go along with a plan of Lucy to arrange a threesome with Letherbridge with the object of robbing him. Honey and Lucy get in the four-by-four in K-Street. Honey attacks Letherbridge while he is driving to the pre-arranged location. The four-by-four crashes; Lucy gets out, pursued by Honey who stabs her and, with Letherbridge's help, tips her into the storm drains hoping that she will be carried away. Mollel becomes concerned that Honey may try and kill his mother who wants to have Mollel's son live with her because he is a somewhat distant dad. He gets back to his mother's house via the good offices of the GSU who have cordoned off the area where his mother lives from Lavington – a middle range, middle class and expatriate neighbourhood – where Honey is clearly preparing to kill Mollel's mother. Mollel gets his mother and his son, Adam, out – again via the good offices of the GSU – and leaves Honey to her fate at the hands of the non-Kikuyu mob raging through the area.

The novel, for me, was more engaging than Brownlee's and there is enough local content in it so that it is not entirely unbelievable. Mollel and Kiunga's moving around Nairobi, eating and having a beer or two ring true – the usual form is to buy six Tuskers at once and line them up for steady drinking. The Nalos' evangelical activities also reflect reality. I do however find the assumption that the police are committed to using what might be called normal police procedures to attempt to solve crimes and that they rarely resort to illegalities far-fetched. There are too many very well documented and attested cases of the police shooting suspects (or not even suspects) in Nairobi for a novel about police procedures in Nairobi to ring true when this is never alluded to – Crompton's police informant was hardly likely to tell him all about that. In that respect Ngugi's (2011) *Nairobi Heat*, which features a considerable amount of killing by the police, is more realistic. Again, although there was considerable violence in Nairobi in the aftermath of the 2007 elections, and the blurb about the book sets the investigation against that backdrop, it never really intrudes on the investigation except with respect to the activities of the GSU, which again come through as much more restrained than they are in practice. In reality, they are not much more than an armed and uniformed set of government thugs. And is it entirely realistic to assume that in the midst of major post-election violence, an investigation into the killing of a prostitute would have continued? There is not then any social commentary in the novel; no using the novel as a way of commenting on and drawing attention to the gross socio-economic inequities which exist in Nairobi or the incompetence, illegalities and proven political partiality of the police. Is it unfair to comment that Crompton lives in Nairobi, clearly enjoys living there, wants to go on living there and writing best-selling novels based on what must be stated to be unrealistically legal police practices in the city?[16]

The final book on crime set in Kenya that I will review can be quickly disposed of. It is *Code Orange* by Ralph Palmer (2010).[17] I did not enjoy reading this novel and I nearly gave up half way through. Most of the expatriate Kenyan-based novels tend to be less good in their second half than their first half and I just couldn't see my way to subjecting myself to its second half. But just as with reviewing a case, even the worst judgments must be read through to the end, so I struggled on.

In this novel two Kikuyu students steal the top secret file detailing British/US machinations to rig the 2007 Kenyan elections from the house of a British civil servant who found the file on a commuter train and decided to keep it in his house. (One of the students is having a liaison with the civil servant's wife, who shows him the file.) The students take the file back to Nairobi to negotiate its sale to both main sides of the elections – the Kikuyus and the Luos – for an astronomical sum. The second half opens without any reference to the first half and consists mainly of describing the efforts of the Deputy Chairman of the Kenyan Electoral Commission to avoid being arrested and killed by the ruling group that had got back to power. The Chairman of the Commission having already committed suicide by

16 It is not as if Crompton is unaware of the injustices that pervade the governance of Kenya. See Crompton (2013a).

17 The basic storyline – the loss of a top secret government file on a London commuter train outlining an Anglo-American plan to interfere in the 2007 Kenyan elections to ensure that the 'right' person was elected President – is not so far-fetched as to be wholly unlikely, but its working out thereafter is wildly improbable.

jumping out of the 13th floor of Nyayo House in Nairobi – notorious in real life as housing Moi's torture chambers in the basement. The novel details the deputy Chairman's travels to Kampala, London, Kampala and to Nairobi where, after finally giving his evidence to a Commission of Inquiry comprising three Commonwealth judges into the elections which shows how the elections were rigged, he is killed by a sniper employed by a general – it's not clear what position this general holds but he employs hit squads to get rid of the government's enemies.[18] The three judges of the Commission of Inquiry are then blown up by a bomb planted on the plane taking them to Masi Mara (a Kenyan game park) and all their papers are burned or eaten by goats. However, one notebook of the Chairman survives that details the rigging of the elections. It is obtained by the British civil servant who purloined the secret file in the first place and who is fortuitously on holiday in Kenya. In some mysterious fashion the notebook comes into the possession of the senior official who had originally left the secret file on the train (and had been promoted from Secretary to the Cabinet to be Trade Commissioner in the EU by the prime minister as the price for keeping silent about other top secret files he had found in the Waterloo left luggage office while he was searching for his file). The British government doesn't seem too displeased with the outcome of the election. In the very last two pages, the two students from the first half of the book are back in England waiting to take possession of the red Mercedes they have bought with their ill-gotten gains.

What general conclusions may be drawn from this review of Kenyan crime novels?[19] First, I have to say that these novels may not be particularly representative of Kenyan crime fiction;[20] they are all by expatriates, including, no doubt controversially, Ngugi (referred to by Matzke (2012) as African-Diasporic). Second, the one novel that gets closest to the realities of Kenya as it then was is *Murder at*

18 During both Kenyatta's and Moi's presidency, political opponents of the presidents were assassinated, the most high profile being Tom Mboya in 1969 during Kenyatta's presidency and Robert Ouko, the Foreign Secretary, in 1990 during Moi's presidency. The killers have never been brought to justice. Moi appointed a Commission of Inquiry into Ouko's death but suddenly wound it up, when it was getting quite close to how Ouko had come to be killed. And see too UN Human Rights Council (2009) Report, which on this matter at least, unfortunately rings true.

19 I am not going to discuss le Carré (2001). It is set in Kenya but it is about international criminal activities and dishonest dealings relating to pharmaceutical use and testing in Kenya and elsewhere and not about Kenyan crime, although deaths do take place in Kenya which marginally involve the Kenyan authorities.

20 Nine authors are listed in African Crime Fiction Written by Authors from Kenya (Keil 2012) which include Huxley, N'gweno and Ngugi. Mwangi wrote *Assassins on Safari* (Duchi 1983) under the pen name of David Duchi. The remaining six include Ralph Palmer listed as being from Ireland and Kenya. Oddly, the list does not include Meja Mwangi's (1973) *Kill Me Quick*, the first of his Nairobi trilogy which I think would be regarded as a crime novel by most commentators. Kurtz (1998) does discuss Mwangi and draws attention to the full length study by Johansson (1992). See also, Kehinde (2004) and Kurtz (1993).

Government House by Huxley (1988) who by then had lived in Kenya for 25 years and no doubt had the entrée both to colonial government and settler circles. Kurtz may have dismissed her as writing for an expatriate non-African audience but it was an audience that would have picked up on her overt criticism of colonial officials and settlers. Third, no doubt because the authors I have reviewed are expatriate or diasporic-African, all the novels lack any kind of cutting edge political or social commentary, or any kind of critical commentary on police procedures; they exist in a political and social vacuum. Fourth, all the novels, with the exception of Ngugi's (2013a) *Black Star Nairobi*, accept as a given, without any overt criticism, the British-style police and justice system imposed on Kenya at the outset of colonialism that excluded customary systems of criminal justice. One would expect that of Huxley's book, where the Canadian nationality of the detective investigating the governor's murder is emphasised, so marking his impartiality from the colonial establishment. But perhaps the most overt and 'colonial' example of this phenomenon is in Brownlee's *Machete* where the Kenyan detective is assisted by an ex-Scotland Yard detective and regular police procedures are contrasted with the primitive and brutal African procedures for dealing with dishonest behaviour. This is in marked contrast to Nigerian attitudes to the colonial systems of criminal justice as discussed in Manji's (2000) article and Dolin's (2007) chapter, especially the latter.

It is finally worth drawing attention to one Kenyan 'pure' crime novel which raises political issues but which I have not read: *A Friend in Court* by Muroki Ndung'u (2004):[21]

> A young lawyer, Rosaly Gakeni, resigns from a prosperous law firm in the capital in order to start her own company in her home town Nakuru. The first case she has to deal with demands from her to cross the limits of her profession and actually find out the organisers of assaults against local farmers. After long and dangerous investigations, it is revealed that the assaults were organised by high-ranking politicians from the ruling party (in the novel named UKN)[22] in order to press the farmers into supporting the party at the coming elections. The immediate organisers and executors of the assaults are taken to court and Rosaly, in a brilliant 'female Perry Mason' manner pins them to the dock and they are sentenced.[23] However strong Rosaly is, as a professional and as a personality, she also needs help and consolation from her devoted male assistant, Gareth Maitika . . . the two lawyers are not led by

21 The novel, although discussed by Rinkanya (2012) is, oddly, not noted in Matzke (2012). Nor is Ndung'u listed in Keil (2012).

22 In reality KANU, the Kenya African National Union.

23 I have to express some reservations about this outcome. High-ranking politicians in the ruling party in Kenya do not appear in any dock in Kenya let alone being pinned and sentenced. Nor is it likely that they will appear at the ICC.

> the perspective of material benefits – in fact, they did not charge their clients, representing the interests of the farmers, even a penny – but by the fact that they are doing something useful for the country, for its people, for the law and democracy.
>
> (Rinkanya 2012, p. 191)

4 Crime fiction in South Africa: an introduction

I now want to consider four writers who write on South African crime. In the list African Crime Fiction Written by Authors from South Africa (Keil 2012),[24] 78 names are listed and one hundred and 77 titles. Of those listed three have black African names and write in English and one has a black African name and writes in Zulu.[25] Clearly to do justice to South African crime fiction would require a book of which there would appear to be none.[26] I am going to discuss Malla Nunn, a diasporic-African based in Australia, Deon Meyer, probably the best known South African crime writer,[27] Angela Makholwa, and Diale Tlholwe in order to contrast their approach to crime writing with the approach of the writers of Kenyan-based crime fiction that I have discussed above.

Malla Nunn's (2009) book, *A Beautiful Place to Die*, was a revelation after reading a succession of Kenya-based novels. It is set in 1950s apartheid South Africa and involves the murder of a South African Afrikaans police captain, Pretorius, whose family more or less controls the small rural town of Jacob's Rest on the border with Mozambique. The story is set at the time when the legislative process, undertaken by the Nationalist government elected in 1948, putting in place full-blown apartheid was just beginning. Whites, coloureds and blacks live in separate areas. Only one detective, Emmanuel Cooper, an English ex-army immigrant, is sent from Johannesburg by major Van Niekerk to investigate the murder, a decision regarded by the dead man's sons as an insult. Within the town there is a new white Afrikaans recruit to the police, Hansie Hepple, and a black police constable,

24 The list includes Michael Stanley, the pen name of two authors who write crime novels set in Botswana, and Tom Sharpe, author of the Wilt books set in and around Cambridge, an Englishman deported from South Africa in 1971 after the publication of his two crime novels, *Indecent Exposure* (Sharpe 1973) and *Riotous Assembly* (Sharpe 1971) satirising apartheid. Oddly, as Stephen Berrisford, a South African colleague has pointed out to me, neither J.M. Coetzee (1999) *Disgrace* nor Gordimer (1998) *The House Gun* are noted though both are crime novels with a good deal of discussion of police procedures.

25 Annoi Dlovu appears to be a black African name but is the pen name of a white female writer.

26 See however Rautenbach (2013); Warnes (2012); Primorac (2012); Davis (2012) and Matzke (2012). For a wider ranging article, see Comaroff (2004).

27 His books are to be found in the crime section of Waterstones in Gower Street. I have read three of his novels, *Blood Safari* (Meyer 2009); *Devil's Peak* (Meyer 2012a); and *Trackers* (Meyer 2012b), the last two featuring Benny Griessel, detective and recovering alcoholic. Meyer writes in Afrikaans and his novels have been translated into English and 16 other languages.

Shabalala, who as the story unfolds turns out to have been very close to the captain and, consequently, knows a lot about his family and background that he is reluctant to disclose. Another key person is Mr Zweigman, 'the old Jew', who runs a dry goods store for Kaffirs and coloureds but is in fact a trained and qualified surgeon and refugee from Germany, a fact which he keeps hidden from the town, although the murdered captain knew of his qualification and had referred some people to him.

There is immediate tension between the murdered captain's sons and Cooper, and more generally between the different groups within the town. Then, because the captain's wife is a daughter of one of the major theoreticians of apartheid, Frikkie van Brandenburg, the Special Branch decide that the murder was political and send two sadistic officers to take over the investigation. The Special Branch assumes all along that the murder was committed by a black political agitator. Cooper is required to report all his findings to the two Special Branch officers and relegated to investigating a snooper who had been preying on coloured women at night. Cooper isn't interested in political expediency and has never been one for making friends. He may be modest, but he radiates intelligence and does not intend to kneel before those in power. Instead, he strikes out on his own, following a trail of clues that lead him to uncover a shocking forbidden love and the imperfect life of Captain Pretorius, a man whose relationships with the black and coloured residents of the town he ruled were more complicated and more human than anyone could have imagined. While the Special Branch thugs are beating a false confession out of an African 'agitator' they have captured crossing the border, Cooper and Shabalala uncover the real murderer. This turns out to be the captain's youngest son who conceives of himself as having a mission to purify the races and had discovered his father's sexual relationship with a young coloured woman; and he is also the snooper. At the outset of his unauthorised investigation Cooper gets beaten up by the sons of the captain, overseen by the Special Branch thugs who add their own professional beating. However, he is subsequently also rescued by the older sons of the captain who discover their father's activities from documents in the youngest son's room and recognise the correctness and justice of Cooper's investigations and conclusions. He is taken to Zweigman to be put together again.

Nunn's (2011) second novel *Let the Dead Lie* is a much darker book than her first, involving more police corruption, double dealing and double crossing, and more interracial relationships. Rather than being set in a small rural town, the action takes place in Durban, just before the coronation of Elizabeth II in June 1953, mainly in and around the docks and involves the murder of a poor white street boy, Jolly Marks. The same basic characters appear, Cooper, Van Niekerk, Shabalala, Zweigman, but they are joined by: Mr Khan, a major Asian crook into both legitimate and illegal business – drugs, fencing goods stolen from ships docking in the harbour; a person referred to throughout the book as 'the tradesman' – Cooper's word for him – who is either Special Services or Security Services; Nicolai and Natalya Petrov, two Russians; and various other characters of different races and colours.

At the end of *A Beautiful Place to Die* (Nunn 2009), Cooper had been shown to be the son of a mixed marriage. At the beginning of *Let the Dead Lie* (Nunn 2011), rather than wait to be exposed as non-white and get Van Niekerk into deep water with the Special Branch, he has resigned from the police and is working in the docks in Durban. He comes across the murder scene of Jolly Marks and begins, without any authority, to investigate it. Mysteriously his European landlady and her African maid are both murdered and he is set up and arrested as the murderer. Enter Van Niekerk, who has been transferred from Johannesburg, and the tradesman. Cooper is released into the tradesman's custody and given 48 hours by Van Niekerk to find the murderer(s) of Jolly Marks. At this point, the Petrovs enter into the story. It transpires that Nicolai Petrov was a senior member of the KGB and Natalya Petrov was one of Stalin's favourite actors. After Stalin's death, Nicolai defected to the UK with Natalya. Nicolai was then sucked dry by the British secret services, with the idea of then trading him back to the USSR in return for a captured British spy. The Petrovs escaped to South Africa and the book is the story of Cooper's gradual realisation of this situation, with the tradesman, probably Van Niekerk and a British officer sent to South Africa to recapture the Petrovs, putting obstacles in his path. With no more than minutes to spare, the denouement is that Cooper lets Nicolai, who has been diagnosed by Zweigman with an inoperable brain tumour and given very little time to live, be recaptured by the British officer and the tradesman without a fight. In the process, however, Cooper gives a good roughing up to the tradesman who turns out to be the triple murderer, but will never be brought to justice. Natalya is allowed to remain in South Africa. Van Niekerk gets promoted to colonel and receives the goodwill of the head of the Security Branch. As the pay-off for letting Nicolai go without a fight, Cooper gets his detective branch ID and race identification card classifying him as European; and Shabalala, who has broken most of the racial laws in helping Cooper, is promoted to a native detective constable. At the end of the book, the two sadistic Special Branch officers who had beaten up Cooper turn up as part of the tradesman's team and clearly strongly disapprove of Cooper's police and racial restoration.

Nunn is a person who, and whose parents, lived in apartheid South Africa on the 'wrong' side of the dividing line between whites and the rest; her novels have the authenticity of that life. She is extremely aware, knowledgeable and clearly highly critical of the realities of police practice and procedure in apartheid South Africa, of the relationships between black and white police, of the policing of the different communities within an apartheid town, of the moral dilemmas of Zweigman, of the brutalities of the Special Branch, and of the complexity of relations between Afrikaaners – the 'white tribe' of Africa – and Africans. Her novels, exceptionally well written and structured, politically, socially and morally acute are totally different from the novels of Ngugi, Brownlee and Palmer. In particular, in common with Huxley and Crompton, she is aware that the better detective novel concentrates on only one or a very few deaths; multiple killings as in Ngugi, Brownlee and Palmer detract from rather than add to the drama.

A fair amount has been written by Deon Meyer[28] so rather than adopt the approach hitherto used in this chapter of summarising a novel and then commenting on it, I will draw attention to some of the socio-political features of Meyer's works as noted by the commentators. Davis (2012) makes the point that:

> Although Meyer's novels are thrillers first and foremost, they do develop credible characters with real psychological depth. In all the books the protagonists are flawed characters struggling with their personal lives . . . Since Meyer's novels are set firmly in the period of transition from the old to the new South Africa, between the apartheid and post-apartheid societies, the pasts of the characters assume particular importance . . . Since Meyer is writing out of a country which is passing through such significant times it is perhaps to be expected that one of the more interesting facts of his fiction is the manner in which he portrays the New South Africa. His work demonstrates how the writer of thrillers need not eschew the opportunity to raise important social issues . . . The South Africa we encounter in *Blood Safari* is a country of game reserves, not only of the vast and famous Kruger National Park, but also of smaller, privately run parks . . . Two issues are of particular concern in this remote rural setting: land claims and ecology. And as Meyer shows they are not only interlocked but frequently in conflict . . . Remarkably for a thriller, Meyer allocates considerable space to the articulation of different points of view on ecological questions . . . Deon Meyer has proved himself a master of the thriller. He knows how to pace the action, create suspense and weave an intricate plot . . . He addresses issues of importance in the New South Africa whether these concern drugs, crime, child abuse, environmental protection or the preservation of wildlife.
>
> (pp. 56–60)

Warnes (2012) draws attention to other aspects of Meyer's novels:

> There is a striking correlation to be drawn between the proposals of South African criminologists like Altbeker, and what crime novelists themselves explore in their fiction. Specifically, both return to the figure of the detective as an antidote to disorder, violence and uncertainty . . . [U]nder Jackie Sebeli [former South African Commissioner of Police] . . . the unfortunate detectives had come to be seen as 'unfashionable; relics, almost of a bygone age'.
>
> [Altbeker 2007, p. 139]
>
> With uncanny timing, just at the point when the inadequacies of preventative policing and the loss of investigators start to be most keenly felt, the detective

28 See footnote 27.

> returns to South African literature with a vengeance . . . his work touches a variety of themes – from apartheid-era corruption to the challenges of transformation, to topics in contemporary architecture and music – but constant throughout is the figure of the detective.
>
> Sometimes private eyes, sometimes policeman, the white male agents of detection in Meyer's novels . . . are bodyguards, defenders of the vulnerable, who symbolically negotiate the threat and disorder of post-apartheid South Africa for their middle-class author and readers. But these characters are themselves damaged, and in need of rescue . . . Not unlike his contemporaries, J.M. Coetzee, Damon Galgut and Ivan Vladislavić, Meyer 'narrativises' the dilemma of middle-aged white men caught between traumatic pasts and a future which appears to have little use for them . . . But unlike the alienated anxious mood of a Coetzee or a Galgut, Meyer's novels are indefatigably optimistic . . .
>
> Crime fiction is a narrative art in which the hermeneutic journeys of the detective-hero are mirrored by those of the reader of the novel . . . In the context of post-apartheid South Africa, the particular resources that this genre offers make it possible for writers to exercise both readerly and socially-responsive reflexes: to write in a way that feels appropriately 'new', attracting a wide and diverse range of readers, while maintaining some of the commitment to political and social conscientising that has long been a feature of South African literatures . . . Far from being apolitical, then, the post-apartheid crime thriller should be read as negotiating – in the ambivalent sense of the word – the threat and uncertainty that many feel to be part of South African life, creating fantasies of control, restoration and maintenance and reflecting on the circumstances that gave rise to this unease.
>
> (Warnes 2012, pp. 986–7, p. 991).

One matter, however, that is not mentioned in these discussions of Meyer is his portrayal of relationships between black and white police; these are rarely as explicit as the other matters discussed by Meyer in his work. It is difficult to believe that they are as unproblematic in practice as they are portrayed in his fiction. What these discussions of Meyer's work, however, do point up in an embarrassing fashion is the shallowness of Kenyan-based crime fiction. I am not impressed by Ngugi's explanation of why he has chosen the genre for his writing or his justification of the violence in *Black Star Nairobi*:

> I do have this attraction to the form because with the form you can do so much. Not only can you tell a very, very entertaining story . . . but you can explore societal issues. In this case I look at the war on terror, the violence coming from the war on terror, the post-electoral violence . . . It allows you to look at very, very extreme situations, extreme violence, a society just about to explode in a way that I don't think you can do with realist fiction.
>
> (Ngugi 2013b)

However, there were no societal issues explored in the book. The violence was too often gratuitous and, as noted above, unrealistic even in a Nairobi where police violence and killings of innocent persons is far too prevalent. Nor was the storyline sufficiently realistic to enable one to relate to it. Although I do not know South Africa in any real sense compared to my knowledge of Nairobi, I could get a much better feel of the realities of South African post-apartheid urban society and of its policing by reading Meyer's novels than I could by reading Ngugi's novels set in Nairobi.

I turn now to two crime novels by black South African writers, *Red Ink* by Angela Makholwa (2007) and *Counting the Coffins* by Diale Tlholwe (2011). These books are very different to Meyer's books and, I would think, novels by other white South African crime writers. They are both set in Johannesburg (Jozi) but in a Jozi inhabited by and familiar to black South Africans. The characters are almost exclusively black with whites having no more than small 'walk on' parts.

In *Red Ink* (Makholwa 2007), the main person around whom the story revolves, Lucy Khambule, is a partner in a PR firm who agrees to write up the story of Napoleon Dingiswayo, a serial killer imprisoned in C-Max, the High Security wing of Pretoria's prison. Napoleon has a brother Sifiso who takes a dislike to Lucy. Both brothers have a Sponsor, KK Mabote, a beneficiary of Black Economic Empowerment (BEE), and formerly involved in the freedom fight but now a dodgy businessman. The Sponsor used the brothers to undertake various killings for him, with Napoleon a rapist and Sifiso the killer, Napoleon agreeing to take the rap for the others. Lucy's business partner and her boyfriend are both killed, with police detective Morapedi investigating the murders. Morapedi's investigation follows the law and correct police procedure, even if he is a little slow on the uptake. KK Mabote gives orders to Sifiso to get rid of Lucy as there is a risk that she will disclose the full story of the relationship between the brothers and KK. There is a knife fight at Lucy's flat and Sifiso is killed. After Sifiso's death, KK skips the country. Napoleon is besotted with Lucy and the last sentence of the novel is that he has escaped from prison.

In *Counting the Coffins* (Tlholwe 2011), the main character is Thabang Maje, member of Security Consultants and Private Investigators (SCPI), with the other central characters being Thekiso, a lawyer who has never practised, and Ditoro, an ex-policeman. Other characters in the novel are: Tabang's wife, Lesogo, a business woman managing property developments; a journalist friend, Tokoloho Mohaji (Tolo); and the main villain, Sandile Nkosi, whose drunken son crashed into Thabang's wife's car killing one of his newborn twins. Sandile was a police informer under the old regime but has reinvented himself as a property developer who has half-built a four-storey shopping mall. He has conned a lot of people out of their savings to invest in his shopping mall, never having had any intention to finish it but rather to keep the money conned from the 'investors'. SCPI are hired to get the money back. Thabang and Tolo discover a fair amount about the scam, the investors and others involved. Tolo's father, a professor, was also part of the scam but it turns out that he was partly instrumental in getting SCPI involved in getting the money back from Sandile. SCPI decide not to do anything about the professor. 'Professor Mohapi isn't a bad man. He might associate with crooks and phonies but he is still a good man . . . why pull him down and crush him. We have so few real good people left as it is' (Tlholwe 2011, p. 139). The story is how SCPI set about getting the money back for the investors using unconventional means – not wholly illegal but taking the kind of short cuts the police cannot. They find out as much as they can about Sandile's other activities, particularly a very dubious club-cum-brothel-cum-under-age-pornographic film studio where lots of well known politicos and others in the public eye go and film underage Kenyans who fled from post-2007 Kenya and were then trafficked into South Africa and are being sexually abused and filmed by the politicos. SCPI, using some of their part-time 'helpers', raid the club, take money, porn films and drugs, and set up a meeting with Sandile with a view to ensuring that he gives back the money to the investors with interest. Ditoro tips off his ex-mates in the police to raid the venue, pick up the drugs and arrest Sandile. However, Kono, an ex-Angolan guerrilla who seems to be behind Sandile and the scam, has arranged for the half-finished mall to collapse killing Sandile and burying the drugs, but he is also killed during the police raid.

In both books there is an undercurrent of cynicism about BEE, those who helped the former regime but have managed to reinvent themselves (and usually get away with it), and dishonest politicians. There are references to continued killings – 'isolated cases cropping up for years now' as former stooges from the old regime are disposed of, with such persons 'seeking anonymity not notoriety. So the struggle continues. For some it never really ended' (Tlholwe 2011, p. 170). There is little about police practice or procedures in either book and in *Counting the Coffins*, some fairly critical comments about the law.[29] The political criticisms are ones unlikely to be voiced by crime novels written by white South Africans.

The context of the social function of the crime fiction genre in South Africa may be noted, although again I see the following comment as referring very much to white South African crime fiction. Rautenbach (2013) summarises the position:

> Proponents of the social function of the genre maintain that it acts as a means of Aristotelian catharsis by presenting a familiar version of reality, while refracting it and providing the resolution and closure which so many South Africans deeply crave: it acts as a Perseus's mirror . . . allowing South Africans to make sense of rampant and often disorientating crime while remaining shielded from it. Orford has also often stated that fiction about crime in South Africa is essentially a study of why it is such a violent place – a 'whydunnit' rather than a 'whodunit' . . . In this sense, the resolution achieved by the

29 Tlholwe began law studies at Fore Hare in 1980 but did not return after one of the mass expulsions of students at the university.

> end of the story may be merely superficial (a victory over a single antagonist), leaving the greater social issues unresolved. Crime fiction Orford argues, acts as a study of the social motivators within the intricate system of crime and punishment, providing unique insight into its society. Crime fiction is useful, she says, because 'the only literary protagonists that could traverse South Africa's stratified society with any kind of plausibility were cops and journalists'.
>
> Similarly, Deon Meyer has stated that 'crime fiction can never be a panoramic window on society, it can only be a small window with a restricted view.'

There is then a growing critical literature on and about South African crime fiction focusing not only on whether it merits being seen as literature but also on its socio-political role. That cannot be said of Kenyan-based crime fiction. Kurtz, for instance, does not even refer to crime fiction as such in his overview of the post-colonial Kenyan novel. This might be because he, like many literary critics, does or did not regard crime fiction as meriting serious consideration as literature but also possibly because when he was writing his book in the mid-1990s such crime fiction as there was in Kenya was nowhere near as socially penetrating as South African crime fiction.

5 Crime novels from Botswana: a brief note

A characteristic of all the novels discussed in this chapter is that they have been written by non-lawyers; indeed, by persons with no practical experience of a criminal justice system. This is why a brief note from Botswana is apposite since the two authors to be discussed here – McCall Smith and Unity Dove – are both lawyers. Taking McCall Smith first, he is the author of the phenomenally successful *The No. 1 Ladies' Detective Agency* series which has now reached 12 books and seems to have stopped.[30] I am not sure that any of these books can be regarded as crime novels, despite the main protagonist of the series Mma Ramotswe being referred to as the Miss Marple of Botswana. I have read four of the novels and they have always struck me as much more like 'Citizens' Advice' type or 'lay preachers' type novels than crime novels, where good and sensible advice is dispensed to a variety of persons with personal problems none of whom seems to have committed any criminal offence which should involve the police. I have no doubt that that kind of advice is widely available in most African countries and would be dispensed by a variety of persons: chiefs, retired officials of one kind of another, and yes, possibly private detectives; nor would I be surprised if some of those persons seeking advice had committed some kind of offence but preferred not to go the police

30 The first book in the series was so-called and was first published in 1998 (McCall Smith 1998).

with the hassle that it would inevitably involve. But when all is said and done, it's difficult to see such activity as crime and so difficult to see novels about such activity as crime novels.

Unity Dow on the other hand is a judge in the High Court and formerly a noted lawyer in private practice in Botswana who single-handedly fought the Botswana government in the courts and won a notable victory that brought about a change in the constitution relating to the laws on citizenship, allowing women to pass their nationality on to their children (Dow 1995). The novel I will discuss is her second novel entitled *The Screaming of the Innocent* (Dow 2002), which involves a ritual murder. It is clear from the reading of the novel that this type of murder does take place in Botswana. The main protagonist is Amantle Bokaa, a Tirelo Sechaba Participant, a TSP or national service worker, who is sent to a clinic in a remote part of Botswana, where, in cleaning out a store cupboard, she stumbles on a pile of bloody clothes that were the clothes of a young child murdered in that area many years ago in an assumed ritual murder, which had never been solved and had been more or less hushed up.

The main thrust of the novel is the way she and a law firm headed by a female lawyer support the villagers in forcing the powers that be to reopen the case and admit that it was a ritual murder that had been hushed up. Four men had been involved in the murder. An old man in the village had been involved too as the butcher forced to cut up the body of the young girl and he recounts to Bokaa the story of the murder. He names the four men involved; the fourth named is the Minister of Safety and Security who led the government delegation to the village to pacify the villagers on the reopening of the case and had taken charge of the pile of bloody clothes so they could be given to the government pathologist. Those who had helped the villagers quickly realise that all their lives are in danger as they 'had been tricked by the smooth talking Minister . . . and had failed the villagers as the evidence that they had guarded for days was once again in the hands of the enemy' (Dow 2002, pp. 214–15). And there, tantalisingly, the novel ends.

The novel does contain some descriptions of work in the state prosecutor's office, a private lawyer's office and how the police operate, particularly the relations between the more senior and the more junior police; most of these descriptions have the ring of truth about them. The novel also has, as one of its main themes, the battle of the female protagonists against the evil of male abuse. Indeed, all of Dow's novels are intensely social and political. Thus *Far and Beyon'* (Dow 2000) tells the story of a Botswanan family's struggle to cope with the devastation of HIV and poverty. Reeling from the loss of a second son to AIDS, Mara turns to traditional magic to fight the curse she believes is destroying her family. Her children, Mosa and Stan, increasingly reject such beliefs, choosing instead to fight the powerlessness and oppression that have made the family so vulnerable to HIV. In the process, they must challenge adult authorities and scrutinise the ways in which they unwittingly consent to the forces that constrict them. *Juggling Truths* (Dow 2003) tells of the Botswanan childhood of Monei Ntuka, shaped by stories from her mother, father, and grandmother as well as from the colonisers and the Christian church about the tensions between modernisation and tradition in postcolonial Africa. *The Heavens May Fall* (Dow 2006) is the story of a fiery up-and-coming lawyer at the Bana-Bantie Children's Agency in Mochudi, Botswana, Naledi Chaba, whose caseload is bulging with stories of rape and abuse. All these are very different from the Kenyan novels and from McCall Smith's idealised version of Botswanan society.

6 Wilson's Bruce Medway novels set in West Africa

Before attempting to arrive at some broad conclusions in this chapter, I want briefly to refer to Robert Wilson's Bruce Medway novels, crime fiction set in West Africa. I read the four books in this series when they first came out in the mid-1990s, long before crime fiction in Africa began to be a subject of academic interest. I remember at the time thinking that they were very realistic in their depiction of West Africa (where I had lived in Nigeria, in the mid-1950s, and worked as a consultant in Kano in the 1970s, visited as an academic at the University of Lagos in 1987, and visited Ghana as a UN official in the early 1990s). I would need to go back and re-read the books to make any comments on their depiction of police procedures and crime but Wilson (n.d.) himself provides an excellent summary of what he was trying to do in these novels which is well worth quoting:

> These four African books are the product of 10 years of travelling, living and working in Africa. But why did I make them crime novels? A screenwriter friend of mine was taking time out to write some crime novels and when he read my travel stories he said: "You'll never sell these as they are, but if you wrote them as crime novels, now that would be different." I hadn't read crime since I was a kid so he told me to start with the classics like Raymond Chandler and proceed to more modern writers like Elmore Leonard.
>
> Reading Chandler was the revelation. I loved that 'noir' voice that developed out of the black and white gangster movies of the 1930s and 40s. I realised that there were similarities between 1940s California and 1990s West Africa. They both had extremes of poverty and wealth, both were riven by political corruption, both were full of people on the make. It came to me that I could create my own African 'noir' voice but that I would have to find a hero who was not a private eye. That would not ring true in West Africa. And so I developed Bruce Medway: fixer, negotiator, debt collector and investigator. He's an Englishmen who's fetched up on the West Coast of Africa after a trip across the Sahara and needs to make some money. He sets himself up as a freelance manager, supervising the unloading of ships, arranging labour and transport, getting stuff through customs and, when people don't pay for the goods he's delivered, he collects the debts for his employers. It's a seedy lifestyle which is mitigated by his relationship with Heike, a beautiful German aid worker, and his friendship with Bagado, a Nigerian/Beninois detective whom he meets on one of his cases. Whereas Bruce has a rather flexible

moral attitude because he finds himself inexorably attracted to bad guys, Bagado and Heike have far greater certitude with which they attempt to keep Bruce on the straight and narrow.

I think these novels have been neglected by critics writing on African crime fiction.

7 Tentative conclusions

> If you have little or no academic experience in literature studies you are going to miss the central fact that without some sort of general theory showing a necessary connection between law and literature culturally, the connection is always strained if not meaningless . . . It seems to me that if law and literature have anything to say to one another directly, it is through discourse whose focus is first, law as an anthropological construct reflecting culture, including imaginative culture; axiomatically, law as narrative, or as a vehicle of this cultural expression, and finally, justice in human society as the narrative's core subject.
>
> (Miller 2013, p. 7, p. 9)[31]

What is my general theory showing a connection between African law and crime and literature which informs this paper? It is that authors of criminal law novels set in Africa would likely use the genre to show the connection between law and society, particularly where, as is the case in all Anglophone African countries, the law is the law imposed by the colonial power some one hundred plus years ago and the society still exhibits many of the traditional traits upon which this law was imposed.[32] The novel provides as good a way of exploring and discussing the interaction between imposed law and existing society or, in the case of South Africa, between the old and the new South Africa, as any anthropological or political study. Does this mean that African crime novels that do not undertake this voyage of exploration are in some way a failure? I do not think so but I do think that, given the general theory, it is a valid criticism of the authors of such novels that they have written a superficial book and it is permissible to try and explore why that might be so.

31 See too Manji (2003). Through a study of *Achebe's Arrow of God*, Manji discussed:

> Achebe's treatment of the administrative and political power exercised by the colonial state and showed that the novel's focus is not simply on the form of power vested in chiefs by the colonial state but also on the epistemic or discursive authority exercised by the colonial administration. The task of demythologising law and colonialism has been undertaken by lawyers, social scientists and novelists alike.

This then seems to be her central theory.

32 This applies as much to Liberia as to those countries colonised by European powers in the nineteenth century, notwithstanding that the colonisers were freed slaves from the USA, are still there, and are still effectively in power.

Before doing so however, and as an example of the kind of discussion that my general theory aspires to, it is relevant to refer to and comment on Dolin's (2007, chap. 7) chapter in his *A Critical Introduction to Law and Literature*: 'Rumpole in Africa: law and literature in post-colonial society'. In this chapter, Dolin discusses John Mortimer's defence of Wole Soyinka's holding up of a radio station in Ibadan, in the Western Region of Nigeria, to prevent a victory speech recorded by the then Prime Minister of the Western Region, Chief Akintola, for an electoral victory gained through malpractice and political intimidation, and the substitution of an alternative recording by Soyinka calling on Akintola to 'get out and take with you your renegades who have lost all sense of shame' (p. 167). Soyinka surrendered to the authorities and was brought to trial:

> Mortimer was briefed by Amnesty International and was admitted to practice in Nigeria for the eventual trial. Together with distinguished Nigerian defence lawyers, he succeeded in obtaining an acquittal in a well-conducted trial . . .
>
> In *Clinging to the Wreckage,* Mortimer remembers the Soyinka defence as a personal revelation of the integrity of the legal system . . . he was most deeply impressed by the fairness and thoroughness of the trial, while all around, the country was in political turmoil. By seeming to symbolise the rule of law, it renewed his commitment to common-law advocacy:
>
> 'Driving away from Ibadan that night, I had the unoriginal thought that British law might, together with Shakespeare, Wordsworth, Lord Byron and the herbaceous border, be one of our great contributions to the world.'
>
> (Mortimer 1982, 152–3)
>
> In adopting the language of imperialist mythology, Mortimer is perpetuating it, even though he is not seeking to defend the empire. Furthermore, his conjunction of literature and law in this context cannot be detached from the colonial past. His praise is juxtaposed against the image of a night of knives: [Mortimer had referred to being stopped at a level crossing where he could see the 'flash of knives and machetes and the cries of the wounded'] English law is still represented as the light in the darkness of African savagery . . . The coupling of literature and law by Mortimer repeats, in the post-colonial age one of the central devices of the imperialist project. It implies a continuing local need for the civilising functions of European culture. By constructing the colonised people as barbaric, it affirms the self-identification of the English as rational.
>
> (Dolin 2007, p. 169)

Mortimer used his experience for one of his Rumpole scripts: *Rumpole and the Golden Thread* where Rumpole is in the fictional Central African state, Neranga, to defend a politician against a criminal charge. Rumpole repeats in a more humorous and cynical fashion the defence of the British system of criminal justice and, as Dolin notes:

> assumes that in court he is on utterly familiar territory, but this assumption proves fatal to his client. The forms of English criminal procedure are followed minutely, but the process is viewed by the other participants not as an end in itself, but as an instrument of the will to power.
>
> (Dolin 2007, p. 176)

Wole Soyinka's novel of 1965, *The Interpreters* (Soyinka 1965), is a linguistically rich and sharply satiric representation of the new, hybridised culture of post-colonial Nigeria.

> [It] unmasks the superficial and self-serving heritage of English law in the immediate post-colonial period in Nigeria, the dispensability of its values and concepts from ordinary understandings of reality . . . in retrospect, the radio-station trial remains an isolated, even exceptional occurrence . . . [For Soyinka] 'justice is the first condition of humanity. The golden thread of Western law is only one element in this evolving struggle to rid the post-colonial nation of the totalitarianism and violence of colonial governments.
>
> (Dolin 2007, pp. 180–1)[33]

Dolin also notes that Chinua Achebe's (1958) classic novel *Things Fall Apart* is an unmasking of English law as an instrument of imperial power.

Another way of approaching these conclusions is via the literary canon of noir crime fiction. Bill Pronzini (2009) summarises noir crime fiction in a way which is easy for a non-literary critic to understand:

> The noir crime story deals with disorder, disaffection and dissatisfaction. Throughout the genre's seventy year history, this has remained a constant and central tenet. The typical noir character (if not the typical noir writer) has a jaundiced view of government, law and power . . . If he is on the side of the angels, he is probably a cynical idealist; he believes that society is corrupt but he also believes in justice and will make it his business to do whatever is necessary to see that justice is done . . . In the noir world, extremes are the norm. Clashes between good and evil are never pretty and good does not always triumph nor is justice always done.
>
> A quality noir story . . . must be reflective of the times it was written, providing an accurate honest and realistic depiction of the locale and of the individuals who inhabit that locale.

33 The quotation is from Soyinka (1972), p. 95.

> Even more important it must offer some insight into the moral and social climate of its time . . .
>
> Even though it involves some type of violent crime, it must not use unmotivated violence or violence for the sake of sensationalism.[34]

It is difficult, if not impossible, to see any of the Kenyan novels discussed in this or indeed any of the novels set in South Africa as being examples of noir crime fiction or as containing any of the kinds of analysis that Achebe or Soyinka adopted with respect to the police and criminal justice system imposed by the British or adopted by the apartheid regime in South Africa. They appear to have little or no overt or covert socio-political theme running through them. This is to be expected of the novels written by English authors – Huxley, Brownlee, Crompton, Palmer – who in varying degrees, would have seen nothing but good in the imposition and application of English law and police procedures in Kenya. However, it is perhaps somewhat surprising in the novels written by African authors Ng'weno, Ngugi, Malla, Makholwa, Tlholwe, Meyer. Both Ngugi and Malla are diasporic-African; Ng'weno lives and works in Kenya; Meyer, Makholwa and Tlholwe live and work in South Africa. Perhaps Unity Dow's novels come closest to noir crime but I would need to read more of them to be sure of that.

Ng'weno adopts, on the whole, a friendly approach to police procedures; perhaps in the mid-1970s that was still the perceived Kenyan attitude to them although, as we have seen, Ng'weno had the reputation of treading carefully in criticising Kenyan institutions in his role as editor of the *Daily Nation*. Nor perhaps would his academic background as a nuclear scientist have given him the necessary intellectual tools to adopt a critical approach to social or legal institutions. Insofar as Ngugi adopts any approach to police procedure, it is at best a cynical one, at worst an anarchic one where in *Black Star Nairobi* (Ngugi 2013a), police procedures are totally ignored in favour of killings with no questions asked. Violence for the sake of sensationalism sums up this novel; the very antithesis of noir. Is that really the image that the police have in Kenya today amongst Kenyans? After reading the UN Human Rights Council Report (2009), it is likely that it is and, if it is, then Ngugi can be said to be accurately portraying Kenyan police non-procedures.

Malla Nunn comes through as the most perceptive of the African authors. She sums up her attitude to Africa as follows:

> A locust plague in Mali, a firebombed church in Kenya, another warlord hiding in the hills with a cache of AK47s and machetes; Africa is still a mess. No

34 An excellent discussion of noir crime fiction is Forshaw (2013). Forshaw draws attention to many Scandinavian authors' willingness to address corruption in the police, something absent in the African novels discussed here, though perhaps hinted at in Nunn's (2011) *Let the Dead Lie*.

> matter how many books I write about her, I will never have the power to fix her. I'm not immune to the human misery unfolding in Libya or Somalia or, most especially, Swaziland, my spiritual home . . . I can no longer judge my own writing in terms of its ability to save Africa. Instead, I can invite readers into an exquisite, wild part of the world where exciting things happen. I can tell stories where despite the obstacles, people fight for each other and for justice. Now, when I stand on a craggy mountainside high above a river in Swaziland (whether I'm really there or just in my imagination) I feel no shame, just the deepest kind of love.
>
> (Nunn 2012)

This is a million miles from the evident feelings for Kenya that Ngugi seems to have and no doubt explains why, notwithstanding the storyline of *A Beautiful Place to Die* (Nunn 2009), while there is justifiable criticism of apartheid as applied to policing in South Africa, there is no criticism of South Africa as a country. But there is no exploration in her book of whether police procedures absent apartheid are acceptable or an alien imposition. Perhaps it is too much to expect of the author and it must be noted that I have read only two of her novels.

In some respects, Meyer represents the most interesting of the African writers. He has the fullest discussions of police procedures in his books and I cannot detect in these discussions any overt or covert criticisms of police procedures from a social or political angle. There are criticisms – of bureaucracy, of pressures from politicians and higher up the police chain of command to solve cases – particularly in *Thirteen Hours* (Meyer 2010)[35] where an American student traveller is being chased by persons who were smuggling people into South Africa, killing them and running an illegal donor organ operation while the student's father is putting pressure on the American consulate in South Africa to put pressure, in turn, on the police. There are also criticisms of lack of transport and so lack of instant police backup when needed, but no socially or politically adverse criticisms of the way the police and the criminal justice system operate. Again, it may be unrealistic to expect that of an Afrikaans author; Meyer grew up in an apartheid society and has clearly come a long way in his acceptance of the new South Africa as his books demonstrate. He would however be quite unlikely to feel that the police and criminal justice system was an alien and imposed one in the way Achebe and Soyinka considered it to be from a Nigerian perspective. For Makholwa and Tlholwe, the law and police procedures are peripheral in their novels; in this respect, their novels may reflect the existing black African perception of these matters; in the apartheid era, these matters were as far as possible steered clear of or, if that was not possible, suffered under. Now, they are there but not particularly obtrusive.

35 Originally published in Afrikaans as *13 Uur* (2008) Human and Rousseau.

My final conclusion is this: just as there is no such phenomenon as African land tenure – there are the different land tenure systems in the 53 sub-Saharan African countries – so too I think that there is no such phenomenon as African crime fiction; as we dig deeper into the crime fiction of different countries in Africa, we will discover that there are as many African crime fictions as there are countries in Africa. My title to this paper has been changed from its original one to reflect that likelihood.

References

Achebe, C. (1958) *Things fall apart.* London: Heinemann.

ACLCCL (1963) *African Conference on Local Courts and Customary Law: record of proceedings of the conference held in Dar es Salaam, Tanganyika, 8th September, 1963–18th September, 1963.*

Akiga (1939) *Akiga's story; the Tiv tribe as seen by one of its members.* Translated from Tiv by R. East. London: Oxford University Press.

Alexander, G. (1936) *Tanganyika memories: a judge in the Red Kanzu.* London: Blackie and Son.

Altbeker, A. (2007) *A country at war with itself: South Africa's crisis of crime.* Johannesburg: Jonathan Ball.

Brownlee, N. (2010) *Machete.* London: Piatkus.

Coetzee, J.M. (1999) *Disgrace.* New York: Viking.

Comaroff, J. and J. (2004) 'Criminal obsessions, after Foucault: postcoloniality, policing and the metaphysics of disorder', *Critical Inquiry*, 30(4), pp. 800–24.

Crompton, R. (2013a) 'Murder in Kenya: PW talks with Richard Crompton'. Interview with Richard Crompton. Interviewed by Lenny Picker for *Publisher's Weekly*, 22 March. www.publishersweekly.com/pw/by-topic/authors/interviews/article/56473-murder-in-kenya-pw-talks-with-richard-crompton.html (Accessed: 21 June 2013).

Crompton, R. (2013b) *The honey guide.* London: Phoenix.

Dathorne, O.R. and Feuser, W. (eds.) (1969) *Africa in prose.* Baltimore: Penguin Books.

Davis, G.V. (2012) 'Old loyalties and new aspirations: the post-apartheid crime fiction of Deon Meyer', in Oed, A. and Matzke, C. (eds.) *Life is a thriller: investigating African crime fiction, selected papers from the 9th International Janheinz Jahn Symposium, Mainz 2008.* Köln, Rüdiger Köppe Verlag, pp. 51–62.

De Smedt, J. (2009) ''No Raila, no peace!' Big man politics and election violence at the Kibera grassroots', *African Affairs*, 108(433), pp. 581–98.

Dolin, K. (2007) *A critical introduction to law and literature.* Cambridge: Cambridge University Press.

Dow, U. (2000) *Far and beyon'.* North Melbourne: Spinifex.

Dow, U. (2002) *The screaming of the innocent.* North Melbourne: Spinifex.

Dow, U. (2003) *Juggling truths.* North Melbourne: Spinifex.

Dow, U. (2006) *The heavens may fall.* North Melbourne: Spinifex.

Dow, U. (ed.) (1995) *The citizenship case: the Attorney General of the Republic of Botswana vs Unity Dow: court documents, judgements, cases and materials.* Gaberone: Lentswe La Lesedi (Pty).

Duchi, D. (1983) *Assassins on safari.* Nairobi: Longman Kenya.

Forshaw, B. (2013) *Nordic noir: the pocket essential guide to Scandinavian crime fiction, film and TV.* Harpenden: Oldcastle Books.

Gordimer, N. (1998) *The house gun.* New York: Farrar, Straus and Giroux.

Hailey, L. (1957) *An African Survey Revised 1956; a study of problems (sic) arising in Africa South of the Sahara.* Revised 1956. Oxford: Oxford University Press.

Herskovits, M.J. (1962) *The human factor in changing Africa*. New York: Alfred A. Knopf.
Hill, M.F. (1961) *Permanent way. Vol. 1: the story of the Kenya and Uganda Railway*, 2nd edn. Nairobi: East African Railway and Harbours.
Himes, C. (1957) *A rage in Harlem*. Reprint. London: Penguin Classics, 2011.
Himes, C. (1965) *Cotton comes to Harlem*. Reprint. London: Penguin Classics, 2011.
Hunter, G. (1962) *The new societies of tropical Africa: a selective study*. London: Oxford University Press.
Huxley, E. (1988) *Murder at government house*. New York: Viking.
Johansson, L. (1992) *In the shadow of neocolonialism: a study of Meja Mwangi's Novels 1973–1990*. Stockholm: Umeå.
Kehinde, A. (2004) 'Post-independence disillusionment in contemporary African fiction: the example of Meja Mwangi's Kill me quick', *Nordic Journal of African Studies*, 13(2), pp. 228–41.
Keil, S. (2012) *Guide to the African Crime Fiction Project*. https://libraries.indiana.edu/guide-african-crime-fiction-project (Accessed: 21 June 2013).
Kurtz, J.R. (1993) 'Mwangi, the Mau Mau historian', in Mwangi, M. (2008) *MejaMwangi.com*. www.mejamwangi.com/rogerkurtzreview.html (Accessed: 25 June 2013).
Kurtz, J.R. (1998) *Urban obsessions, urban fears, the postcolonial Kenyan novel*. Trenton NJ; Asmara, Eritrea: Africa World Press Inc.
le Carré, J. (2001) *The constant gardener*. New York: Scribner.
Mair, L.P. (1934) *An African people in the twentieth century*. London: Routledge.
Makholwa, A. (2007) *Red ink*. Northlands: Pan Macmillan.
Manji, A. (2000) '"Like a mask dancing": law and colonialism in Chinua Achebe's *Arrow of God*', *Journal of Law and Society*, 27(4), pp. 626–42.
Manji, A. (2003) 'Law, literature and the politics of culture in Kenya', *Social Justice and Global Development Journal*, 2. www2.warwick.ac.uk/fac/soc/law/elj/lgd/2003_2/manji/ (Accessed: 21 June 2013).
Matzke, C. (2012) 'Of guns, ghosts and gangsters: a preliminary checklist of African and African-diasporic crime novels in English', in Oed, A. and Matzke, C. (eds.) *Life is a thriller: investigating African crime fiction, selected papers from the 9th International Janheinz Jahn Symposium, Mainz 2008*. Köln: Rüdiger Köppe Verlag, pp. 203–12.
McCall Smith, A.M. (1998) *The no. 1 ladies' detective agency*. Edinburgh: Polygon.
Mengiste, M. (2013) 'What makes a real African?', *The Guardian*, 8 July.
Meyer, D. (2009) *Blood safari*. Translated by K.L. Seegers. London: Hodder and Stoughton.
Meyer, D. (2010) *Thirteen hours*. Translated by K.L. Seegers. London: Hodder and Stoughton.
Meyer, D. (2012a) *Devil's peak*. Translated by K.L. Seegers. London: Hodder.
Meyer, D. (2012b) *Trackers*. Translated by K.L. Seegers. London: Hodder.
Miller, J. (2013) *The structures of law and literature: duty, justice, and evil in the cultural imagination*. Montreal: McGill-Queen's University Press.
Mortimer, J. (1982) *Clinging to the wreckage: a part of life*. London: Weidenfeld and Nicolson.
Mwangi, M. (1973) *Kill me quick*. London: Heinemann.
Ndung'u, M. (2004) *A friend in court*. Nairobi: Focus Publications.
Ng'weno, H. (1975) *The men from Pretoria*. Nairobi: Longman Kenya.
Ngugi, M.W. (2011) *Nairobi heat*. Brooklyn: Melville House.
Ngugi, M.W. (2013a) *Black star Nairobi*. Brooklyn: Melville House.
Ngugi, M.W. (2013b) 'Searching for clues in a dangerous Nairobi'. Interview with Mukoma wa Ngugi. Interviewed by Jacki Lyden for *NPR*, 13 July. www.npr.org/2013/07/13/200832498/searching-for-clues-in-a-dangerous-nairobi (Accessed 15 July 2013).

Nunn, M. (2009) *A beautiful place to die*. London: Picador.

Nunn, M. (2011) *Let the dead lie*. London: Picador.

Nunn. M. (2012) 'The challenges of writing about Africa', *Huffington Post*. www.huffington post.com/malla-nunn/writing-africa_b_1628637.html (Accessed: 21 July 2013).

Oed, A. and Matzke, C. (eds.) (2012) *Life is a thriller: investigating African crime fiction, selected papers from the 9th International Janheinz Jahn Symposium, Mainz 2008*. Köln: Rüdiger Köppe Verlag.

Palmer, R. (2010) *Code orange*. Nairobi: Akis Investment.

Pepper, A. (2003) 'Black crime fiction', in Priestman, M. (ed.) *The Cambridge companion to crime fiction*. Cambridge: Cambridge University Press, pp. 209–26.

Primorac, R. (2012) 'Nation, detection, and time in contemporary Southern African fiction', in Oed, A. and Matzke, C. (eds.) *Life is a thriller: investigating African crime fiction, selected papers from the 9th International Janheinz Jahn Symposium, Mainz 2008*. Köln: Rüdiger Köppe Verlag, pp. 21–34.

Pronzini, B (2009) '*What is noir crime fiction?*', *Noir Con*. www.noircon/info/2009/07/what-is-noir-crime-fiction.html (Accessed: 21 July 2013).

Rautenbach, A (2013) 'Crime fiction in South Africa: the history, the hype and the "genre snob" debate'; *Litnet*. www.litnet.co.za/Article/crime-fiction-in-South-Africa-the-history-the-hype-and-the-genre-snob-debate (Accessed: 21 July 2013).

Rinkanya, A.N. (2012) 'Rewriting gender in Kenyan crime fiction', in Oed, A. and Matzke, C. (eds.) *Life is a thriller: investigating African crime fiction, selected papers from the 9th International Janheinz Jahn Symposium, Mainz 2008*. Köln: Rüdiger Köppe Verlag, pp. 185–92.

Ross. A. (2011) 'A vivid portrait of Nairobi undone by a very weak crime story'. Review of *Nairobi heat*, by Mukoma Wa Ngugi. www.amazon.com/review/R1PXUOOJ5838Z2/ref=cm (Accessed: 21 July 2013).

Sharpe, T. (1971) *Riotous assembly*. New York: Viking.

Sharpe, T. (1973) *Indecent exposure*. London: Secker and Warburg.

Soyinka, W. (1965) *The interpreters*. London: Collins.

Soyinka, W. (1972) *The man died: prison notes 1967–69*. London: Rex Collins.

Stanley, M. (2010) 'Michael Stanley's top 10 African crime novels', *The Guardian*, 30 June. www.theguardian.com/books/2010/jun/30/michael-stanley-african-crime (Accessed: 25 July 2013).

Tlholwe, D. (2011) *Counting the coffins*. Cape Town: Kwela Books.

UN Human Rights Council (2009) *Report of the Special Rapporteur on Extrajudicial, Summary or Arbitrary Executions, Philip Alston: addendum: mission to Kenya*, 26 May. A/HRC/11/2/Add. 6. www.refworld.org/docid/4a3f56432.html (Accessed: 21 July 2013).

Warnes, C. (2012) 'Writing crime in the new South Africa: negotiating threat in the novels of Deon Meyer and Margie Orford', *Journal of Southern Africa Studies*, 38(4), pp. 981–91.

Wilson, R. (n.d.) 'The Bruce Medway books'. www.robert-wilson.eu/medway/index.html (Accessed: 25 July 2013).

Index

Printed in Great Britain
by Amazon

56711867R00111